THE IMPACT OF LIBERALIZING INTERNATIONAL AVIATION BILATERALS

The Impact of Liberalizing International Aviation Bilaterals

The case of the Northern German region

Edited by
DAVID W. GILLEN
HOLGER HINSCH
BENEDIKT MANDEL
HARTMUT WOLF

Routledge
Taylor & Francis Group
LONDON AND NEW YORK

First published 2001 by Ashgate Publishing

Reissued 2018 by Routledge
2 Park Square, Milton Park, Abingdon, Oxon OX14 4RN
711 Third Avenue, New York, NY 10017, USA

Routledge is an imprint of the Taylor & Francis Group, an informa business

ISBN 13: 978-1-138-73497-5 (hbk)
ISBN 13: 978-1-315-18681-8 (ebk)

Contents

List of Figures

List of Tables

List of Contributors

Science Applications International Corporation

Holger Hinsch	Project Coordinator
Jonathan Harvey	ALM Model Development
1710 SAIC Drive, MS T3-8-2	Phone: +1 703 676 4628
McLean VA, 22101	Fax: +1 703 821 7938
USA	email: holger.hinsch@saic.com

Prof. Dr. David W. Gillen	Economic Impacts
University of California at Berkeley	
Institute of Transportation Studies	
109 McLaughin Hall # 1720	Phone: +1 510 642 2637
Berkley, CA 94720 – 1720	Fax: +1 510 642 1246
USA	email: dgillen@euler.berkeley.edu

MKmetric Gesellschaft für Systemplanung mbH

Dr. Benedikt Mandel,	Airport Choice Model Development
Oliver Schnell	Airport Choice Model Development
Durlacher Allee 49	Phone: +49 721 961 60 0
76131 Karlsruhe	Fax: +49 721 961 60 99
Germany	email: info@mkm.de

Institut für Weltwirtschaft

Hartmut Wolf	Policy Analysis
Düsternbrooker Weg 4	Phone: +1 510 642 2637
24105 Kiel	Fax: +1 510 642 1246
Germany	email: h.wolf@ifw.uni-kiel.de

Wirtschaftsbehörde der Freien und Hansestadt Hamburg

Dr. Hans-Martin Niemeier	
Alter Steinweg 4	Phone: +49 40 428 41 1468
20459 Hamburg	Fax: +49 40 428 41 2879
Germany	email: hans-martin.niemeier@ wb.hamburg.de

Hamburg Airport

Dr. Thomas Immelmann	
Director Corporate Communications	
Flughafenstrasse 1-3	Phone: +49 40 5075 3600
22335 Hamburg	Fax: +49 40 5075 1876
Germany	email: timmelmann@ham.airport.de

Preface

Air transport is one of the most dynamic industries in the world. Over the 1994-98 period it has been growing at 6 percent annually. A key driver of this dynamic process has been the increased liberalization of the old restrictive aviation system. No doubt, overall the outcome of air liberalization has been a story of success. However, one cannot ignore the negative side of liberalization, and pose the question, 'how the negative side effects of liberalization might be minimized by economic policy'?

The process of economic liberalization results in two divergent trends for regions without a major hub airport:

Globalization, especially the internal EU-market, enhances trade, but also the competition between regions. While the 20th century ended with globalization of capital, the 21st century will be one of factor mobility. Locations that have high levels of accessibility, meaning air transport, will gain relative to those that do not since the most important factor, labor with embodied human capital, will be attracted to such destinations.

Liberalization of air transport has increased inner European traffic. Most European airports provide more flights of a better quality to other destinations than 15 years ago. However, most European regions with second tier airports have lost, almost completely, all the direct intercontinental flights they had under the old restrictive regime.

These two divergent trends create a puzzle to be addressed by economic policy. Liberalization has intensified competition among regions and increased the volume of direct intercontinental flights, but at the same time has driven those flights to regions with hub airports. How should regions with secondary airports effectively compete? Shall they demand restrictions to a further liberalization in order to keep or gain intercontinental flights?

The study for the State Ministry of Economic Affairs and Hamburg Airport on the regional economic effects of liberalization of bilateral agreements provides a clear and very positive answer to this puzzling questions. In a nutshell, the present status of liberalization is incomplete as restrictive bilateral air service agreements have contributed to the formation of airline alliances who tend to concentrate traffic at their respective hubs. A further liberalization is needed as secondary airports such as Hamburg Airport would obtain improved air services to intercontinental destinations leading to more passengers, positive effects on economic welfare and employment, and fewer negative environmental impacts. The main political conclusion of the study is therefore that to gain first - mover advantages and to not lose substantial traffic to neighboring countries, it is essential to liberalize first and move to open skies directly and rapidly. The results of this extensive analysis have been intensively discussed with the Department of Transport and the respective ministries of the 16 German federal states. At their meeting in September 27th and 28th, 2000 the head of these ministries agreed that the criteria of economic welfare should be the guiding criteria in bilateral air service agreement negotiations, and that first mover advantages should be gained by a faster liberalization. The State Ministry of Economic Affairs hopes that other regions in Europe as well as in other parts of the world will accept the logic and strength of arguments pro liberalization of the study findings. The Ministry will continue to emphasize, and to support even more strongly than before, a liberal policy in that respect at the federal and EU-level.

Senator Dr. Thomas Mirow
Free and Hanseatic City of Hamburg
State Ministry of Economic Affairs

List of Abbreviations

ACI	Airport Council International
ADV	Arbeitsgmeinschaft Deutscher Verkehrsflughäfen
AEA	Association of European Airlines
ALM	Air Liberalization Model
APEC	Asia-Pacific Economic Cooperation
AR	Aviation Revenue
ASA	Air Service Agreement
BMV	Bundesministerium für Verkehr
CAB	Civil Aeronautics Board
CRS	Computer Reservation System
DLR	Deutsches Zentrum für Luft- und Raumfahrt
EBM	Economic Base Multiplier
ECAC	European Civil Aviation Conference
EU	European Union
FFP	Frequent Flier Program
GATS	General Agreements on Trade in Services
GDP	Gross Domestic Product
IATA	International Air Transport Association
ICAO	International Civil Aviation Organization
IO	Input-Output
LC	Liberalization Club
MFN	Most Favored Nation
OAG	Official Airline Guide
OD	Origin-Destination
OECD	Organization for Economic Cooperation and Development
OLC	Open Liberalization Club
TFP	Total Factor Productivity
UC	Unit Cost
WLU	Work Load Unit
WTO	World Trade Organization

1. Introduction

Background

This study came about over the course of a two-year period as many countries and regions were investigating the impacts of liberalizing bilateral air service agreements (ASAs). In particular, The European Economic Community, Transport Canada, the Department of Transportation in Australia and New Zealand commissioned several studies that expanded the scope of knowledge regarding the impact of ASAs.

Many of these studies had a national focus and determined the extent to which a country's approach to international aviation policy affected the success of its national carriers, air travelers, tourism industries and economies in general. This particular study extends the reach of previous analysis by looking at intra country impacts of ASAs. In particular, it investigates the impact of national policies on specific airports and regional economies in Germany.

For Europe, this type of analysis is of particular importance. Over the past decade, the European gateways of choice; London's Heathrow International Airport, Amsterdam's Schipol International Airport, and Germany's Frankfurt International Airport have become increasingly burdened by sustained growth in international air travel. As such, many air carriers, and national aviation policy makers, are contemplating the extension of direct international airport access to other cities with the appropriate infrastructure.

This study investigates the impact of open designation of airports in Germany on Northern Germany. In so doing, it considers a number of interrelated questions, as follows:

- To what extent do ASAs impact the route choices of international air carriers?
- What is the likelihood that liberalized ASAs will impact 'second-tier' European airports?
- To the extent that traffic increases at these airports, what is the level and mix of the new traffic that is generated?
- What impact will this new traffic have on the local economy, through increases in employment and income at airports and tourism activity?

The Terms of Reference for this study describe the main study tasks, the basics of the analytical approach and the subsequent sections of the study.

Terms of Reference

This study fulfills multiple objectives related to evaluating the potential impacts of air transport liberalization for the German economy and travelers. The terms of reference for the study, dually funded by the Hamburg International Airport and the State of Hamburg, is divided into the four main tasks described below. These tasks provide a comprehensive view of the institutional and regulatory environment affecting international air travel, the economic implications of changing the rules governing international travel and the policy and airport strategy considerations that arise because of these changes.

Task 1: Determine the Impacts of Bilateral Agreements on German Economy

This task reviews international air travel in the context of the current economic environment. It further investigates national and regional economic data to understand the incremental impacts of increases in international air travel and changes in the distribution of air travel within Germany and throughout Europe. Chapter 2 of this study provides the context in which to consider bilateral changes by describing the international airport system and its importance to Germany. Chapter 3 summarizes the analytical framework used to estimate economic impacts and Chapter 5 presents the results in form of welfare gains, increased airport revenue, and employment impacts.

Task 2: Assess Bilateral Agreements in Liberalized EU Aviation Market

This task analyzes the institutional and regulatory framework within which Germany participates in the international aviation arena. It looks into the past to understand the evolution of this framework and assesses the differences among various countries. Chapter 2 reviews the current and historical regulatory and institutional context that future changes will be judged against. It also summarizes conventional understanding of liberalization and open skies as it relates to the various countries under study.

Task 3: Evaluate Qualitative and Quantitative Impacts of Liberalizing International Aviation ASAs

This task provides an understanding of the nature and order of magnitude of the impacts associated with liberalizing air service agreements. The estimates of these impacts in turn inform the broad public policy and airport strategy recommendations. This study uses a combination of qualitative and quantitative techniques to assess the impacts of bilateral international aviation liberalization. It also investigates the full range of impacts from changes in the total number of passengers carried to the number of employees and income generated by a specific airport.

Task three has two major sub-tasks. The first, models bilateral ASA changes by evaluating the impact of changes in ASAs on the 'full' price (fare and non-fare factors) paid for airline services and the resulting impacts on consumer and producer surplus. ASAs in some circumstances affect the relative values of accessing air transportation services. This study specifically investigates the impact of changes in access on destination choice and route choice. Both choices affect the relative airport shares of traffic and the potential for incremental traffic. This sub-task contains the following steps:

I. Define Network Changes. Collect data on current flows of passenger and aircraft traffic between the countries selected, including all potential routings and airport destinations. The network following liberalization is also defined to identify potential routings and airport destinations that do not exist today.

II. Develop Operating Data Sets. This step develops comprehensive data sets to reflect all operating characteristics of the carrier route combinations in question (i.e., frequencies, fares, aircraft types etc.).

III. Model Simulation. This step simulates the aviation environment before and after the shock of changing a bilateral ASA between Germany and another country.

The second sub-task models the Impacts of liberalized ASAs on the Northern Germany/Hamburg economy and involves three steps. It translates the air transportation effects resulting from liberalization from the above sub-task (i.e., increase in passenger travel) into economic impacts for the region (i.e., tourism, employment, income and taxes). This sub-task involves implementing a standard economic impact methodology using regional specific data sets related to employment and income.

Task 4: Policy Recommendations

The final task of the study consolidates all of the quantitative, qualitative and international regulatory/institutional analysis into concrete policy and strategy recommendations for the State of Hamburg and the Hamburg International Airport.

Overview of Study Methodology

From the outset of this study, one of the objectives was to combine the best available theoretical and quantitative methods and techniques in the field of international aviation economics. This study benefits from the work of many of its team members on similar projects. It is also the first time that a combination of aggregate level trade theory techniques have been combined with detailed microeconomic network allocation models to evaluate the impact of changes in ASAs.

Figure 1.1 presents an overview of the study methodology that combines quantitative as well as qualitative analysis to arrive at the final study results. The first stage in the methodology defines the input database that is 'shocked' in the analysis. This baseline database was developed using 1997 as the benchmark. This is the last full year in which all of the required data was available on a consistent basis.

The second stage of the methodology combines the results of the regulatory and institutional analysis surrounding the bilateral ASAs with an assessment of network shocks, i.e., the degree to which changes in ASAs affect the variables in the evaluation models. These analyses are fed into two separate models. The first is an aggregate level trade theory based model that evaluates the impact of changes in a bilateral (i.e., airline or airport designation, fares) on total air travel between two countries. The second disaggregate model allocates this traffic to the various possible destinations within these countries based on operating characteristics of airlines and the preferences of consumers.

In the end, the results of both models are combined to arrive at the key impact indicators. The first series of outputs are related to economic welfare impacts, i.e., the extent to which consumers benefit from improved airfares or access to alternative destinations or airlines. The second outputs relate airport impacts (e.g., increases in movements by aircraft type and revenues). The third relates to airlines to the extent that market shares and profitability may change after an ASA has been changed. And, the fourth combines all of these indicators into a roll-up of the impacts on the region.

Figure 1.1: Overview of Study Methodology

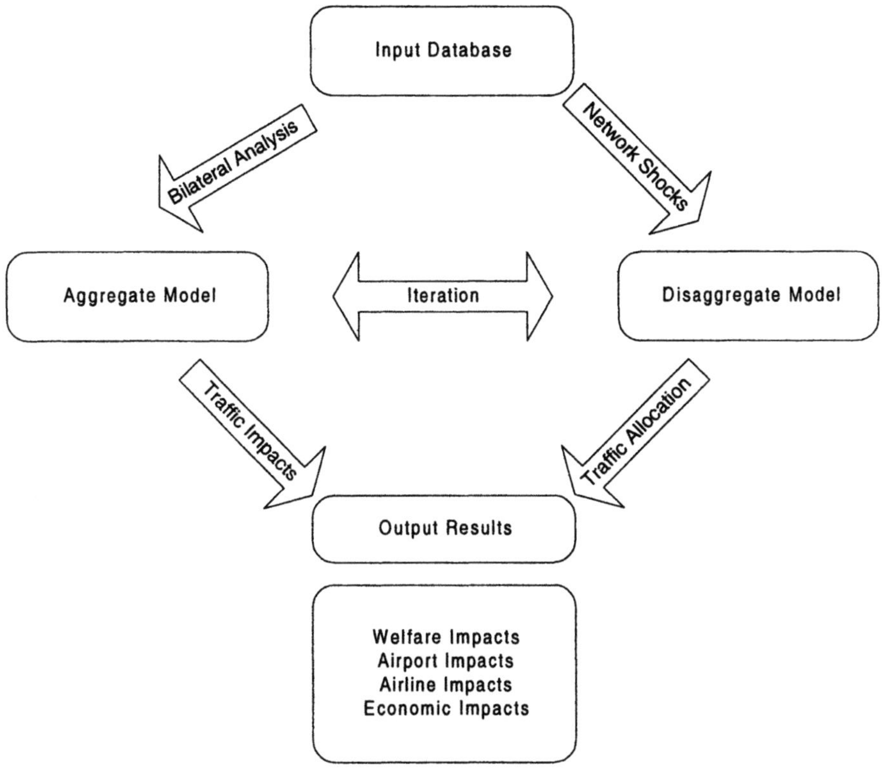

Study Outline

The next section of this study investigates the institutional and regulatory framework, which has and still governs international air travel in Germany. Chapter 3 provides a detailed presentation of the analytical methods used to generate the results in Chapter 5. Chapter 4 discusses the data collection effort and data sources and lastly Chapter 6 presents the policy and strategy recommendations that follow from the results.

2. Institutional and Regulatory Framework and General Analysis of the Effects of Air Service Agreements

Introduction

The international air transport system has undergone substantial institutional changes in the last two decades. Having been dominated since World War II by a dense network of bilateral air service agreements (ASAs) which contained and typically still contain tight regulations of market entry, fares and capacities, more and more air transport markets have been subject to liberalization since the end of the 1970s. Three events in international air transport are of particular importance for the evolution towards liberalized markets. First, the thorough liberalization of air transport within the European Union (EU) that has developed as a part of the Single European Market Program. Second, the US 'open skies' strategy that liberalized bilateral agreements with major trading partners. And third, the recent move to multilateral intra-regional liberalization in other parts of the world like South America (Andean Pact of 1991 and Fortaleza Agreement of 1997), Africa (Banjul Accord of 1997, CEMAC, COMESA and Yamoussoukro II, all of 1999), the Caribbean Community (in effect from 1998), South East Asean (CLMV Agreement of 1998) and The Middle East (Arab Civil Aviation Commission 1998).[1]

As a result of the move to liberalization European international air transport is now governed by two different classes of institutional regimes each covering different geographical areas. While intra-EU air transport is completely liberalized, most international air transport links to countries outside the EU are still governed by more or less restrictive bilaterals. An important exemption from this rule is air traffic to and from the US, as several European countries have liberalized ASAs as a response to the open skies-initiative of the US government, providing US carriers with traffic rights in Europe in exchange for traffic rights for European carriers to additional gateways in the US.

The increasing complexity of different institutional arrangements leads to several interrelated questions. First, how does the coexistence of different institutional frameworks affect the national air transport systems, and, as second-round effects, the accessibility of the national economies as a whole as well as of their regions? And what are the consequences for social welfare? Second, how does this coexistence affect the room to move for national air transport policy? And third, what consequences emerge for the design of national air transport policy? This chapter is devoted to answer these questions for the case of Germany from a general point of view. It starts with a description of the recent development path of world and German air transport markets, the main determinants of air transport and airport operations, the existing regulatory regimes in the industry, and recent changes in these basic determinants. The information presented in this chapter renders the necessary background for the later analysis of the role of bilaterals in correcting market failures and as instruments for strategic air transport policy. The first part of the analysis is devoted to the social welfare effects of aviation. The second part turns to the specific case of Germany.

The International Air Transport System

Since the end of World War II world air transport markets have been characterized by an almost steady increase of demand for air transport services. Recently, they have also been influenced by changing economic conditions for the provision of air transport and related infrastructure services, in particular in view of major changes of the institutional framework, which governs the international air transport system. This chapter provides background information on the state of, and recent trends in, the international air transport system, which may have direct implications for the optimal design of German air transport policy.

Growth and Composition of World Air Traffic

Commercial air transport is a rapidly growing industry. Since the end of World War II almost rather steady growth rates have been recorded for aggregate ton-kilometric performance of commercial airlines world wide, although markets have somewhat matured during the last three decades, and although the almost world-wide recessions at the beginning of the 1980s, the Gulf War of 1990/91, and the Asian currency crisis of 1998 each brought about a temporary sharp decline of growth rates. The Gulf war[2] resulted in the only contraction of world air transport so far; however, this was only short-term, and in the following years aggregate air transport performance soon recovered (Figure 2.1). Growth rates are expected to remain high in the years to come: Average growth is forecasted at more than 5 percent per year between 1998 and 2001 by the International Air Transport Association (IATA), and at more than 4 percent up to the year 2010 by the Airports Council International (ACI).[3]

Figure 2.1: Aggregate World Growth Rates Air Traffic of Commercial Carriers, 1982-1998[a]

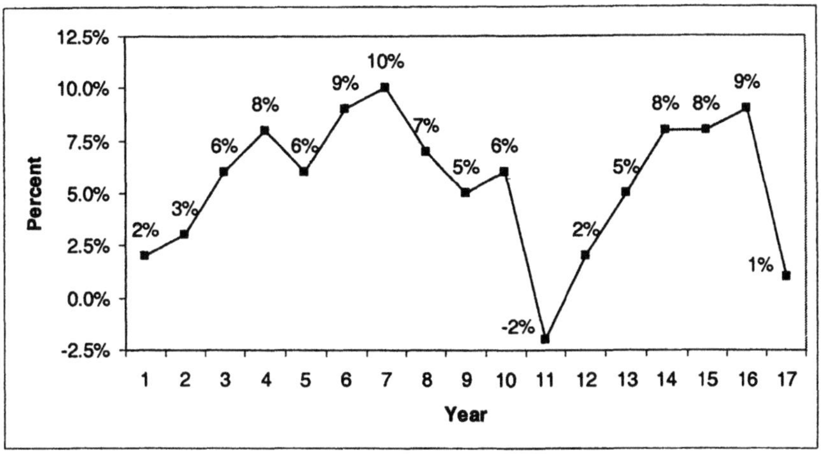

[a)] World Traffic is measured in tonne-kilometers performed by commercial airlines.

Source: ICAO (various years).

Commercial air transport is provided both on scheduled and on charter services, with the first one by far dominating the aggregate figure. In 1997 more than 90 percent of ton-kilometric performance worldwide was on scheduled flights. It should be noted that scheduled carriers are engaged in the non-scheduled (charter) market as well, providing more than 60 percent of all charter services in 1997 (Table 2-1).

Table 2-1: Composition of Aggregate World Air Traffic of Commercial Carriers 1992-1998[a]

	1993	1994	1995	1996	1997	1998
				– per cent –		
All services						
Scheduled services	94.6	94.6	93.8	93.7	94.1	n.a.[b]
Non-scheduled services of scheduled carriers	2.7	2.9	3.8	3.7	3.7	n.a.[b]
Non-scheduled services of non-scheduled carriers	2.7	2.5	2.4	2.6	2.2	n.a.[b]
Total	*100.0*	*100.0*	*100.0*	*100.0*	*100.0*	
Scheduled Services						
International	62.0	63.3	64.5	65.2	66.1	66.3
Domestic	38.0	36.7	35.5	34.8	33.9	33.7
Total	*100.0*	*100.0*	*100.0*	*100.0*	*100.0*	*100.0*

[a] World air traffic is measured in tonne-kilometres performed. — [b] n.a. = non available.

Source: Own calculations according to ICAO (various years).

International scheduled services' performance is growing markedly more rapid than that of domestic services. In 1998 they accounted for nearly two thirds of total scheduled performance. Correspondingly to the rise of the share of the international sector, domestic services steadily declined since the early 1990s.

World air transport is dominated by passenger services (Figure 2.2). Freight transport is mostly carried as a by-product of flights predominantly dedicated to passengers, whereby cargo is transported as belly load of aircraft.[4] Notwithstanding, airfreight has shown above-average growth rates in the 1990s.

Figure 2.2: World Scheduled Air Transport by Type of Traffic, 1990-1998[a]

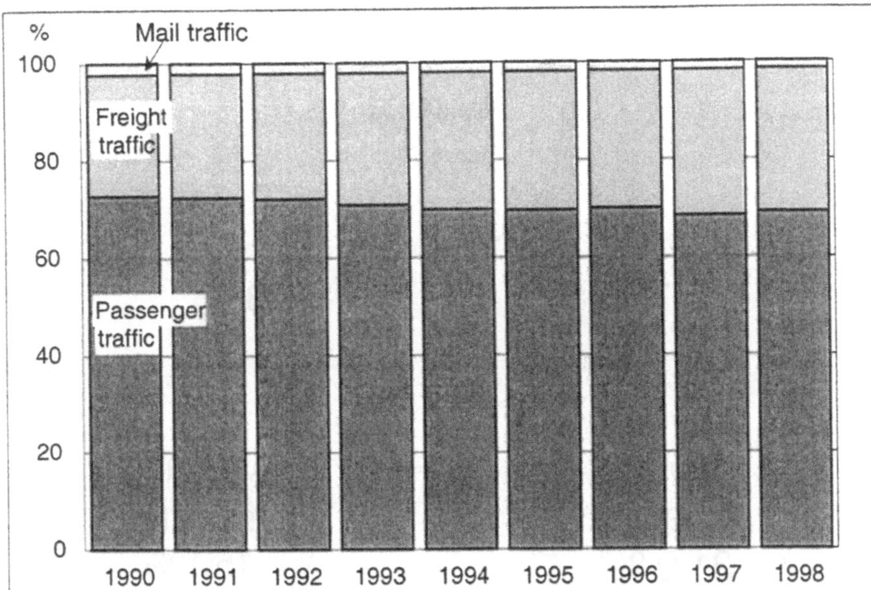

[a]Scheduled air traffic is measured in tonnes-kilometres performed.

Source: Own calculations according to ICAO (various years).

As regards the regional composition of world air transport (Figure 2.3), intra-regional traffic in North-America is clearly dominating all other traffic flows, thus making this region and, in particular, the US domestic market the largest individual marketplace. In 1998 intra-North American traffic flows accounted for 31 percent of total IATA members' passenger traffic performance. This came near the combined figure of all traffic flows within Europe plus all flows on intercontinental air linkages between Europe and the other major trading blocs. Given the average distances within and between the blocs, the volume of Europe's intercontinental air traffic by far exceeds intra-regional flows. In contrast to Europe, intra-regional traffic flows in the Asia/Pacific region, which accounted for more than one and a half of the European share in world air transport, were only slightly less than that region's intercontinental traffic. In sum, intra- and interregional transport performance between and within these three main regional blocs accounted for no less than 83 percent of the world total figure.

Figure 2.3: Major World Air Traffic Flows, 1998[a]

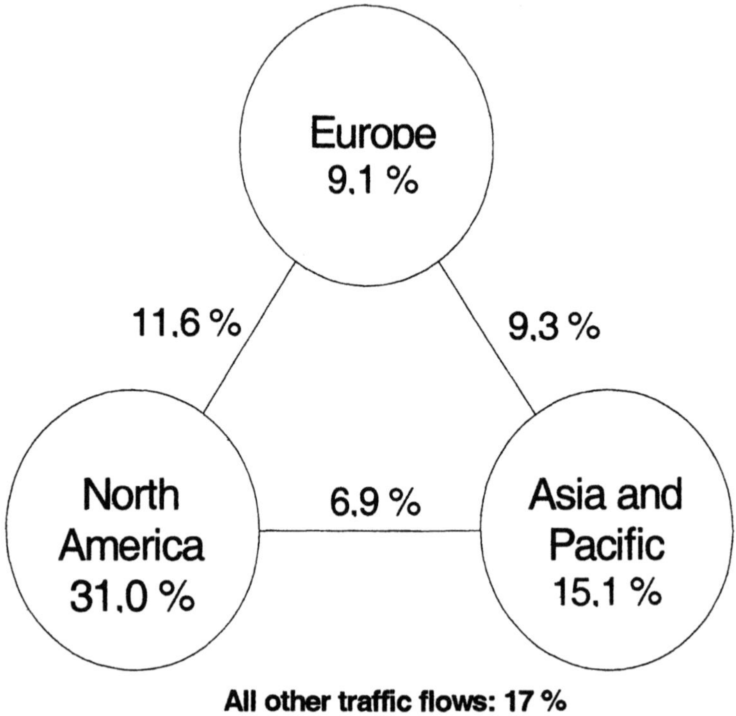

[a]Traffic flows are measured by revenue passenger-kilometres flown by IATA-airlines.

Source: Association of European Airlines (1999: 4).

For Europe, the dominance of intercontinental traffic is clearly reflected in the major European carriers' performance records. In 1998 the members of the Association of European Airlines (AEA) provided more than half of their scheduled passenger-kilometers and even almost three quarter of their scheduled freight ton-kilometers on North Atlantic routes and on routes to and from the Far East and Australia (Table 2-2). Hence, access to the attractive intercontinental markets is crucial for the economic success of any major European airline.

Table 2-2: International Scheduled Traffic by AEA-Member[a] Airlines, 1998

Region	Revenue passenger-kilometers	Freight tonne-kilometres	Revenue passenger-kilometers	Freight tonne-kilometres
	million		– percent –	
Within Europe	120 255	937	24.8	3.8
North Atlantic	149,678	8,906	30.9	36.3
Mid Atlantic	34,415	1,362	7.1	5.6
South Atlantic	21,342	1,426	4.4	5.8
Far East/Australia	100,572	9,035	20.8	36.8
Sub Sahara/Africa	37,848	1,747	7.8	7.1
North Africa/Middle East	20,272	1,110	4.2	4.5
Total of AEA-airlines	*484,837*	*2, 523*	*100.0*	*100.0*

[a] AEA-member airlines are: Adria Airways, Aer Lingus, Air France, Air Malta, Alitalia, Austrian Airlines, Balkan Bulgarian Airlines, British Airways, British Midland, Cargolux, Croatia Airlines, CSA Czech Airlines, Cyprus Airways, Finnair, Iberia, Icelandair, JAT Yugoslav Airlines, KLM Royal Dutch Airlines, Lufthansa, Luxair, Malev, Olympic Airways, Sabena, SAS, Swissair, TAP Air Portugal, and Turkish Airlines.

Source: Airline Business (March 1999: 77).

The importance of access to international traffic for European airlines is also reflected in the fact that, although in 1998 the three largest airlines of the world (measured in total tonne-kilometres) were all registered in the United States, the top two in terms of international scheduled traffic were European carriers (British Airways and Lufthansa), with another two European carriers among the top five (Air France and KLM).

Not surprisingly, the geographical distribution of world air transport is also reflected by the airport sector. In 1998 the top three airports of the world (in terms of work load unit)[5] were U.S., while the four largest engaged in handling international traffic (in terms of international passengers) were all European (London-Heathrow, Frankfurt, Paris, and Amsterdam) (Figure 2.5).

Figure 2.4: World's Largest Airlines, 1998

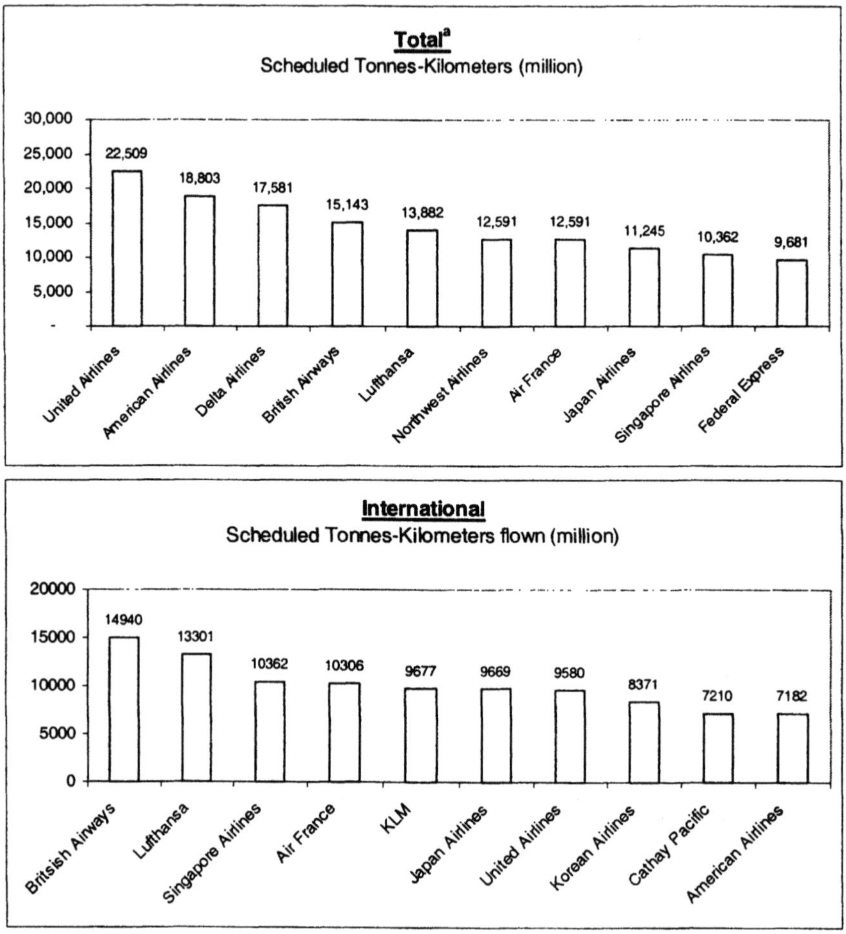

Source: International Air Transport Association (1999: 32-33).

[a]Total = International + Domestic

Figure 2.5: World's Busiest Airports, 1998

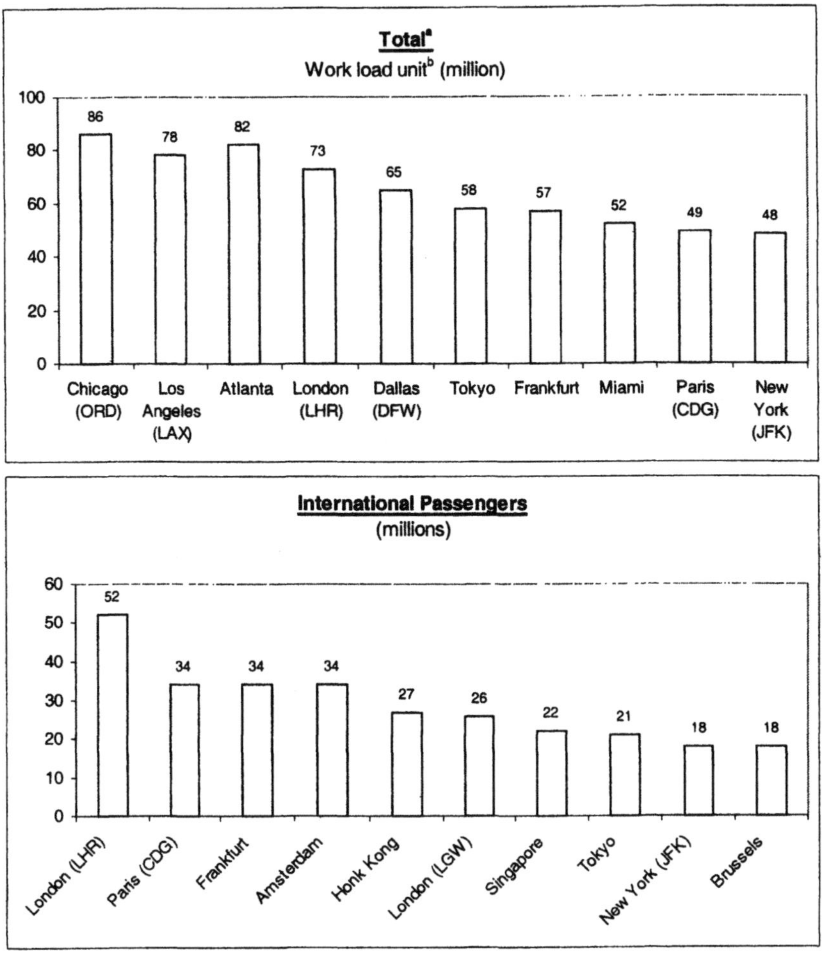

Source: International Air Transport Association (1998: 15).

The airports at London, Frankfurt, Paris, and Amsterdam did also provide the highest connectivity rates (in terms of flight frequency offered at these airports) to intercontinental traffic flows compared to other European airports. (Table 2-3) All of major airports are located at the geographical center of Europe, with only rather short distances in between (in terms of aviation geography).

Table 2-3: Top European Airports Serving Intercontinental Markets, 1998

	City	Airport	Country	Flights per day
Top European Airports in Traffic Relations with North America				
1	London	Heathrow	UK	175
2	Frankfurt	Rhein-Main	Germany	90
3	Paris	Charles de Gaulle	France	82
4	London	Gatwick	UK	74
5	Amsterdam	Schiphol	Netherlands	68
6	Brussels	National	Belgium	31
7	Zurich	Zurich Airport	Switzerland	29
8	Madrid	Barajas	Spain	26
Top European Airports in Traffic Relations with Asia/Pacific				
1	London	Heathrow	UK	75
2	Frankfurt	Rhein-Main	Germany	64
3	Paris	Charles de Gaulle	France	42
4	Amsterdam	Schiphol	Netherlands	33
5	Zurich	Zurich Airport	Switzerland	23
6	Istanbul	Istanbul	Turkey	13
7	Vienna	Schwechat	Austria	12
8	Copenhagen	Copenhagen	Denmark	11

Source: Airline Business (June 1999: 70).

Growth and Composition of German Air Traffic

Growth of German air transport followed — and is still following — roughly the pattern of world air transport markets (Figure 2.6). In terms of workload units, it showed an average annual growth of nearly 30 percent during the 1950, 18 percent during the 1960s, nearly 5 percent in the 1970s and the 1980s, and four percent in the period between 1990 and 1998.[6] Forecasts of future growth of air passenger traffic up to the year 2015 are in the range of 4-5 percent a year (Vill 1998: 76), which would mean an increase from 111 million passengers in 1996 to 234-280 million passengers.

Figure 2.6: Growth Rates of German Air Transport 1982-1998

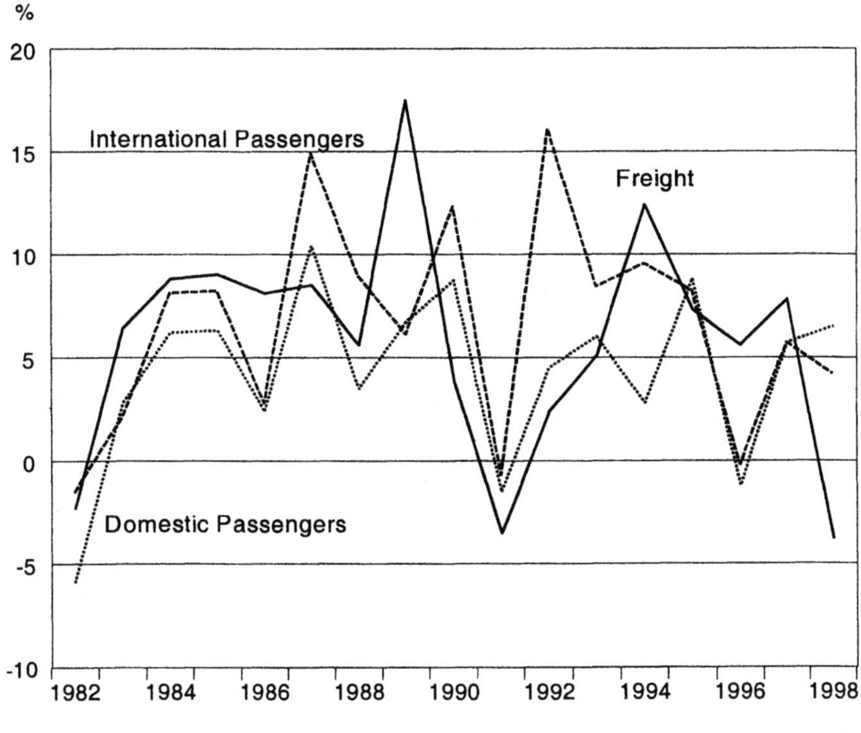

Source: Statistisches Bundesamt (various issues).

Like the major world air transport markets also German air traffic is clearly dominated by passenger services. More than 80 percent of all work load units are carried on flights which are predominantly dedicated to passengers, most of them on scheduled flights. Prior to the liberalization of EU air transport markets in 1993, about a quarter of all passengers originating in Germany flew on non-scheduled flights. This share dropped to less than 10 percent once liberalization had become effective, partly because former charter airlines entered scheduled markets, partly because charter flights were substituted by scheduled flights in leisure travel, and partly because transport performance of scheduled services boomed as a consequence of liberalization (Table 2-4).

Table 2-4: Traffic at German Airports by Type 1990-1998[a]

	1980[a]	1985[a]	1990[a]	1995	1996	1997	1998
			–percent –				
Type of service[b]							
Passengers[c]	83.2	82.4	82.1	83.3	83.2	83.6	84.9
Freight	14.1	14.8	15.2	13.9	14.2	14.4	13.4
Mail	2.7	2.8	2.7	2.8	2.6	2.0	1.7
Total	*100.0*	*100.0*	*100.0*	*100.0*	*100.0*	*100.0*	*100.0*
Type of passenger service[c]							
Scheduled	75.9	75.5	77.7	91.5	91.5	90.1	92.3
Non-scheduled	24.1	24.5	22.3	8.5	8.5	9.9	7.7
Total	*100.0*	*100.0*	*100.0*	*100.0*	*100.0*	*100.0*	*100.0*
International	56.8	59.4	62.5	67.2	68.4	68.5	68.2
Domestic	43.2	40.6	37.5	32.8	31.6	31.5	31.8
Total	*100.0*	*100.0*	*100.0*	*100.0*	*100.0*	*100.0*	*100.0*

[a] Western Germany. — [b] Calculations are based on work load unit. — [c] Calculations are based on number of Passengers boarding/off-boarding at German airports.

Source: Own calculations according to Statistisches Bundesamt (various years).

Given the relatively short distances between the main centers of economic activity in Germany and the well-developed ground transportation systems, most German air transport is performed on international routes, which also showed above average growth. (Table 2-4). The most important international air transport links (in terms of number of WLU) are those with other member states of the European Union. In 1998 passenger traffic within the EU accounted for more than half of all international passengers to and from Germany, with another 20 percent accounting to links to other European countries. With regards to intercontinental traffic, the North Atlantic represents the most important geographical market for German air carriers, closely followed by the Asia/Pacific region. Around 10 percent of all passengers on flights originating in Germany in 1998 were transported to destinations in North America, with the United States being the prime destination, the corresponding figure for the Asia/Pacific region being more than 8 percent (Table 2-5).

Table 2-5: Air Traffic to and from Germany by Origin/Destination Region, 1980-1998

Region	1980	1985	1990	1995	1996	1997	1998
			– percent –				
Passenger traffic[a]							
EU[c]	56.7	56.5	55.0	53.6	53.0	53.1	56.7
Rest of Europe	15.7	14.8	15.8	18.7	19.3	19.7	19.8
Canada	1.5	1.6	1.3	1.3	1.3	1.2	1.2
United States	11.2	11.9	10.9	9.6	9.5	9.4	7.9
Rest of America	2.0	1.4	2.3	3.0	3.0	2.9	2.7
Africa	5.9	5.4	5.6	5.5	5.5	5.5	4.5
Asia	6.6	8.1	7.8	7.9	7.9	7.9	7.1
Australia	0.4	0.3	0.5	0.4	0.4	0.4	0.1
Total	*100.0*	*100.0*	*100.0*	*100.0*	*100.0*	*100.0*	*100.0*
Freight traffic[b]							
EU[c]	25.3	25.0	25.5	21.2	22.5	24.1	22.9
Rest of Europe	5.9	5.8	5.3	7.6	7.7	7.6	6.8
Canada	1.0	2.4	2.7	2.4	2.5	2.1	2.2
United States	26,3	24.8	24.2	24.6	24.4	25.1	25.6
Rest of America	3.2	5.2	4.8	4.0	3.9	3.8	4.6
Africa	6.8	8.2	5.3	5.2	5.0	4.6	4.6
Asia	31.5	31.4	31.3	34.3	33.5	32.3	33.1
Australia	0.0	0.9	0.9	0.7	0.6	0.3	0.3
Total	*100.0*	*100.0*	*100.0*	*100.0*	*100.0*	*100.0*	*100.0*

[a] Passenger traffic is measured in number of air journeys to and from Germany.— [b] Freight traffic is measured in freight tons carried to and from Germany. — [c] Austria, Belgium, Denmark, Eire, Finland, France, Greece, Italy, Luxembourg, Nether-lands, Portugal, Spain, Sweden, and the United Kingdom were counted as members of the EU throughout the entire period 1980-1998.

Source: Own calculations according to Statistisches Bundesamt (various years).

Regarding air freight, the shares are more evenly distributed among continents: In 1998 roughly one third of air cargo was carried to and from Asia/Pacific, while another third was carried within Europe and a quarter on routes to and from North America.

Traffic Distribution among German Airports

The German airport system is characterized by a relatively wide geographical dispersion of airports throughout the country, reflecting the polycentric structure of the German economy. In 1997, a total of 28 airports provided services for scheduled flights (Figure 2.7). However, despite the great number of airports, traffic is concentrated at four airports, with Frankfurt/M., Munich, Düsseldorf and Berlin accounting for more than two thirds of all air traffic (measured in work load unit, WLU) to and from Germany in 1998 (Figure 2.8). The airport of Frankfurt/M. alone recorded 40 percent of total WLU in 1998, a share of about one third of all passengers traveling by air, and two thirds of all air freight handled in Germany.

Economic Impact of the Air Transport and Airport Industries

The *direct impact* of the air transportation system on the national economy may be demonstrated in terms of national accounts. In 1990, German air carriers and airports combined accounted for 0.5 percent of German GDP.[7] In 1996, the total workforce of airlines and airport companies combined accounted for approximately 66.000 employees, with another 135.000 persons employed at non-affiliated companies providing complementary services which were located at the airports' sites (ADV 1997: 137). This represented 0.5 percent of the national workforce.[8] Hence, on the national layer the direct impact may be regarded as being relatively small compared with other branches. At the regional level though, the direct contribution of the air transportation system to economic activity is in many cases very significant, especially for airports handling international traffic. For instance the Hamburg International Airport provides more than 12.000 jobs and is one of the largest companies in the region. In 1991, the Frankfurt airport ranked third in terms of the total number of workers employed at one place of work in Germany (Meier 1991: 48).[9]

Figure 2.7: Location of German Airports, which handled Scheduled Traffic in 1997

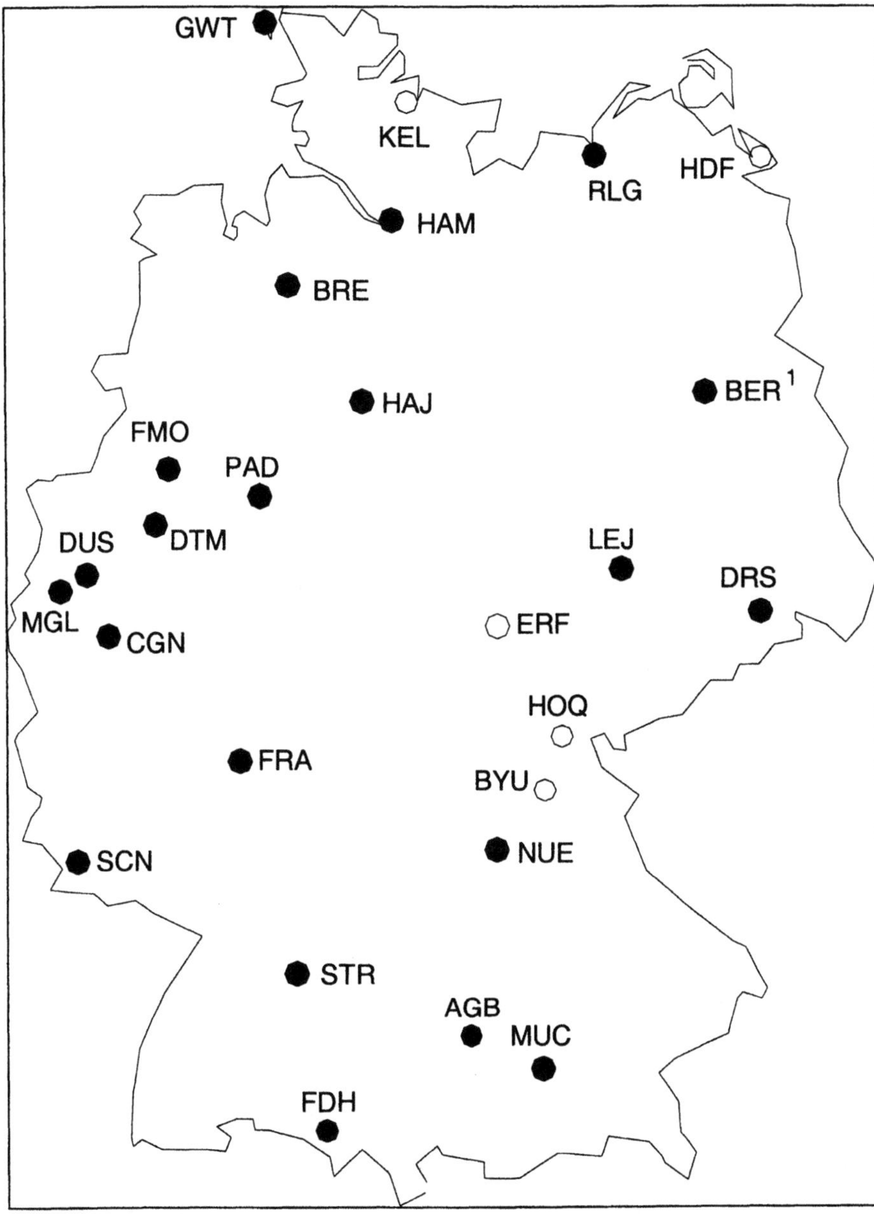

Source: ADV (1997: 11).

Figure 2.8: Market Shares of Airports in the German Airport System in 1998

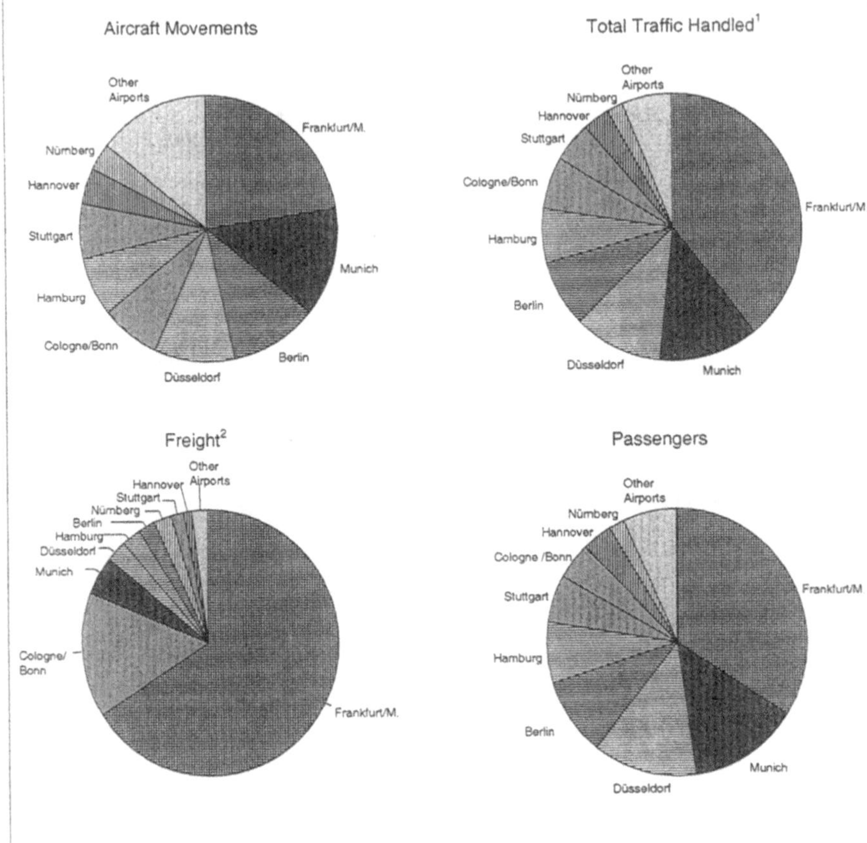

[1]Total Traffic Handled measured in Work Load Unit. - [2]Freight measured inTonnes.

Source: Own compilation according to Statistisches Bundesamt (1998).

The *indirect impact* of air transport on the national economy must be regarded to be far greater than is expressed in the above figures. The German economy is to a high degree export-oriented. Thus, accessibility of the world's goods and service markets by German firms as well as accessibility of Germany by foreign investors is a crucial determinant affecting the development of the national economy. The already growing importance of efficient air transport services for the economy as a whole is not only reflected by the fast growth of business travel, but also of air cargo, which could increase its share in trade in high valued goods substantially relative to other transport modes: In 1995 (as well as in 1980)

German air carriers transported only a share of 0.1 percent of German imports measured in cargo-tons, however the value of air cargo contributed 10 percent (1980: 7 percent) to total value of all imports.[10]

According to a number of studies which investigated the factors that determine the position of German regions within the process of locational competition for mobile capital, firms operating in dynamic international markets regard easy access to excellent air transport links among the most important locational factors when deciding on where to make direct investments.[11]

Demand and Supply of Air Transport and Airport Services

Air transport depends on complementary services provided by airlines and airports.[12] The operational characteristics of both industries as well as the characteristics of demand for their services all have a fundamental impact on the optimal design of national air transport policy. This sub-section outlines the relevant characteristics of demand for air travel and the economics of airlines and airports.

Demand for Air Transport Services Two broad classes of passengers have to be distinguished according to their travel purposes: Business and leisure travelers. In the early 1990s, nearly two thirds of all passengers on flights originating at German airports were business travelers, while in domestic services their share was reported to be even higher, at around 85 percent (Baum and Weingarten 1992: 14).

The demand for air services of *business travelers* is often characterized by an urgent need for travel to distinct locations at rather short notice; while their travel expenses are typically not borne personally, but by their companies. Therefore, this demand tends to be relatively inelastic with respect to price, while it usually reacts more sensitively to non-price features, such as frequency and reliability of airline' services, and whether the destination to which the traveler has to fly can be reached by direct flights or only by connecting ones. All of these features have an impact on the time span, which is needed to reach the final destination. (Table 2-6).

Table 2-6: Ranking of Determining Factors of Carrier Choice by Business Travelers

Rank	Factor	Index[b]	Rank	Factor	Index[b]
1	Schedule	8,27	7	Cabin Staff	6,38
2	Safety	8,03	8	Advance Seat Selection	6,33
3	Punctuality	7,22	9	Cheapest Avail. Fare	5,54
4	Comfort and Legroom	6,84	10	Lounge Access	5,45
5	Efficient Check-In	6,79	11	Onboard Food/Drink	5,25
6	Frequent Flyer Scheme	6,59			

[a] Data based on the views of 5.250 business travelers worldwide. Their countries of residence were: USA (17 percent), Australia (12 percent), Italy (12 percent), France (10 percent), Germany (10 percent), Japan (9 percent), Hong Kong (8 percent) and Singapore (8 percent). – [b] On a scale from 0 to 10 points.

Source: Airline Business (July 1997:67).

Not only because of the low price elasticity of business travel, but also because business passengers tend to travel considerably more often than leisure passengers do, the market for business travel generates revenue substantially above the average and is therefore very attractive to airlines. Lufthansa, for example, has stated that around two thirds of all business travelers flying on that airline in the mid-1980s took at least 5 flights per year, and, although they represented only 8 percent of that carrier's customers, they generated more than 20 percent of its revenue (Grande 1985: 40).[13]

In order to give business travelers incentives to use the services of a specific carrier (or network) repeatedly in a longer period of time, most airlines offer their customers loyalty bonus schemes. Regular customers either get volume-based price discounts or various non-price benefits of frequent-flyer programs (FFPs). Because the transfer of such benefits between different passengers (or at least between different firms) is typically prohibited, FFPs may create a lock-in effect and tie members of those schemes to dedicated airlines and their respective route networks. As a result, those airlines get a competitive advantage vis-à-vis rivals that offer the most frequent flights and the greatest number of connections at the respective airports, and hence give travelers the biggest opportunities to earn bonus miles.

In contrast, most *leisure travelers* privately bear their travel expenses, and usually are far more flexible in planning their journey. They may even have a choice among different destinations which may serve a given travel purpose. Since they travel, on average, less frequently than business passengers do, the airlines' loyalty schemes are of minor importance to them when deciding on which carrier to fly. For all these reasons, leisure travelers attribute the highest priority to low fares when choosing the airline, and even when deciding on the transport mode to use (Table 2-7).[14]

Table 2-7: Ranking of Determining Factors of Transport Mode and Carrier Choice by German Leisure Travelers

Rank	Factor	Rank	Factor
1	Cheapest price	5	Comfort of travel
2	Accessibility	6	Quality of baggage handling
3	Speed of travel	7	Safety
4	Schedule		

Source: Baum und Weingarten (1992: 14).

Transport needs of *freight forwarders* differ according to the type of cargo to be shipped. Perishable cargoes or goods with short life cycles are rather price insensitive, but depend on a high quality of service. Short travel times and a great number of connections rank among the most important determinants of demand, with the latter gaining further importance the more geographically dispersed the forwarders' transport needs are: Dealing with just a few air service providers, with each of them operating on a large geographical scale not only tends to reduce transaction costs of creating sustainable logistical networks, but also leads to higher transport volumes shipped by each of the carriers, thereby facilitating negotiations with carriers on rate discounts and quality upgrades with respect to cargo handling. In contrast, freight forwarders who do not depend on the speed of transport but more on a reliable just-in-time delivery of cargo to their customers, may be more flexible when choosing among different transport modes and carriers, and hence are more price sensitive.

Airline Operations One of the key features of the *airline industry* is the existence of integrated route networks centering on one or a few hubs, which serve as interchange points for connecting traffic. The prominent role which hub-and-spoke systems have gained in air transport is due to factors on the supply as well as on the demand side of transportation. First, the production of air transport services is characterized by considerable economies of aircraft size. This means that (in general) the larger the aircraft employed for a given flight is, the lower will be the average costs per available seat-km provided on that flight (Doganis 1991: 144 ff.). However, this technical effect will only be transformed into real cost advantages for airlines if they manage load factors to be sufficiently high to compensate for the higher costs of employing larger aircraft. In order to reach high load factors, airlines consolidate traffic from various directions ('spokes') on 'hubs' by networking of routes, by this way realizing economies of scope and traffic density, which may be transformed into a cost advantage vis-à-vis rivals.[15] When designing their route networks, airlines usually take into account complementary routes by other carriers (including those that are engaged in ground transportation) which my serve as feeder links for the hub. As has already been mentioned, the group of high-yield passengers is particularly inclined to a carrier with short travel times. Hence, the efficiency of a hub operation depends not at least on the 'connectivity rate' of the hub, which is the number of connections available to passengers within a certain time span.

Second, by means of consolidation of traffic at hubs airlines might be able to serve markets which do not generate enough OD traffic to make operation viable for direct travel and cargo shipping on a stand alone basis, but whose operation may become remunerative if they are additionally used by connecting passengers and transshipped cargo from other spokes of the network. Therefore, hubbing helps airlines to acquire more traffic and to reach a bigger size of their networks which may (although economies of scale are of minor importance in the airline industry)[16] be transformed into a competitive advantage because it makes marketing strategies like frequent flyer programs more effective. The attractiveness of such programs for travelers does not only depend on the benefits offered to regular customers but also on the size and geographical scope of the network covered by bonus schemes. The more connections an airline is able to offer to its customers, the more likely it is that she can meet the demand preferences of a maximum number of travelers by a highly attractive variety of destinations, making it for the traveler easier and more convenient to deal just with a single or a few airlines.

Third, hub-and-spoke networks might also enable airlines to provide higher frequencies than would otherwise be economically justified and therefore to attract more high yield traffic because of the same economies of density effect as mentioned before.

However, hubbing may also cause some disadvantages to airlines: First, passengers normally prefer direct flights to connecting flights, not only because connecting flights usually require more time for the whole journey than direct flights do but also because flight connections might be missed and baggage might be lost when changing planes. Therefore, time-sensitive passengers are often willing to pay a fare premium for direct flights, which represents the airlines' opportunity costs of offering only connecting ones. Second, the efficient operation of a large hub requires fine-tuned flight schedules in order to minimize passengers' connecting times at the hub airport, and also might lead to periods of considerable traffic peaks which require an extensive size of ground handling facilities which are underutilized at off-peak times.

Airport Operations Although several studies estimating cost structures of airports exist, there is no clear evidence as to whether economies of scale are of any significance in the airport industry.[17] A recent empirical study by Doganis et. al. (1995) provides empirical evidence that average costs of airport operation decrease as long as the volume of traffic handled does not exceed five million work load units per year, however, they fail to distinguish between economies of scale and those of traffic density.[18] In fact, whether economies of scale can be exploited by an airport operator depends not at least on the location of the airport's site: Near the center of an urban agglomeration the costs of capacity expansion can often be expected to be prohibitively high due to high opportunity costs of land use and environmental damage. At a location more distant from the center these costs will usually be considerably lower. Hence, a general answer to the question if economies of scale exist is not possible.

However, since most of the costs of airport operation are fixed in the short term, there is no doubt that considerable economies of traffic density exist in this industry as long as an airport has not reached its declared capacity at least at times of peak traffic: As long as an airport remains underutilized, almost any additional traffic will lower average costs of operating the infrastructure facility. But as an airport gets more and more overloaded, diseconomies of traffic density might occur, not only with regard to direct costs of airport operation, but also with regard to those costs which airport customers have to bear: A delayed flight will not only entail discomfort for passengers of that flight, but the delay may spill over to other connections which are provided within the same route network. Therefore it may also generate costs for passengers riding on other spokes of the network. Furthermore, at higher levels of congestion airlines may find themselves forced to provide additional aircraft at that airport's site as a reserve in order to buffer delays and to guarantee seamless traffic flows within their route networks. As these strategies increase the carriers' costs of providing services at that airport, the airport may lose attractiveness especially for hub operations.

Not only the aggregate volume of traffic handled by an airport, but also traffic composition has a significant effect on airport unit costs. The higher the share of international passengers is, the higher are the average costs of airport operation. The reason is that handling international flights requires substantial additional terminal space for customs, health, immigration services and the like than operations for domestic flights.[19] However, higher average costs will be overcompensated by additional revenues. Average revenues increase even more with a rising share of international passengers than average costs because not only does revenue generated by shops and other concessions in the terminal area increases significantly as the throughput of international passengers increase, but also became the handling of international flights generates above-average revenue due to higher landing fees and other aeronautical charges (Doganis 1992: 52). Hence, it may be very appealing option for an airport to attract international traffic and especially to become a hub for international markets.

The chances of an airport to attract international traffic and may be to become even a hub's location depend on:

- The geographical location of the airport's site;
- The quality of its infrastructure services; and on
- Institutional factors.

Following high-yield passengers' preferences for direct flights, airlines prefer to perform their hub operations at airports, which are located in geographical areas with a high density of population and a high regional level of real income. At such locations, attractive direct flights can be offered to many business travelers without losing the (network-) advantage of hubbing.[20] In addition, an efficient hub operation requires short and timely connections, making both the declared minimum as well as the average connecting time likely to be realized important determinants of airlines' decisions on hub locations (ADV 1997: 56). Hence, the quality of infrastructure services is important for competition between airports for hub functions. The institutional framework is important in so far as regulations may restrict airports' ability to attract traffic, because airlines may lack adequate traffic rights to serve the airports they would prefer in the absence of regulation.[21]

In Europe the distances between the main hub airports which serve as main gateways for intercontinental traffic are rather modest, as has already been mentioned. Moreover, all major hubs are located in geographical areas with dense population and high-income levels. As Table 2-8 demonstrates, minimal and average connecting times at Frankfurt airport are comparable to those at other European gateways. Hence, the quality of service and, in particular, the regulatory framework under which air transport services are offered have to be regarded as the main determinants of competition among airports for connecting traffic.

Table 2-8: Minimum and Average Connecting Times at Major European Gateways

Airport	Pas. in 1996	Share of connecting passengers	Minimum connecting time (min.)		Aver. Con. time[a]
	(mill.)	(percent)	Intra-European	Inter-continental	(min.)
Amsterdam	27,7	40	40	50	200
Frankfurt/M.	38,7	48	45	45	133
London-Heathrow	56,0	35	45–60[b]	45–60[b]	170
München	15,7	15	35	35	94
Wien	9,1	20	30	30	120
Zürich	16,3	32	40	40	148

[a]Average connecting time refers only to operations of airlines operating a hub at the respective airport. – [b]Terminal 1: 45 minutes, Terminals 2 and 3: 60 minutes.

Source: ADV (1997: 56).

Regulatory Framework for Air Transport in Germany

The regulatory provisions for international and domestic air transport in Germany have changed remarkably during the last two decades. In the following sections a brief overview on the history and current state of affairs of the regulatory framework for air transport between Germany and the rest of the world, as well as for the domestic market will be presented.

International Air Transport to and from Germany In order to understand the implications of the design of national air transport policy for the direction of international traffic flows it is important to analyze the mutual interrelationship between the tightly regulated start-up system which emerged after World War II and still governs many international air transport routes on the one hand, and the meanwhile liberalized system within the European Union on the other. Hence, this chapter will describe the traditional regulatory system and the path to liberalization, which led to the current institutional setting.

The Traditional Regulatory System for Air Transport The regulation of *scheduled air transport services* can be traced back to the Chicago Conference of 1944, when representatives of fifty-two states met to discuss the future design of the institutional framework for world air transport. The participating states could not agree on the establishment of a multilateral market order for world air transport. Instead, the principle of sovereignty of the nations over the airspace of their countries, which had first been established by the Paris convention of 1914, was maintained.[22] The conference participants agreed on the definition of 'freedoms of the air' (Table 2-9). These freedoms define airlines' rights to provide air transport services. Within this framework only the 1st and 2nd freedom rights were granted on a multilateral basis according to the 'Transit Agreement' of 1944. The granting of 3rd and 4th freedom, and in particular of cabotage rights, became subject to bilateral negotiations between the states at each end of the route.[23] The exercise of 5th freedom and 7th freedom rights is also subject to bilateral air service agreements (ASAs), but represents a special case, because airlines which operate such services need permission from all three states which are linked by 5th freedom rights.

Usually, the task of negotiating the legal design of bilateral air transport relationships is performed by the national ministries of transport of the respective states. In Germany the responsibility lies at the Federal Ministry of Transport. Although the Chicago conference of 1944 has led to the creation of the International Civil Aviation Organization (ICAO) as a supra-national institutional body to deal with issues of international air transport, its authority was (and is still) limited as a forum to discuss mainly technical aspects of the provision of air transport such as security standards.

Table 2-9: International Air Transport Freedom Rights

Freedom Rights	*Definition*
1st	the right of an airline of one country to fly over the territory of another country without landing
2nd	the right of an airline of one country to land in another country for non-traffic reasons, such as maintenance and refueling, while en route to another country
3rd	the right of an airline of one country to carry traffic from its country of registration to another country
4th	the right of an airline of one country to carry traffic from another country to its own country of registration
5th	the right of an airline of one country to carry traffic between two countries outside its own country of registration as long as the flight originates or terminates in its own country of registration.
6th	the right of an airline of one country to carry traffic between two foreign countries via its own country of registration (this is a combination of third and fourth freedoms)
7th	the right of an airline to operate stand-alone services entirely outside the territory of its home state , to carry traffic between two foreign states
8th (cabotage)	the right of an airline to carry traffic between two points within the territory of a foreign state (cabotage)

Source: OECD (1997); ICAO (1998).

Two years after the Chicago conference the United States and the United Kingdom signed the so-called 'Bermuda (I) Agreement'. This agreement set the legal framework for the bilateral air transport relationship between both countries. It soon became, and still serves as, a prototype for ASAs throughout the world, including those, which were signed by Germany.

ASAs typically grant substantial economic rights which can be grouped into four categories (Kasper 1988: 50 ff.; Gillen 1997: 102 ff.):

- Designation,

- Market access,
- Capacity/frequency controls,
- Air fares approval.

For each of these categories there exists a great variety of possible arrangements. Designation refers to the number and identity of airlines that may serve a route. Existing arrangements range from very restrictive which allows for single designation of one airline to fully liberal agreements which allow any carrier to serve a route. Usually, the agreements limit foreign ownership of the designated airlines, and a majority stake has to be hold by domestic residents. This prevents third party circumvention of bilateral ASA provisions. In between these extreme cases, ASAs can be found which call for multiple, but nevertheless limited designation.

Market access defines traffic rights as well as specifies landing points. Almost all ASAs grant 3rd and 4th freedom rights. Therefore the restrictiveness of an ASA should be measured by 5th freedom, cabotage rights and the number of landing points the airlines can serve. The most restrictive ASAs are characterized by granting neither 5th freedom nor cabotage rights and by limiting access to only a single origin/destination point at each end of the route. Less restrictive ASAs provide for limited 5th freedom rights or/and multiple landing points in one or both respective countries. The most liberal ASAs give airlines open access to all airports in both countries, and do not only refrain from restricting 5th freedom traffic, but also grant the right of unrestricted cabotage to the airlines.

Capacity/Frequency Controls refer to the quantity of services that airlines can provide. Possible arrangements range from predetermination of capacity and frequency, normally with an equal share of both of the designated carriers on each route which is served under the terms of the ASA, to the complete absence of such controls. In between these extremes, agreements can be found which allow for an increase of capacity/frequency subject to regulatory approval. Sometimes a 'country of origin rule' is implemented, which restricts a government's disapproval to traffic originating in its own country.

In terms of fare setting, national authorities are legally responsible for the regulation of air fares under this regulatory framework. They usually delegate this task to the designated airlines, which use 'Tariff Conferences' organized by the International Air Transport Association (IATA) as a platform to negotiate air fares on their own. The respective national authorities usually approve the resulting airlines' agreements on air fares. Very restrictive ASAs call for strict agreement on airfares by all carriers serving the respective city pairs. Sometimes airlines are also obliged to pool revenues (Doganis 1991: 30 ff.). Relatively moderate ASAs are characterized in this respect by double disapproval of the governments in both countries that are linked under the terms of the ASA. This means that an air fare proposal will be automatically accepted as long as neither government rejects it. Liberal agreements do not contain any restriction on airline price competition.

Regulatory Reforms[24] In the late 1970's the traditional system of regulating international air transport by means of restrictive bilateral ASAs came under growing pressure from a number of sources, including:

- New developments in domestic air transport policy in the U.S. which spilled over to other countries including Germany;
- New competitive pressures by some Asian airlines; and
- The formation of the European Single Market extending the free-trade regime to services.

The new air transport policy of the United States rested on two closely related events. The first was the implementation of the US Airline Deregulation Act of 1978, which led to almost complete deregulation of the US domestic air transport market. The resulting competition led to productivity gains of US air carriers and fare reductions for travelers. The second event was the 1978 US Civil Aeronautics Board's (CAB) 'Show Cause Order' that proposed the withdrawal of anti-trust immunity for IATA air fares conferences. Initially, the CAB had threatened to prevent all airlines from participating in air fare coordination meetings for routes to and from the US. Subsequently this was limited to only US air carriers in return for approval to some liberalization of air fare setting by other states. In 1982 the US and the European Civil Aviation Conference (ECAC) agreed on a 'Memorandum of Understanding' which introduced flexibility in price setting for airlines operating on the North Atlantic market. This replaced strictly pre-approved air fares by 'air fare zones' within which air carriers were allowed to adjust prices without taking recourse to the IATA conferences and also without approval of national authorities.

The US government also searched for productivity gains in the international arena. They signed liberal ASAs with a few strategically located countries, which to a certain extent, pressured more restrictive states to agree to liberalization of their markets in order to prevent traffic diversion away from their air carriers and airports. In 1978 the United States and the Netherlands signed a new ASA which was intended to reduce the role of governments in matters of capacity, frequency and air fares, and which gave the airlines from both countries the freedom to engage in effective price and capacity competition. Similar ASAs were signed between the U.S. and Germany and Belgium. Both granted air carriers of these countries more landing points and extensive 5th freedom rights including 'break of gauge rights', that allowed the airlines to change from a larger to a smaller aircraft in the other countries territory on a through service (Doganis 1991: 55 and 1993: 52).[25] However, cabotage still was (and is) not allowed.

Because US airlines could leverage their sizeable domestic market to feed international flights, European carriers, including Lufthansa lost considerable market share in the North Atlantic market. In addition, these airlines came under growing pressures by some Asian airlines which did not participate in the IATA air fare conferences but were able to offer high quality services at relatively low fares and thus compete successfully against their European counterparts.

Additional pressure resulted from the progress of European economic integration. With the formation of the Internal European Market the free trade regime was extended to transport services. The traditional system of tight regulation of air carriers' access to intra-European air transport markets could no longer be upheld and had to be replaced by a more liberal one.

As a consequence of these pressures, intra-EU air transport has been gradually liberalized since the mid-1980s. In 1984, Germany and the United Kingdom signed a new ASA, which gave the designated air carriers of both countries freedom to engage in limited price competition and also granted the airlines more landing points in each country. The results were a decline of prices of 'advance-purchase' discount tickets, the introduction of the business class as a new product of air carriers, and new services from airports which had not been served before (Sichelschmidt and Wolf 1993: 169 ff.). Since 1987, the European Commission implemented three 'Liberalization Packages'. These packages brought about a gradual removal of regulations with respect to price, market access and capacity/frequency. In 1993 international air transport between EU countries was almost completely liberalized. In 1997 all cabotage restrictions were also removed. Since then, EU air carriers have been granted all air freedom rights within the EU.

In the 1990's the German government took also steps to liberalize ASAs with some other countries outside the EU, particularly with some countries of the former East Bloc. Moreover, in April 1996 a new 'Open Sky-' ASA was signed with the United States. This agreement granted unlimited market access to international routes between these countries and total freedom in price setting. However, these agreements fell short of granting cabotage rights. With this movement towards liberalization, about 80 percent of international air traffic to and from Germany (measured in terms of passengers) must now be regarded as being freed from tight regulatory controls (ADV 1997: 67).

Likewise, nine other European countries signed open skies-agreements with the U.S. between 1992 and 1995, among them Austria, Belgium, Denmark, Finland, Iceland, Luxembourg, Norway, Sweden, and Switzerland. Talks between the United States and the U.K. on an open skies-agreement are underway as a prerequisite for the proposed British Airways-American Airlines alliance (Oum 1998: 128).

In contrast to the scheduled air transport sector, air charter services between Germany and other Western European countries had been governed by fairly liberal regimes since the 1950s. These regimes were based on the ECAC 'Multilateral Agreement on Commercial Rights in European Air Charter Services' of 1956. This agreement granted charter air carriers unrestricted access to foreign markets as long as there would be no conflict with the interests of the scheduled carriers. The German flag carrier Lufthansa was, and still is, engaged in charter operations through its subsidiary Condor, which is one of Germany's biggest operators of charter flights. This liberal stance helped to evolve a dense network of air charter links from Germany mainly to Greece, Portugal and Spain, which are prime destinations for German tourists. Charter air traffic gained a significant market share especially in the Western European air transport market, with 45 percent of all passengers on routes between Germany and other EU-countries carried on charter flights in 1993. Since the liberalization of the intra-EU air transport market for scheduled services, some charter airlines are also engaged in scheduled markets, mainly by selling single seats on frequently operated flights which predominantly serve package-tour markets.

As a result of the liberalization steps taken on various markets, international air transport to and from German is now governed by two fundamentally different regulatory regimes with respect to different geographical areas of the world. While Intra-European and also North Atlantic air traffic to and from Germany is now almost completely liberalized (North Atlantic and Eastern Europe bilaterally), German air transport relationships with other parts of the world are still subject to more or less tight regulation.

Domestic Air Transport and Airport Sector Domestic air transport in Germany was also subject to tight economic regulation until the end of the 1980s.[26] As in many other countries, the national air transport policy aimed at protecting Lufthansa as the state-owned flag carrier both on international markets and on domestic routes. Other carriers were not allowed to operate services within the national borders. Furthermore, air fares were subject to approval by the Federal Ministry of Transport. This transport policy enabled Lufthansa to cross-subsidize unprofitable routes between regions which only generate low density air traffic. In fact, this policy resulted in a state-protected monopoly for Lufthansa as the sole provider of scheduled air service within Germany.[27]

The tight domestic policy was terminated in 1988 though the regulatory system in a legal sense remained intact: Aero Lloyd and German Wings were designated as additional providers of domestic air services in addition to Lufthansa. Though legally the Federal Ministry of Transport is still responsible for regulation of German air traffic, it has since then refrained from exercising its regulatory powers. De facto, domestic air transport is now completely liberalized. After German reunification the special political status of Berlin was abolished and restrictions for German airlines to serve this city were removed.

In order to prevent abuse of monopoly power by airport authorities, landing fees of German airports are subject to price regulation by the transport ministries of the Länder. German regulatory provisions do not legally bind regulators to use specific regulatory procedures when deciding on airport charges. However, the Länder as regulators have agreed to sign a memorandum which recommends base regulatory decisions on airports costs (Arbeitsgruppe Verwaltung und Recht 1980). Hence, in practice airport regulation takes the form of cost-plus regulation, thus giving the airport authorities little incentives to reduce costs.

Not only prices, but also the allocation of the airports' runway capacity is under regulation. In order to ration scarce capacity at high density airports slots are allocated to the airlines according to a mechanism which is based on guidelines set by IATA.[28] A system of pre-specified priorities is used against which competing demands for slots are weighted. The most important of these priorities is the historical precedence ('grandfather right'). An airline having used a slot last year will receive it again in the future as long as it does not sacrifice it on a voluntary basis. Airlines are allowed to barter with slots, however, regular slot trading which involves monetary payments is not allowed. Because a slot cannot be capitalized when leaving a market, airlines are very reluctant to give up grandfather rights, not taking into account the social opportunity costs of their own operations. At the same time, potential entrants which do not already possess attractive slots cannot enter markets at high density airports. This limits potential competition on the air transport markets. For the same reason competition is also reduced between airports, as the prohibition to sell slots in combination with the opportunity to earn scarcity rents at regulated high density airports creates a lock-in effect for grandfather airlines (Wolf 1999).

Recent Trends in Air Transport Regulation and Operations

The last decade has brought about significant changes for air transport. Not only has steadily increasing demand led to severe problems of airport congestion, but also the regulatory framework under which airlines and airports operate has altered its character fundamentally as a result of the liberalization of major air transport markets in the world. Airlines have adopted new strategies to respond to these challenges.

Liberalization of Intra-EU Air Traffic and Accessibility of Foreign Hubs

As long as restrictive bilaterals governed intra-EU air transport the accessibility of the majority of German airports for foreign airlines was heavily restricted for several reasons: First, as German air transport policy aimed at supporting Lufthansa, foreign air carriers rarely got traffic rights to link secondary German airports to their hubs. The sample of specified landing points for which 3rd and 4th freedom rights were granted was rather limited. Second, capacity restrictions in an ASA typically did not refer to single routes but regulated capacity on all air transport links between the two countries. Accordingly, airlines of the trading partner which would have liked to develop a new route often had to reduce capacities on already existing links in order not to violate overall capacity restrictions. In practice, this proved to be a high barrier to develop new transborder air transport links. Third, 5th freedom rights were seldom granted to foreign airlines. This limited opportunities to connect secondary airports of Germany to foreign hubs in third countries as a sequel of already existing international flights and thus to build efficient networks. By these restrictions, national air transport policy aimed at preventing diversion of connecting traffic away from Frankfurt as the main gateway for international traffic from and to Germany, and to support Lufthansa as the national 'flag carrier'.

The liberalization of intra-EU air transport gave airlines new opportunities to restructure their networks and to develop new routes. Especially new entrants were, and still are, very active in developing new air transport links by direct flights between secondary airports and also between secondary airports and foreign hubs. This gives connecting passengers more opportunities to choose between alternative transfer points (Boss, Laaser, Schatz et al. 1996: 152 f.). As a consequence of the new regime, flight frequencies between secondary airports in Germany and European hubs increased substantially. As high-yield passengers prefer high flight frequencies, the threat of traffic diversion has grown substantially. Hence competitive pressure between airlines' networks as well as between European hub airports has increased considerably.

The Emergence of Strategic Airline Alliances The last few years have seen the emergence of a growing number of strategic alliances between airlines from all around the globe which coordinate several aspects of their operations including the building of integrated networks which are operated by several partner airlines. According to Knorr (1998a: 79), the number of such agreements rose from approximately 200 in the year 1990 to 400 in 1996. More than half of all air carriers worldwide are said to be engaged in one or even several of such agreements.

Airline alliances differ with respect to the geographical area they cover as well as with respect to those aspects of production of air transport services on which the partner airlines cooperate. Regarding geography, big alliances involve airlines from several continents and therefore operate on a global scale. In 1997 the biggest alliances in terms of passenger traffic were 'Star Alliance' and 'One World', which each accounted for about one fifth of worldwide international passenger air traffic that year. Both alliances involve several European carriers, with British Airways, Deutsche BA, Finnair and Iberia all being members of One World, while the Star Alliance centers around the Lufthansa-United partnership with British Midland and SAS also being European members of Star. Other global alliances in which European airlines participated were the Delta-Swissair- and the KLM-Northwest-Group.

Smaller alliances concentrate on specific geographical areas, such as markets within Europe or even operate only in domestic markets. E.g. the Air France-Eurowings partnership was designed to feed traffic originating in Germany into Air France's hub at Paris, and the Lufthansa-Cimber Air partnership was designed to feed traffic from regional airports in Germany into Lufthansa's hub at Frankfurt/M.

While such agreements between airlines may cover several aspects of the airlines' logistics and distribution, at the heart of many alliances lies the objective of coordinating schedules and fares as well as marketing efforts. One of the key features of many alliances is code sharing which means that travel across the networks of several carriers is ticketed as if it would be one flight. Also travel on flights provided by only one partner of a codeshare agreement may be ticketed under the code of another partner airline. Another characteristic of many alliances is joint frequent flyer programs of the partner airlines.

What gives many alliances their strategic character is that they serve as means to open new markets for the partners by:

- Circumventing legal restrictions on market access;
- Making marketing strategies more effective by raising the size of the integrated network the partners serve; and

- Lowering costs for airline partners by generating favorable feeder relationships between airlines and increasing capacity utilization (i.e. load factors).

Code sharing may help to circumvent legal restrictions on market access because it allows carriers which do not hold traffic rights to benefit from the services provided by their code-share partners who have gained the needed market access rights. Selling seats on the partners' flights under one flight code is a way to get indirect market access, even if direct access is denied because of restrictive ASAs. Similarly, access to slot-controlled airports is made possible. As under current regulation airlines are not allowed to engage in monetarized slot trading, code sharing may sometimes be the only way for airlines who do not possess attractive slots at congested airports to start economically viable services.

Alliances may make marketing strategies of carriers more effective for several reasons. First, as has already been stated, a larger network offered by an airline also increases the attractiveness of its frequent-flyer program and therefore might generate additional high yield traffic. Second, because code sharing allows carriers to sell seats under their own code on flights that are operated by their partners, they can offer higher frequencies and more direct flights than would otherwise be possible so that even more additional traffic might be attracted. And third, the partners' co-operation with respect to the design of through fares might avoid the problem of double monopolization, thereby allowing them to offer more attractive fares and earn higher revenue.[29]

Alliances may also lower the costs of provision of air transport services as a consequence of joint purchase, maintenance and capacity planning and close coordination of flight schedules. Furthermore, they enable airlines operating predominantly on either an intercontinental or a regional scale to exploit economies of traffic density without setting up their own feeder operations, so that each partner can concentrate on those operations which can be offered at a comparative advantage. Closely related to this, vertical alliances may help to reduce transaction costs which otherwise might occur if upstream and downstream production of connecting transport services are both integrated into one firm. Intra-firm integration of vertically linked services typically results in low-powered incentives for employees whose relationships are governed by internal control mechanisms instead of the mechanisms of the market.

To sum up, airline alliances may help to enhance the efficiency of the production of air transport services by the partners, give them a competitive advantage vis-à-vis non-alliance affiliated air carriers, and enable airlines to gain access to markets which would otherwise be denied to them because of legal or economic barriers.

Airport Congestion The steady growth of demand for air transport as well as the concentration of air traffic at a few main airports has led to severe capacity constraints at many European airports. According to a study by the Stanford Research Institute (1990), sixteen of the major European airports are already congested at least at times of peak demand or will reach complete capacity utilization in the next decade. The nature of the problem is not uniform across airports. While some airports suffer from congestion because of inadequate apron and terminal capacity, others are burdened with lack of runway capacity. Operational restrictions, which are due to apron and terminal shortages, would in general not pose big problems to overcome. Expanding the capacity of runway systems may be much more difficult because of strong political opposition based on environmental considerations. In Germany, runway capacity is almost operated at its declared limit for most of the day at Frankfurt/M. and Düsseldorf.[30] These airports are suffering from negative economies of traffic density.

General Assessment of Bilateral Regulation

In essence, the function of bilateral air service agreements is to regulate international air transport in order to prevent alleged sector-specific market failures on air transport markets and/or to generate rents for the national economies by a strategic trade policy approach. This section will analyze

- If there is a need to regulate air transport markets on the grounds of the public interest to be protected against inefficient outcomes on deregulated markets, and, if so, if the bilateral policy approach represents an appropriate means to control for market failures; and
- The prospects of success of a strategic trade policy approach in terms of social welfare of the national economy in general and with special regards to Germany. The analysis is based on a qualitative assessment rather than on a comprehensive formal analysis, although it will, in particular with regards to the analysis of the prospects of a strategic air transport policy encompass some modeling of social welfare effects of bilateral regulation, thus paving the way for the comprehensive econometric modeling that will be presented in the succeeding chapters.

We will start with the introduction of the proposed kinds of general arguments in favor of regulating international air transport. Then we will turn to the question whether liberalized air transport markets tend to fail to produce efficient outcomes, and whether bilateral air service agreements are an appropriate policy tool to prevent the proposed market failures. Later on, the prospects of success of a strategic air transport policy will be assessed.

Arguments for Regulating Trade in Air Transport Services

Proponents of regulation of international air transport markets usually raise four main arguments in favor of the system of bilateral air transport agreements:

- First, liberalized air transport markets would fail to realize the maximum of potential benefits to the national economies. Instead air transport markets are supposedly tending to become monopolized by a few airlines which might then exploit their powerful market positions to the detriment of consumers and other sectors of the national economies;
- Second, because access to international air transport links is essential for the well-being of a national economy, air transport policy must prevent any dependency of the nation on the behavior of foreign airlines. Hence, it is claimed, that the operation of a resident carrier is essential for ensuring high-quality access to international markets. Support of the national airline is said to be necessary to guarantee the ongoing participation of the 'flag carrier' in international aviation.[31]
- Third, it is said that bilaterals may offer policy makers opportunities to support their respective national carriers and airports in competition on international markets, although typically at the expense of the trading partners, and hence to generate rents for the national economies.
- A fourth argument asserts that even in those cases where full liberalization of international air transport would be superior in terms of national social welfare, a country may use its sovereignty over the national airspace as a powerful bargaining tool within the framework of bilateral negotiations over traffic rights. By this means rent dilution may be prevented which might otherwise occur if the trading partners support their own national airlines. Hence, bilaterals might create a balance of bargaining power with regard to international air transport affairs.

While the first two arguments aim at correcting market failures, the third and the fourth ones aim at the exploitation of the countries' sovereignty over their respective national airspaces in order to generate or to protect rents for the national economies and thus are motivated by strategic reasons.

Correcting Market Failures through Bilateral Agreements?

Among the two arguments in favor of ASAs as means to correct for sector-specific market-failures, only the first one, i.e. the presumed need for bilaterals as a tool for ensuring competition will be discussed here. The second one, i.e. the alleged indispensability of a national flag carrier as a means of maintaining competitive countervailing power in international air transport can immediately be rejected if competition on air transport markets is assessed to be workable: Even if a country would, in a multi-country open market setting, import all of its air transport services, it would not become subject to monopolistic exploitation by foreign carriers as long as it would ensure open access to all its transport links to foreign destinations to all suppliers willing to enter the markets. Keeping this in mind, we can turn to the first argument.

The appropriateness of ASAs for correcting market failures can be assessed by answering two interrelated questions. First, do fully deregulated air transport markets tend to produce inefficient market outcomes? Second, if the first answer would be 'yes', are bilaterals an adequate tool to correct for market failures? The first question may be answered by referring to the results of the deregulation of domestic US air transport markets under the Airline Deregulation Act 1978, and of the liberalization of the intra-EU aviation markets.

Experiences with deregulated air transport markets Although the deregulation of US air transport after 1978 was limited to domestic markets it may serve as a blueprint for liberalization of cross-border air transport, given the geographical extension of the country, the distances flown in air traffic, and the market size in economic terms (supply, demand and network served). To a certain extent, it has actually been the prime blueprint for European liberalization, when the EU made up its mind to open air transport markets among its member states from 1988 onwards.[32]

When by virtue of the Airline Deregulation Act of 1978 barriers to entry to, and exit from domestic US routes as well as former price regulation were abolished, operators and even some economists feared that market performance and safety records would deteriorate substantially. However, deregulation largely proved to be a success story, although not all problems had been be solved, and new ones appeared.

A variety of advantageous market trends and developments have supported the success of deregulation:[33]

- The number of carriers active in the US market has nearly doubled since deregulation, with an improved division of labor between trunk, regional and commuter carriers, and despite a high failure ratio of more than 70 percent for new carriers.
- The overwhelming majority of passengers can now make use of discount tickets being priced, on average, at less than one third of

standard fares. Fares for the average passenger have substantially decreased in real terms.

- Capacity utilization levels of planes have increased from around 50 to more than 70 percent.
- Route networks in the single carriers' perspective and in an aggregate perspective have become more dense and more efficient, partly because of a restructuring of route-networks (particularly as a consequence of the emergence of powerful hub-and-spoke systems), and partly because of co-operation between different groups of carriers.
- Costs of air transport have decreased substantially. Due to market entry of low cost carriers which have forced incumbents to cut their own costs and improve their productivity, labor costs have been cut by introducing two-tier wage scales (different scales for newly hired and for incumbent personnel) or by changing compensation packages.
- The long-term trend of decreasing accident and fatality rates, which could be observed since the 1960s, has continued after deregulation in 1978. Moreover, the lead of US carriers against the average of all other carriers has remained stable, though the majority of other carriers is much less subject to competitive pressures than US carriers are. Even US regional and commuter carriers, being a source of some safety concern in the past, have meanwhile improved their safety records (Knorr (1997: 112 ff.)).

In contrast to the clear advantages of deregulation, some critics point to a crucial shortcoming which, according to their assessment, might call for certain re-regulation of US air transport: Although aggregate market shares, which measure the degree of market concentration at the national plane, decreased in the first years after deregulation, they rose again in the late 1980s and the 1990s. The share of the largest 8 carriers was 1994: 97 percent of aggregate passenger miles compared to 80 percent in 1978. Throughout the last two decades a series of mergers happened decreasing the number of actual competitors. Furthermore, concentration has also increased at certain hub airports, and there is strong evidence, that air fares for direct flights to and from airports that are dominated by one or two carriers are higher than on other routes (e.g. Borenstein 1992).[34] Critics fear that air transport might end in a narrow oligopoly with weak competitive pressures which would enable incumbents to exert market power, to drive out outsiders and to earn monopoly or cartel rents.

However, the relevance of increased concentration at the national as well as at the airport level to future air transport market performance in the

U.S. may be questioned. Due to the rather small amount of sunk investments which are required at the route level, OD air transport markets are to a high degree contestable by potential competitors as long as market entry is not prevented by administrative barriers.[35] Furthermore, regional disparities in fares ('hub pricing') may reflect a spatially efficient Ramsey-price pattern for complex networks:[36] As competition between different connecting links serving the same OD-markets but operated by different carriers is subject to fierce price competition, carriers might be forced to price these services at short-run marginal costs, while higher air fares for direct flights to and from hubs have to ensure break even of the operation of the integrated network as a whole (Spiller 1989, Kleit 1992). Thus, spatial price differentiation might be expected as an outcome of workable competition at the network level, ensuring stability of efficient route networks.[37] Hence, observation of spatial price differentiation alone is not sufficient to claim market failure. Instead, competition between whole networks rather than between single routes may be the appropriate focus to assess whether deregulation has failed to prevent customers from being monopolistically exploited by air carriers.

The reluctance of US authorities to grant cabotage rights to foreign carriers, which has explicitly been justified by the argument that the large market would enable foreign carriers to build up large networks in the domestic market (Kasper 1988: 88 f.) is clearly at odds with a systematic incontestability of major US carriers' networks. Cabotage rights for foreign carriers would be an additional potential for competitive pressure.

Notwithstanding these qualifications, a high degree of concentration on the national plane might affect competition between carriers as it raises the number of multi-market contacts of the same airlines on different markets. This, in turn, may raise the probability that carriers (implicitly) engage in collusive action (Evans and Kesssides 1994). Moreover, marketing strategies like frequent flyer programs, bonus schemes for travel agents and biased screens of computer reservation systems (CRSs) may raise barriers to entry that potential newcomers' have to face, thus reducing competitive pressures for incumbents. Additional sources of market power might result from the scarcity of slots at high density airports and, probably even more relevant, the scarcity of gates at airport terminals. The limited availability of infrastructure facilities, in combination with the control of these resources by incumbents,[38] reduces contestability of air transport markets. However, these problems do not suggest that deregulation was not successful, but, instead, that deregulation has to be accompanied by effective competition policy measures.

The favorable US experience is largely mirrored by evidence from the effects of liberalization of European air transport markets. European countries in general as well as Germany in particular have likewise witnessed improved air transport at lower costs and prices, as described below:[39]

- The aggregate number of links has increased. This is particularly true for links on which new entrants, former charter carriers or newly founded companies started services in the market, and for links from secondary airports to other member countries;
- Standard fares remained largely unaffected, but fares for discount tickets decreased substantially;
- Market entry by former charter carriers or entirely new firms could be observed on several links, for the major part on newly served routes but also on routes of incumbent flag carriers;
- Flight frequencies have increased on a variety of routes; and
- Former flag carriers have significantly improved productivity.

As in the U.S., potentially adverse effects on competition may be expected from the increasing importance of frequent-flyer programs of incumbents, bonus schemes of travel agents, biased screen of CRSs, and the scarcity of slots at congested airports in combination with the existence of grandfather rights.[40] However, with regard to the first one, in some cases new competitors got access to FFP's of major European airlines by means of co-operation. The role of bonus schemes might be expected to deteriorate in the future, as selling tickets by the internet is likely to become more popular. With regards to CRSs, the European commission has already implemented a code of conduct that limits abuse of CRS-ownership. In an overall view the European experience so far supports the hypothesis that liberalized air transport markets perform better than tightly regulated ones, although the problem of getting access to high-density airports by new entrants still remains.

Summing up, one may contend that competition on air transport markets, although not being perfect, is workable. Hence, there is no need for regulatory control on the grounds of sector-specific market failures. However, effective competition policy may be required to ensure the sustainability of the favorable outcomes on liberalized markets.

Are bilaterals an adequate tool to correct market failures? As policy action may be required to ensure sustainability of competition in the long run, one may ask the second question, i.e. whether bilateral air service agreements are suited to serve as proper instruments of competition policy. Even apart of the high transaction costs that ASAs impose on international aviation[41], the answer to this question tends to be 'no', not only because of the high costs of administering the system of ASAs and especially the inherent inflexibility of bilaterals which typically cannot be quickly adjusted to rapidly changing market conditions, but also because of the growing globalization of the airline industry. The last topic may be demonstrated by referring to the example of global airline alliances.

Although global alliances may enhance the efficiency of air transport for the reasons described above, their long-term impact on competition and openness of world air transport markets is still not clear. On the one hand, growing concentration of world air traffic on a few groups of allied carriers may perhaps raise the probability of implicit collusion between alliances as a result of the enhanced number of multi-market contacts or by creating uncontested 'spheres of influence' of networks. On the other, vertical cooperation between carriers serving predominantly intercontinental resp. regional markets may also enhance competition between networks, as upstream and downstream carriers each depend on efficient feeder services provided by the respective partners, and also as cooperation enables smaller airlines to overcome problems of network size. Hence, with regards to the design of competition policy, potential adverse competitive effects of airlines' cooperation will have to be balanced against their merits for carriers and air transport users. This requires an institutional policy framework that is based to a high degree on a rule-of-reason approach instead of being dominated by per se-rules.

ASAs are not well suited to serve as measures of competition policy. What puts the need for effective control of international air transport markets at odds with the instrument of bilateral agreements is simply the fact, that alliances might help carriers to circumvent tight regulation of access to national air transport markets. It is highly improbable that bilaterals could be applied effectively to cope with perceived competitive problems arising from global alliances being partly formed to undermine their effectiveness. Accordingly, doubts can be raised whether bilateral agreements would be an appropriate tool to prevent competitors being driven out of the market, just because the history of most bilaterals is a story of protecting incumbent carriers against competition rather than protecting competition against incumbent carriers.

In addition, competition policy by means of bilaterals might create externalities on third parties and adverse incentives among market participants. Thus, the task of defining and executing competition policy for global air transport markets should better be centralized at a supra-national layer, for instance under the umbrella of the ICAO or of a newly founded 'liberalization club'. A club charter could provide rules and enforcement mechanism for any required competitive action, even for side-aspects which currently are still regulated in some bilaterals, such as slot allocation regimes or the structure of airport charges. Recent activities of the European Commission, for instance in defining a 'code of conduct' for non-discriminatory listing of flights in computer reservation systems, or in harmonizing the framework for airport charges, are steps in that direction, although they are limited to a regional scale. European legislation for the Single European Air Transport Market replaced bilaterals among member countries without leaving any gap. Accordingly, competencies for competition policy for global air transport markets could be allocated to a liberalization club.

Strategic Air Transport Policy as a Means to Generate Rents for the National Economy

The aim of a strategic air transport policy is to divert rents from foreign economic agents in the air transport business to domestic ones by supporting the various elements of the domestic air transport system at the expense of foreign airlines and airports. However, as will be shown in this section, any strategic air transport policy imposes social costs on the national economy. Hence, policy makers must carefully assess the net welfare effects when deciding on which policy action to take.

In order to fully understand the welfare implications of different market regimes (i.e. regulation vs. liberalization) the analysis presented in this section will take a disaggregated look at the effects of a strategic air transport policy and discuss welfare gains and losses of each affected group of agents separately. To assess the effects of regulation, the concept of 'social surplus' as a means to measure welfare effects will be deployed. Social surplus refers to profits of airlines and airports as well as to consumer rents of passengers and freight forwarders, but is not confined to these groups and takes also into account the effects on sectors (and regions) of the economy which are not directly participating in air transport.

Airlines provide their services within networks of many routes, which are usually closely interconnected with each other. They do not only compete on single OD markets, but also across networks which typically consist of a variety of city pairs. Hence, the question arises how to define the relevant market. This will be done, for the sake of the following detailed welfare analysis, by defining an air transport market as a single city ('OD'-) pair. Thereby it is made possible to investigate the effects of strategic regulation of air transport markets at the route level as well as to take into account network effects in subsequent steps of the analysis. An OD-market comprises both direct and connecting flights; with passengers and freight forwarders taking connecting flights have to make a stopover or a transshipment operation at a transfer point en route.

As was already discussed, German air transport is currently governed by two fundamentally different market regimes. In order to fully understand the implications of the co-existence of both regimes for the optimal design of national air transport policy, the following analysis will be conducted in three steps:

- First, the general welfare effects of regulation will be discussed assuming that market structures are 'exogenous': A market structure is called to be exogenous if public authorities on either end of the link have, by virtue of the respective air service agreement, complete control of all traffic flows between a city pair. Thus policy makers can block any market entry, and no traffic diversion occurs. For instance, exogenous market structures result from the traditional system of very restrictive Bermuda-type bilaterals with single designation and limited access to secondary landing points, and without granting 5th-freedom or cabotage rights to any of the carriers operating in the relevant markets. As long as almost all international world air traffic was governed by air service agreements of the very restrictive kind, the structure of German international air transport markets could roughly be described as exogenous, although some traffic diversion away from the German hub Frankfurt/Main occurred via ground transportation and also via a limited access of foreign carriers to secondary airports based on 3rd/4th freedom rights.
- However, since intra-EU air transport markets have been almost completely liberalized under the Single Market Program, not only German airlines but air carriers from all EU-countries have unlimited access to all airports in Germany. Furthermore, some EU-members have already liberalized, or might in the future liberalize air transport links to countries outside the EU as well. Hence, the threat of traffic diversion in international markets has become much more serious for the German air transport system. Accordingly, the second step of the analysis is devoted to the analysis of the repercussions that the co-existence of different market regimes yields with respect to the optimal design of the national air transport policy. The framework for analysis will be labeled 'endogenous market structures': A market structure is called to be endogenous if traffic flows within an OD-market are not under full control by the bilateral in question. Thus traffic diversion might happen as a result of market entry and output expansion by airlines whose actions are not directly governed by the terms of the respective air service agreement.
- In the subsequent section, we will apply the results and conclusions derived so far to the German case, investigating the degree of endogenity of German air transport market structures by presenting

some pieces of empirical evidence for the actual threat of traffic diversion. This will pave the way for the latter comprehensive econometric analysis that is done in the following chapters.

The modeling that is done at steps 1 and 2 of the analysis is based on the concepts of the new strategic trade theory, recognizing that international air transport markets are imperfectly contestable.[42] In addition we borrow deeply from the work of Brueckner et. al. (1992 and 1994) with regards to the analysis of network effects on air transport markets.

In order to concentrate on the main economic forces that affect the ultimate outcomes of a restrictive air transport policy, the first two stages of the analysis will present a rather stylized picture of the economic and institutional conditions in air transport, which partly abstracts from some basic features of real air transport markets and policies. The following four assumptions will hold throughout the entire analysis:

- First, consumers regard connecting flights to be inferior substitutes to direct ones. Furthermore, non-price preferences for certain carriers might exist.[43]
- Second, strategic policy actions take place without inducing any transaction costs on aviation: Existing bilaterals can be redesigned, even unilaterally, at any time and without any direct administrative costs as well as without any monitoring costs with respect to the enforcement of bilaterals. Furthermore, the mere discretion which might be executed by policy makers does not affect the unconstrained output decisions of the airlines, because it is assumed that none of the airlines' costs are sunk.
- Third, airports are not capacity constrained; i.e. they can accommodate all traffic that will be generated as a result of regulation.
- Fourth, only one price prevails in an OD-market; i.e. different prices for business and leisure travelers as well as different prices charged by different air carriers will not be considered although in practice they may be sustainable as air transport services provided by different air carriers on the same route are not perfect substitutes.

These assumptions will be abandoned in the succeeding step 3 of the analysis, which refers to real air transport markets.

Exogenous Market Structures in Air Transport

As no threat of traffic diversion exists within a framework of exogenous market structures, it is appropriate to limit the analysis of the social welfare effects of strategic regulation first to the case of two countries, from which one represents the 'home country', and the other is called the 'foreign country'. Only one airport is located in each of these countries. It is assumed that two airlines provide services in the relevant market, with one of them being registered in the home country and the other in the foreign country. The former is called the 'flag carrier', and the later the 'foreign airline'. Air transport between both countries is governed by single designation; accordingly, profits of the two airlines do not induce entry by competitors. Within this framework, it will be analyzed how strategic output controls of 3rd/4th freedom traffic generally affect the home country's social welfare. Subsequently, the general effects of regulating access to landing points will also be taken into consideration. This will require the introduction of a third country and a second airport within the home country.

Regulating Third/Fourth Freedom Traffic In order to work out the fundamental effects of strategic regulation and to pave the way for subsequent analysis, the discussion in this section is limited to the case of a single OD-market which links the home and the foreign country. Only the flag carrier and the foreign airline are allowed to operate the route. Both hold only 3rd and 4th freedom rights. Traffic diversion does not occur. Within this framework, which can be deemed to represent the most favorable starting point for a restrictive air transport policy, the disaggregated welfare effects of a restrictive air transport policy by policy makers of the home country will be investigated.

The effects of restricting the output of the foreign airline in the OD-market can be analyzed by comparing a reference scenario of an almost liberalized air transport link with a scenario of tight regulatory constraints as outlined above. The question to be answered is: How will a hypothetical policy shift from a setting of almost full liberalization to another of strategically motivated regulation change social welfare of different groups of economic agents in the home country? To arrive at an answer suppose the OD-market was originally governed by an almost free market regime, which did not impose any restrictions on both airlines concerning capacities and pricing. The market regime diverged from an entirely free design only insofar, as potential new entrants were barred to serve the market because of single designation.[44]

Figure 2.9 may serve as a tool to illustrate the hypothetical market outcome under the reference scenario of the fairly liberal air transport agreement in the first place, and subsequently to analyze the effects of restrictions (price and capacity controls) on the foreign airline's output. The whole graph consists of three areas: quadrants I and II, and the additional graph III. In the *North-Western quadrant (graph area I)* the output of both air carriers in the market as well as the mutual interdependency in terms of duopolistic reaction functions can be found. The horizontal axis measures the output Y_H of the flag carrier, the vertical axis the output Y_F of the foreign airline. The line R_H represents the reaction function of the flag carrier subject to the supposed duopoly situation; i.e. R_H is the geometric locus of the optimal output (quantities of services) which the flag carrier will decide to provide in the market as a function of the foreign airline's supplied output (both airlines are supposed to deploy the quantity of services as their strategic variable). It is upward sloping because the less output the foreign airline produces, the higher is the optimal output for the flag carrier. The reaction function is convex (seen from the origin) because of the existence of economies of traffic density; i.e. the more output the flag carrier provides the lower are the corresponding marginal costs of service provision. This implies that the marginal expansion of the flag carrier's output in reaction to a unit reduction of the foreign carrier's output will be the greater the more output the flag carrier already provides.[45] The same holds for the reaction function of the foreign airline. The market equilibrium for the almost liberal scenario is described by the intersection of both reaction functions resulting in Y_H^* as the output of the flag carrier and Y_F^* as the output of the foreign airline.

The North-Eastern quadrant (II) derives the market price for air travel in the OD-market and also shows the costs per workload unit for each of both airlines. Its vertical axis measures the price p charged for air transport services as well as the average supply costs of each carrier for given quantities of airlines' services, while the horizontal axis represents total market output Y (= $Y_H + Y_F$). The function D_T represents total demand for air transport services in the OD-market, which is the aggregate demand of those air transport customers living in the home country ('residents') plus the demand of those customers living in the foreign country ('foreigners'). D_T exhibits the usual downward sloping because the lower the prices for air travel, the higher is the demand for air transport services in this market. The horizontal axis of the North-Eastern quadrant measures total output in that market, which within the described fairly liberal reference scenario is Y_T^* representing the aggregate of the output of the flag carrier (Y_H^*) and that of the foreign airline (Y_F^*). (The output Y_H of the flag carrier is directly transmitted from quadrant I, while the output Y_F of the foreign airline is mirrored from the vertical axis of quadrant I onto the horizontal axis of quadrant II using the 45^0-line in quadrant II). Y_T^* leads to a price p^* for air travel. The line C represents the function of average costs on which both carriers operate.[46] It is downward sloping because the provision of air transport services is characterized by economies of traffic density.

The separate *Area III* shows the disaggregate demand functions D_H for air transport services by residents and D_F by foreigners respectively.

Figure 2.9: Market Outcomes on a Third/Fourth Freedom Route and Welfare Effects

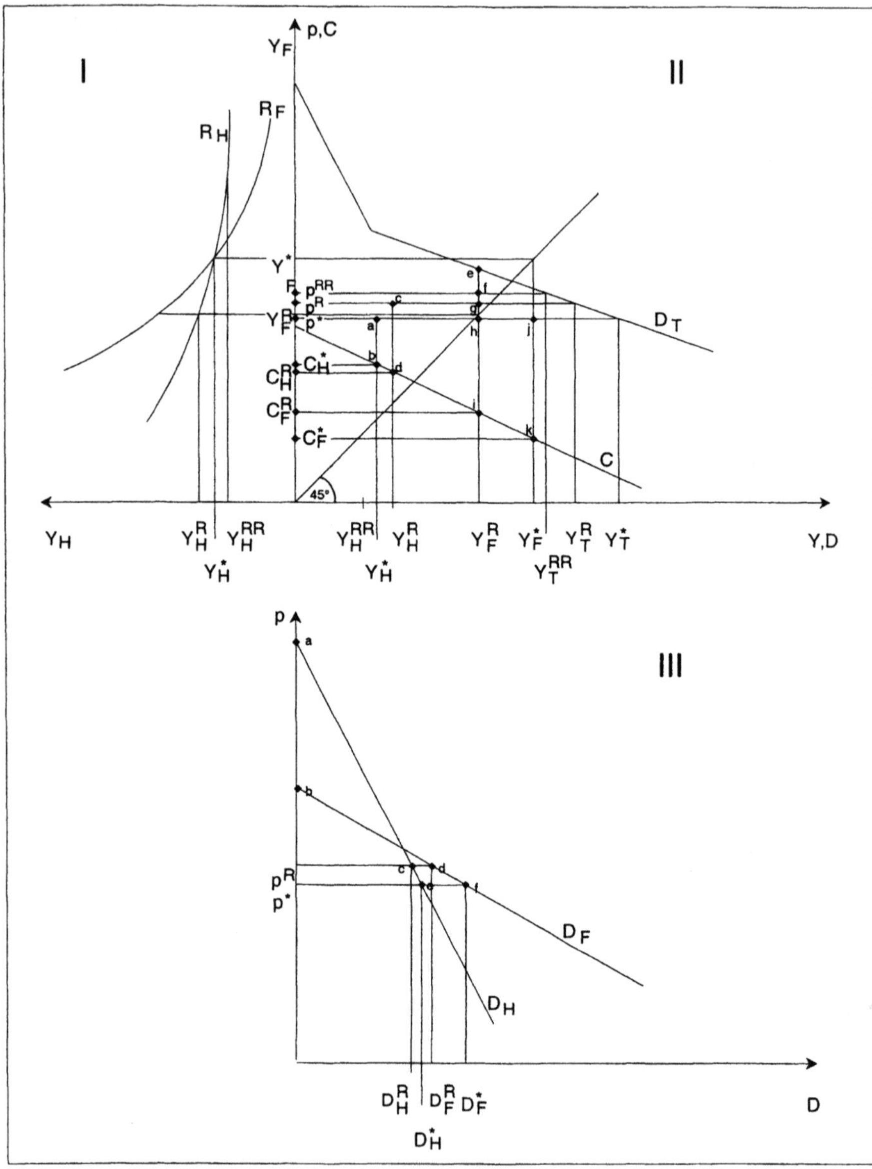

The profits of both carriers can be derived from quadrant II: As an aggregate output Y_T^* of both airlines leads to a price p^* for air transport, and an output Y_H^* of the flag carrier leads to average costs c_H^* for this carrier, the flag carrier enjoys a profit which is represented by the square

'p^*-c_H^*-b-a'. The profit of the foreign airline can be identified as the square 'p^*-c_F^*-k-j' respectively. Area III identifies the rents which residents as well as foreigners receive: Given the equilibrium price p^*, residents' demand for air transport services will be D_H^*, and foreigners' demand will be D_F^*. Hence, residents receive a consumers' rent which is represented by the triangle 'a-p^*-e', and foreigners receive a surplus which can be identified by the triangle 'b-p^*-f'.

After having identified the unconstrained market equilibrium, we can turn to the second step, the comparison with the outcome of a hypothetical restrictive policy approach. Suppose that the home country intends to support the flag carrier by means of some regulation, which forces the foreign airline to contract its output to Y_F^R.

For the sake of analysis of the social welfare effects four groups of economic agents are distinguished who might be subjected to either welfare gains or losses:

- The flag carrier,
- The home airport,
- The residents, and
- Other sectors of the economy, whereby this group also encompass regional interest.

The question is: Will regulation at the expense of the foreign carrier generate a positive net welfare effect for the home economy as a whole? To arrive at an answer, first have a look at Figure 2.9 to derive the expected profit change the flag carrier will realize.

The flag carrier As long as the foreign country does not retaliate, the flag carrier clearly gains from the implementation of regulation: First, because the foreign airline has to contract its output, the flag carrier finds it optimal to expand its service and thus carries a higher volume of traffic. (In Figure 2.9 the flag carrier expands its output to Y_H^R, which can be seen in areas I and II). Second, because of the existence of economies of traffic density the higher traffic volume leads to lower average costs of the flag carrier (in area II of Figure 2.9 the new average costs of the flag carrier are given at c_H^R). Third, if regulation reduces total output in the market, what will be assumed for a moment, the price for air transport will rise. Hence, regulatory action will result in a higher yield per workload unit for the flag carrier. (areas II and III show the new price p^R for air travel in the OD-market. The price is derived from the new aggregated output Y_T^R.). All three effects combined result in a higher profit for this carrier (the new profit is represented by the square 'p^R-c_H^R-d-c').

As can be seen, the profit gain of the flag carrier comes from three sources:

- Cost reductions (because of improved exploitation of economies of traffic density at higher traffic volumes);
- Transformation of former social surplus of the foreign country into profits for the flag carrier (because of the higher price which foreigners have to pay for air transport services and also because the foreign airline carries less traffic); and
- Domestic redistribution of former consumers' rents of residents in favor of the flag carrier (because residents have to pay a higher price for air transport than before).

While the first one reflects improved efficiency of the flag carrier's operations, and while a transformation of former social surplus of the foreign country is also clearly a gain for the home economy, the redistribution of rents at the disadvantage of residents comes not without social costs, even if national policy makers do not care for purely domestic distribution issues. In any case, social costs emerge from 'second -round' effects: First, as domestic residents have to pay a higher price for air transport services as a result of regulation, some of them will choose another transport mode even if that mode's services will be produced at higher social costs than air services. Second, other passengers may abstain from travelling and freight forwarders may reduce the cargo shipped at all, although social opportunity costs of air transport might be lower than the social welfare costs of such reactions. Third, the biased modal split as well as the reduced demand for transportation will have repercussions on other sectors of the economy, as will be discussed later. All these effects combined represent the regulatory burden, which the home country has to bear as a result of restricting the foreign airline's output. Of course, the overall welfare effect of introducing unilateral regulation is only positive for the home economy if the additional profit of the flag carrier outweighs the regulatory burden of the society as a whole.

The amount of profit that the flag carrier receives as a result of regulation is negatively correlated with the price elasticity of demand for air transport both of foreigners and of residents: The less price sensible both user groups react, the more profit will the flag carrier earn.[47] Furthermore, the less elastic residents react to a price change, the less will they substitute air transport by services provided by other transport modes. Accordingly, the less will they abstain from traveling at all. Hence, unilateral regulation is the more attractive in terms of profits of the flag carrier, the less price elastic demand for air transport in the OD-market is.[48]

However, a substantial part of the flag carrier's additional profit comes at the expense of the foreign country: Not only does the foreign airline suffer from a loss of traffic and induced higher average costs (within Figure

2.9 the new average costs of the foreign airline can be identified in area II to be c_F^R), but also foreigners have to pay a higher price for air transport than before if total market output contracts. Hence, the foreign country may have an incentive to retaliate. It could issue a counter regulation, which would force also the flag carrier to lower its output. The result would be a further reduction of total output in the market, which would translate into an even higher increase of price for air transport. But as the market share of the foreign airline also increases, the foreign country might recoup part of the profit which otherwise would be transferred to the flag carrier. (In Figure 2.9 the foreign country restricts, as an example, the output of the flag carrier to Y_H^{RR} which leads to a further contraction of total output in the market to Y_T^{RR} and thus to a higher price p^{RR}, inducing a higher profit for the foreign airline: The new profit of the foreign airline is described by the square 'p^{RR}-c_F^R-i-f', which is bigger than the profit without retaliation 'p^R-c_F^R- i-g'). The incentive for the foreign country to retaliate is the stronger the less sensitive foreigners and residents react to the induced price increase, as a rather low price elasticity of foreigners for air transport services means a rather low burden of retaliation for the foreign economy[49], while a rather low price elasticity of residents means a big gain in terms of social surplus by retaliation. Thus, the incentive to retaliate is strongest in exactly those circumstances that would otherwise favor unilateral regulation by the home country. As a result of retaliation, the flag carrier' s profit shrinks.

Because (a) retaliation diminishes the profit of the flag carrier, while (b) the regulatory burden for the home country is even higher than before, and because (c) the foreign airline likewise suffers from a regulatory burden by bilateral regulation, both countries experience a loss of social welfare and hence are worse off under a tight regulatory compared to a liberal market regime. Unilateral liberalization is, however, not attractive for any one of both countries in the specific setting of this two-country model, because the country that removes regulatory restrictions unilaterally while the other maintains output restrictions for the airline of its trading partner will find itself worse off than under a regime of bilateral regulation.[50] To the contrary, bilateral liberalization would improve social welfare of both countries.

The residents The size of the regulatory burden which the restrictive air transport policy imposes on residents cannot be deduced in general. Several effects might occur, which might work in opposite directions. The change of the residents' rents depends (a) on the incentive of the foreign country to retaliate, as has already been discussed, and (b) on the change of total output in the market. Regarding the latter, the contraction of air transport services induced by regulation is the weaker the more economies of traffic density are realized by the flag carrier as a result of regulation.[51] Total market output might even increase, and price for air transport services could even decrease, if the expansion of the flag carrier's service is strong enough to outweigh the contraction of the foreign airline's service. The latter case would mean that residents would even benefit by regulation.

However, regulation-induced cost savings of the flag carrier might not be as strong as expected, if policy makers should, when implementing the restrictive ASA, have based their expectations on observations of the flag carrier' s cost function under almost free market conditions. Because the restrictive ASA lessens competition between the two airlines in the market, and the market structure cannot change, incentives for the flag carrier to cut costs might be less than under a free market regime. Instead, X-inefficiency might arise. This would mean that the carrier operates on a new cost function with costs for any given output being higher than before.[52]

Indeed, empirical studies by Dresner and Tretheway (1992) as well as by Boss et. al. (1996: 140ff.), that estimated the effect of regulation on the level of air fares in existing international markets, have concluded that competition, but not regulation, tends to reduce discounted air fares, while under the same conditions passengers paying full fares usually enjoy better services in terms of flight frequency. Hence, it is much more likely for domestic residents to lose rents than to gain from regulation. Furthermore, if the foreign country retaliates, domestic residents will undoubtedly lose.

The home airport Regulation of the air transport market usually leaves the home airport less traffic volume to handle. Thus the restrictive ASA will lead to underutilization of airport capacity. Because the airport sector is characterized by considerable economies of traffic density as well, underutilization raises average costs of airport operation. Hence, the airport has to raise its charges in order to break even, which will result in a profit deterioration for the flag carrier, thus reducing the prospects of success of strategic regulation of the air transport market.

Other sectors of the economy The regulation of international air transport markets does not only affect those groups which are directly involved in the airline or airport industry as service providers or consumers, but also has effects on other sectors of the economy. While carriers of other transport modes might, for the above-mentioned reason, benefit from regulation of the air transport market, other sectors of the economy will suffer from a loss of welfare:

- First, the reduction in the volume of air traffic will result in a decreased spending of airlines and airport service providers as well as of foreign passengers in the home country, all of which may lead, via negative multiplier effects, to a reduction of jobs and income in other domestic branches;

- Second, and somewhat related to the first effect, higher costs of access to the home country by air transport might, in the long run, lead to a decrease in foreign direct investment. Furthermore, access to international markets by domestic firms will become more costly. Both will not only lead to additional negative multiplier effects but will also deteriorate the competitive position of the domestic economy on world's goods and services markets;
- Third, if the flag carrier's incentives to cut costs are reduced as a result of regulation, X-inefficiency will increase, which means higher salaries and other (non-monetary) benefits for the flag carrier's employees without any corresponding productivity gain. As a result, the attractiveness of jobs in the airline business will increase compared to other sectors of the economy which compete with the flag carrier for qualified personnel. Enterprises from other sectors might be forced to raise salaries of their employees in order to remain competitive in recruiting qualified manpower. Hence, sector-specific protectionism may lead to higher costs of production in other sectors, thereby further reducing their international competitiveness. Also imports will become more expensive, which will contribute to the regulatory burden of the home country.

Overall assessment of regulation Within the described exogenous market structure, an air transport policy that unilaterally restricts the foreign airline's output may under certain circumstances generate additional profit for the flag carrier. However, this usually comes not only at the costs of residents, but also at the costs of other sectors of the economy. Thus, even if the strategic move of the home country does not induce retaliation by its trading partner, regulation of the market may only enhance the social welfare of the home country, if the loss of consumers' rents and the additional regulatory burden for the economy as a whole does not outweigh the profit gain of the flag carrier. However, as retaliation is the best response strategy of the foreign country in exactly those circumstances that otherwise might eventually generate huge enough profits for the flag carrier to outweigh the regulatory burden of the home country, a social welfare gain for the home country by introducing regulation is unlikely to occur.

Regulating Market Access Market access refers to traffic rights and landing points. Regulations that prevent the foreign airline from exercising fifth freedom and cabotage rights and from serving multiple landing points within the home country aim at securing the flag carrier a solid traffic base by protecting its feeder relationships, and hence, to facilitate this airline to exploit economies of traffic density to the disadvantage of the foreign airline.

This sub-section is solely concerned with the welfare effects of access regulation. Thus, price regulation will not be considered. In addition, as the principal effect of retaliation by trading partners and also the effect of regulation induced X-inefficiency on social welfare were already discussed, they will not be explicitly mentioned here, albeit in footnotes. Instead, the focus is on unilateral regulation.[53]

Fifth Freedom Rights In order to analyze the social welfare effects of regulating fifth freedom rights, a 'third country' has to be introduced into the analytical framework. The airline of the third country will be called 'third airline'. All countries are linked by two spokes a and b, which constitute three markets (Figure 2.10):

- First, the OD-market between the home and the foreign country (served by link a);
- Second, the OD-market between the home and the third country (served by link b); and
- Third, the OD-market between the foreign and the third country (served by the combined links a and b).

Suppose that there is no direct air transport link between the foreign and the third country. A reason could be, for instance, that traffic potential on that link is too small to make it economically remunerative. Instead passengers who travel between these two countries have to make a stopover at the domestic hub. Again air transport on the a- as well as on the c-link shall be governed by single designation.[54]

Figure 2.10: Exogenous Market Structure and Fifth Freedom Rights

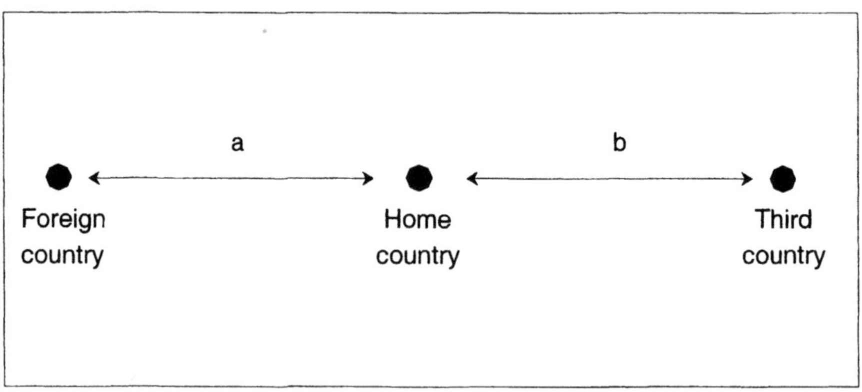

Within this setting, a restrictive ASA is defined here as one that prevents the foreign as well as the third airline to serve the OD-market between the foreign and the third country by exercising 5th freedom rights.

In order to assess the welfare implications of regulation, two cases have to be distinguished:

- First, the foreign and the third airline do not coordinate their services; and
- Second, both carriers do coordinate.

With regards to the first case, only the flag carrier is able to offer online connections and through fares for travel between the foreign and the third country using its 6th freedom right.[55] This transforms into a competitive advantage of this airline vis-à-vis its rivals, and correspondingly, into a higher traffic volume carried by this airline.[56] This in turn, yields a positive economies of traffic density effect for the flag carrier, which can be leveraged into the other markets by consolidation of traffic on the a-respective the b-link, thus generating a positive economies of scope effect in all markets. As a result of regulation, the flag carrier becomes the dominant airline in all markets, although only one market is subject to regulation directly.

However, regulation would fail to generate higher profits for the flag carrier if the foreign and the third airline coordinate their services by forming a strategic alliance, which would enable them also to offer online connections and through fares. In this case, regulation would have no effect at all.

The home airport as well as the residents and other branches of the economy are only affected by regulation if the first case holds. For this case, the regulatory effect on the volume of traffic that the airport handles and the costs of access to the home country depend on several countervailing effects: First, the flag carrier realizes cost reductions because of traffic consolidation. Second, the other airlines have to operate at higher costs. Third, the flag carrier becomes the dominant carrier in all markets and hence might exercise market power. Thus, the net welfare effect is only positive if the cost reductions of the flag carrier outweigh the cost increase of the other airlines, while this effect is strong enough to outweigh the market power effect, which, however, is unlikely to occur as recent experiences with deregulated markets have shown.

Multiple Landing Points and Cabotage Rights In order to study the welfare effects of regulating the access to multiple landing points and granting cabotage rights, a 'hub airport' and a 'secondary airport' within the home country have to be introduced into the analytical setting. Figure 2.11

depicts five possible links between the four airports, constituting five markets:

- The first one is for travel between the foreign country and the hub airport (link a);
- The second one links that country and the secondary airport (link c); and
- The third one is for domestic air services within the home country (link b);
- The fourth and the fifth ones are for services between the third country and the hub airport (link d) respective the secondary airport (link e). In the following, it is assumed that traffic potential in these markets is to small to make airlines' operation economically viable on a stand alone-basis.

A fairly liberal ASA would allow all carriers to serve all routes. To the contrary, the restrictive one is defined here as preventing the foreign airline to serve the secondary airport neither by international nor by cabotage services. This implies, that the foreign airline is constrained to serve only the a-link.

Figure 2.11: Exogenous Market Structure and Multiple Landing Rights

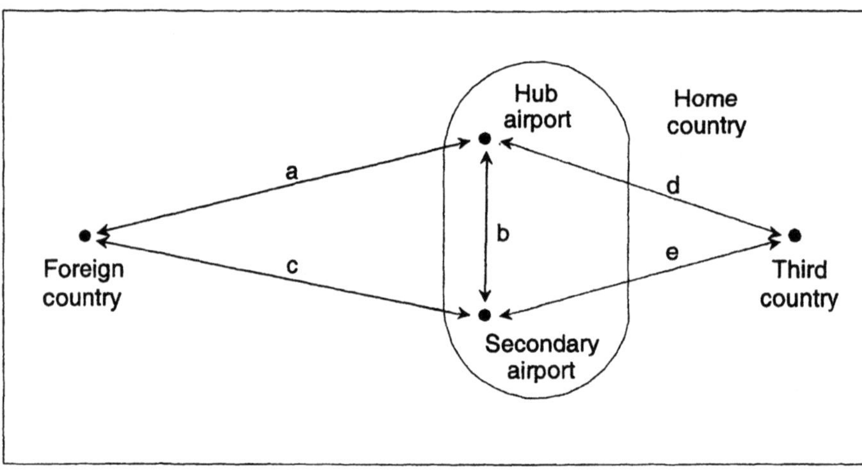

Suppose that regulation holds and that the flag carrier consolidates its traffic at the hub airport in order to exploit economies of scope.[57] This implies, that the c-link is not served at all. Welfare effects of regulation will be analyzed according to the disaggregated pattern of the preceding sub-sections.

The flag carrier The gains for the flag carrier that may be achieved by the strategic protection of the domestic feeder link may come from the same three sources that have been discussed above within the framework of 3rd and 4th freedom traffic, namely improved cost efficiency, transformation of social surplus of the foreign country into rents for the flag carrier, and domestic redistribution of rents of residents to the flag carrier.

Cost efficiency of the flag carrier on the international (a-) route will improve because this airline benefits from superior access to feeder traffic compared to its rival: As the foreign airline is denied the right to offer through or cabotage services, all traffic within the home country is reserved for the flag carrier. Hence, only this carrier is able to provide online connections and through fares for travel between the foreign country and the secondary airport in the home country. Thus it gets a competitive advantage vis-à-vis its rival in this market. This transforms into more traffic carried by the flag carrier than under a liberal regime.

As direct and connecting traffic may be consolidated on the same aircraft serving the international route, thus leading to the exploitation of economies of scope, the superior access of the flag carrier to domestic feeder traffic leverages into a cost advantage for this carrier in the market for direct air services between its hub airport and the foreign country. Thus, the reservation of beyond traffic originating or terminating in the home country generates a spillover effect in favor of the flag carrier with regard to international air services even if this market is governed by free trade.[58]

The residents Different residents may be affected in different ways by restricting the foreign airline's access to secondary airports in the home country. The direction and magnitude of effects will depend on

- The airport at which they prefer to start or end their travel or shipment operation; as well as on
- The net price effect of increased economies of density and enhanced market power for the flag carrier.

Consider first residents who are regular customers of the hub airport and who usually take direct flights between the hub and the foreign country. They are affected by two effects opposed to each other: First, traffic consolidation at the hub lowers the flag carrier's cost of providing direct services on the international route. Second, according to the assumption of still exogenous market structure, the flag carrier becomes the dominant carrier on that route. Again (as in the last sub-section), the net welfare effect for residents usually taking flights from and to the hub airport will only be positive, if the gains of economies of traffic density outweigh the market power effect, so that the cost advantage for direct flights between the hub and the foreign country leads to lower prices for customers. However, as discussed above, regulation is far more likely to result in higher fares.

Another effect is that traffic consolidation at the hub also reduces average costs of flights between the hub and the secondary airport. Again, however, passengers riding on entirely domestic air services will only benefit from this spillover effect, if the net effect of enhanced economies of density and enhanced market power leads to lower air fares. Furthermore, the larger traffic volume which is handled at the hub airport lowers the costs of serving the d-link, and hence, to develop two new markets: The market for air services between the hub airport and the third country, and for services between the foreign and the third country. As a result, residents near the hub airport benefit from enhanced quality of service and better access to more routes.

Second, consider residents who demand international services and who usually make use of the services of the domestic secondary airport. Obviously, they suffer from regulation, because connecting at the hub instead of taking direct flights raises the residents' total costs of flying (including longer travel time and other inconveniences of connecting flights).

Hence, the net welfare effect of regulation in terms of aggregate consumers' rents depends on the net effect of enhanced economies of traffic density and enhanced market power of the flag carrier on air fares, and on the individual price elasticities of demand for air transport services of both groups of residents:

- The weaker the cost effect and the stronger the market power effect are,
- The less price sensible residents near the hub airport are, and
- The more price elastic the other residents react.

The higher is the regulatory burden (in terms of resident's welfare) and the more likely is a social welfare loss for the home country as a consequence of the regulation of the international air transport market, et vice versa.

Considering that airlines prefer to locate their hubs in regions which are characterized by a low price elasticity of demand for air transport services, and also considering that the experience with deregulated air transport markets have shown, that the net effect of potential cost reductions and enhanced market power usually tends to result in higher fares, it is unlikely that the aggregate consumer rents of all residents is positive.

Another point that is to be made here is, that restrictions on the foreign airline's access to the secondary airport prevent competition between both domestic airports to attract international air transport services. Thus, strategic regulation of the international air transport market may create the need for successive regulation of the hub airport's conduct. This may be the case even in a situation where the established hub's position would be naturally contestable in the absence of transport regulation. Regulation imposes additional costs to the economy due to the typical costs of regulation, like the occurrence of productive inefficiency of the airport's operation. These costs have to be weighted against the improved quality of the hub region's transport links.

The airports in the home country Obviously, the national hub gains by regulation, while the secondary airport suffers. Not only does the secondary airport loose traffic to handle, because some potential customers will choose a ground transport mode to reach the hub, while others may abstain from flying resp. shipping air cargo altogether. But in addition, the secondary airport looses all prospects to generate enough feeder traffic for attracting the flag carrier to operate the route to the third country. The second effect probably has more serious impacts on the secondary airport than the first one as it constrains its future development potential.

Another effect is a deterioration of average yield at the secondary airport, not only because of the lower traffic volume that is handled here, but also because handling international flights is usually charged above average (Doganis 1992). In order to secure break even airport regulators will be forced to approve an increase in airport charges. The consequence will be a further reduction of air traffic originating or terminating at this airport. As a follow-up effect, the higher airport charges at the secondary airport will reduce additional profits of the flag carrier generated by regulation of international air transport, thus reducing the social welfare gains for the national economy as a whole.

To the contrary, the hub airport clearly gains from an air transport policy which restricts foreign airlines to serve the secondary airport:

- First, it wins connecting traffic which otherwise would have been flown directly between the secondary airport and the foreign country.
- Second, as a follow-up effect regulation might make it possible to operate a service between the hub airport and the third country, as the larger volume of connecting traffic may increase traffic density on routes.
- Third, as airport charges depend on the size of aircraft and the number of passengers on a given flight, total as well as average revenue of the hub airport increases, while at the same time additional traffic lowers

average costs of traffic handling. Hence, the hub airport earns more profit under regulation of the air transport market than under a free market regime for air transport.

Other sectors of economy Other transport modes clearly benefit from regulation, because some of those passengers and freight forwarders, which have to connect at the hub airport, will choose ground transportation instead of domestic flights to reach the national hub. However, because the shift in the modal split of transport is induced by regulation, it represents a regulatory burden for the economy as a whole.

The effects on other sectors of the economy depend on the location of plants, distribution centers and administrative headquarters of the respective firms. Firms which are engaged in international trade in high-valued goods and services and thus need excellent access to air transport links to their foreign markets but are located near the secondary airport suffer from a location disadvantage as a result of the restrictive air transport policy. Other branches located in the secondary airports' regions may be indirectly affected as well, according to negative multiplier effects.

Firms located in the neighborhood of the hub airport enjoy a competitive advantage in their markets in the first place because of their superior access to international air transport links. In the long run, however, economic activity may tend to concentrate in the hub airport's region, which may yield over-agglomeration in this region. This would, ceteris paribus, induce regional factor prices to increase, as firms have to compete for scarce land and the regional labor force. Higher factor prices induced by the regulation of the international air transport market will partly erode the locational advantage of the hub region and hence might further raise the regulatory burden for the economy as a whole.

Overall Assessment of Regulation As long as market structures are exogenous, the effects of denying multiple landing points and cabotage rights to foreign airlines cannot be deduced in general, as they depend on the concrete circumstances. However, in addition to the national economy's regulatory burden which was already mentioned in the preceding sub-sections, additional social costs occur, which may affect the spatial division of labor within the home country and also affect its position in locational competition. While the flag carrier may gain in terms of additional profit, costs of airport services (which reduces the flag carrier's gain) and factor prices for export oriented industries raise. In the long run, the last effect may lead to a structural shift of the national economy, with a shrinking export sector and an expanding sector for non-tradeables. Policy makers, who have to decide on the design of air transport policy, have to take all the mentioned effects into account, which is not an easy task, because some of the costs will only emerge in the long run and cannot easily be projected at the time of policy action. Hence, the danger of inappropriate regulatory action as a result of imperfect information must be regarded as to be great.

Endogenous Market Structures in Air Transport In contrast to the analytical setting in the preceding sub-sections, airlines' route networks normally link more than just two or three countries. Furthermore, regulated and liberalized markets coexist in world air transport. Thus route networks may cover different but interconnected markets which are governed by different kinds of market regimes, and policy makers must take into account spillover effects of regulating single routes on liberalized ones and vice versa. If, for example, regulated direct and liberalized connecting services within the same market are close substitutes, airlines can circumvent regulation by diverting traffic flows away from regulated to liberalized routes. Because air transport is characterized by economies of scope and traffic density, this may yield repercussions to traffic flows in interconnected markets.

This section extends the preceding analysis by taking the coexistence of different kinds of market regimes governing different but interconnected markets into account. The main focus lies on possible spillover effects of strategic regulation to markets which are governed by free trade. The framework of analysis will be endogenous market structures; i.e. profits earned by incumbents will induce market entry by newcomers. Newcomers can either enter into routes already served by incumbents, or they can divert established traffic flows to new routings.

It is clear that retaliation by the foreign country to regulation usually leaves both countries worse off than under free trade. Therefore, the welfare analysis will not explicitly refer to retaliation albeit in footnotes.[59]

Regulating an International Third/Fourth Freedom Route In the following sub-sections, we will drop the restrictive assumptions which were employed in the preceding analysis step by step, beginning with the option of entry of new carriers into the domestic market (with the international market still being regulated). In a second step, the assumption of single designation on the international leg will be dropped, and in a third step we will consider competition on interconnected routes to a third country.

Competition within Domestic Markets International and domestic markets are interconnected if both use joint routes. To study the effects of regulating an international route on the outcomes within the domestic market three different markets will be considered in this section, namely

- the OD-market between the hub airport and the foreign country (served by link a),
- the domestic market which links the hub airport to a secondary airport in the home country (served by link b), and

- the OD-market that links the secondary airport in the home country with the foreign country (served by the combined links a and b).

The air transport links that are used by the various traffic flows in the current setting are drawn in Figure 2.12.

Suppose that the a-link is governed by single designation. Thus it is only served by the flag carrier and the foreign airline. In contrast to this, the domestic market is fully liberalized, apart from the fact that the foreign airline is neither allowed to carry passengers from and to the secondary domestic airport nor to operate cabotage services. It is served by the flag carrier and domestic independents. The market between the foreign country and the secondary airport is regulated by denying the foreign airline's own operations access to that airport, as well as denying the domestic independents access to international routes. Thus, all international traffic has to pass the hub airport in the home country. The foreign airline and the domestic independents may provide a joint connecting service between the foreign country and the secondary airport, which competes with the flag carrier's service in this market. A joint service may avoids the problem of double monopolization and enables the allied carriers to offer online connections via codesharing.

Suppose that the foreign airline's output on the a-link is restricted because of strategic regulation. In which way does this affect the outcome in the domestic market?

Within this setting, the flag carrier and the domestic independents are asymmetrically affected by regulation. First, because the foreign airline has to reduce its output on the international link, the independents suffer from less international feeder traffic for their services on the domestic link. In contrast, the flag carrier is in an advantageous position as it attracts additional international feeder traffic. Second, because of the larger volume of international feeder traffic, the flag carrier gains a competitive advantage vis-à-vis the independents in the domestic market, reducing the contestability of its domestic service. As a result the flag carrier may exercise market power in the domestic market even if this market is fully liberalized.

Figure 2.12: Interconnected International and Domestic Markets

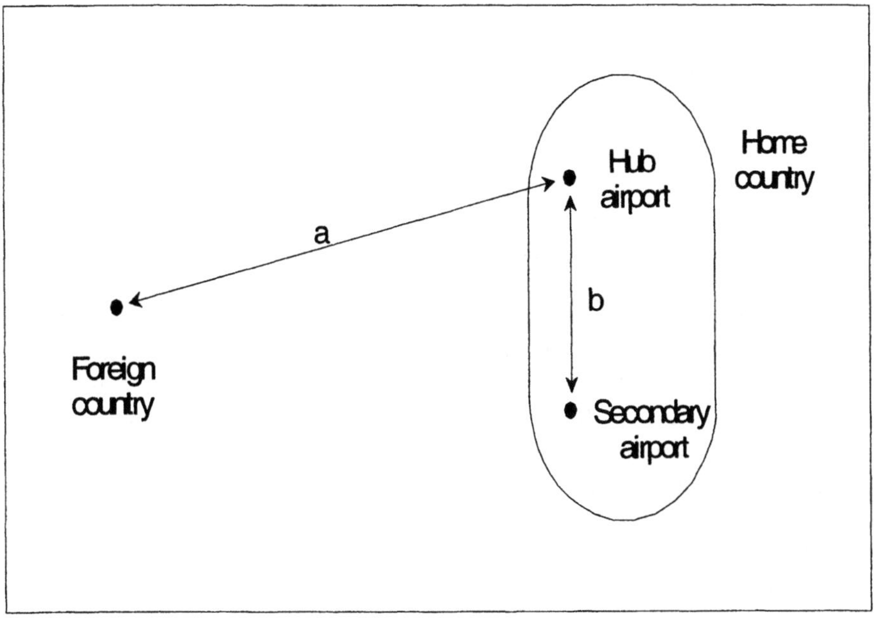

As long that the market power effect is not outweighed by increased economies of traffic density, the airports, the residents, and other sectors of the economy are worse off under regulation than under a free trade regime.

Multiple Designation for the International Market The adverse consequences of regulation of the international market with regard to the domestic market can be avoided, if the home country removes all barriers for independents to enter the international market for direct flights. In this case, the independents' disadvantage in access to international feeder traffic vanishes, and the flag carrier is prevented to earn monopoly rents within the domestic market. In addition, unlimited designation of resident airlines prevents the flag carrier also from earning monopoly rents on international routes. Residents benefit by lower air fares, and, as lower air fares mean more traffic to handle, also the home airport benefits by unlimited designation. Hence, negative consequences of restricting the foreign airline's output in the international market could be balanced by removing all barriers for market entry by independents.[60]

However, compared to full deregulation, this is only a second best solution in terms of improving access of the home country to international air services: On the one hand, the flag carrier is provided to earn monopoly rents (thus regulation fails in this respect), on the other, residents would have to pay higher air fares if the foreign carrier is barred to serve the market while it could operate more efficient than the own airlines.

Competition on Interconnected Routes to a Third Country The coexistence of different market regimes governing different routes within the same international OD-market exerts a threat of traffic diversion to strategically motivated regulatory action by the home country. Competing routes free of regulatory restrictions may serve as a by-pass for any strategically restricted routes. Traffic diversion does not only reduce the prospects of generating profit for the flag carrier by means of regulation of a single route, but it spills over to other markets which are governed by free trade as will be shown in the following.

In order to study the welfare consequences of regulating the OD-market for air transport services between the home and the foreign country in the face of a threat of traffic diversion a greater number of different but interconnected markets than in the preceding section have to be considered. In this sub-section the case of four countries will be analyzed which constitute six international air transport markets. These are linked which each other by five spokes (Figure 2.13):

- The first market comprises all air traffic between the home and the foreign country. The two countries are linked by two different routes, a direct route and a connecting one. Direct traffic between both countries takes place on the b-link, connecting traffic is funneled through the airport of the third country by using a combination of the a- and the c-link.
- The second market represents all air traffic between the home and the third country, which are linked by a direct route on the link c.
- The third market is that of air traffic between the foreign and the third country. Traffic flows use the link a.
- The fourth market comprises all traffic flows between the home and a 'fourth country', which are linked by d.
- The fifth market comprises all air traffic between the third and the fourth country, which flows over link e.
- Finally, the sixth market is constituted by OD-traffic between the foreign and the fourth country, which are linked by two connecting routes, from which one (links a and e combined) uses the third country as a transfer point, while the other (links b and d combined) passes through the home country. It is assumed that no direct traffic is carried between the third and fourth country. This assumption serves the end of elaborating the inter-hub competition between the home and the third country in more detail.

As can be seen in Figure 2.13, all transport links serve multiple markets. For example the a-link carries direct traffic between the foreign and the third country as well as connecting traffic between the foreign and the home and between the foreign and the fourth country.

Figure 2.13: Interconnected International Markets

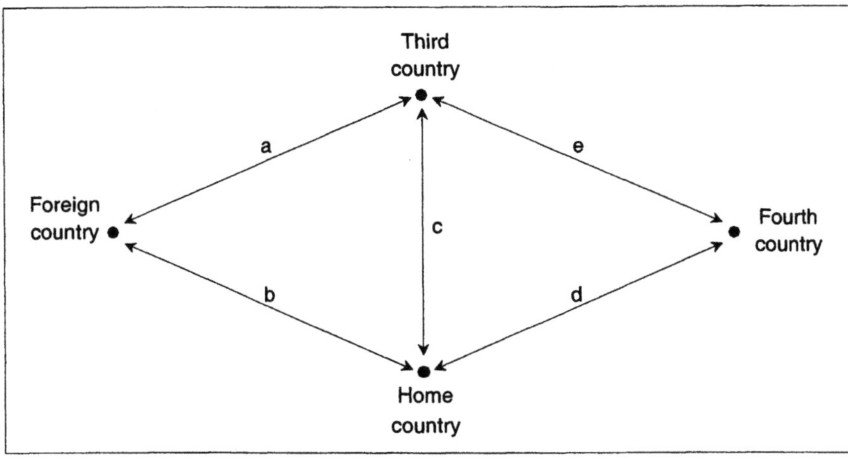

Suppose that only services between the home and the foreign country provided on the b-link are subject to regulation. All other routes are liberalized. What will be the effects of restricting the foreign airline's output on the b-link in terms of social surplus for the home country? In order to bring out the consequences of traffic diversion, in the following direct and indirect effects of regulation will be distinguished: While the former comprise only those effects that would occur if the regulated market would be isolated from other markets, the latter comprise repercussion effects that will be generated by spillovers of regulation to other markets.

In the following it is assumed that the already described market power effect of regulation in favor of the flag carrier always outweighs the traffic density effect, so that regulation always leads to a higher air fare on the regulated route.

Direct effects in the OD-market between the home and the foreign country

The direct effects of regulation with regard to the OD-market between the home and the foreign country are as follows: First, a reduction of the foreign airline's output that leads to a higher price for air travel on the direct route may induce some passengers to substitute direct by connecting flights. These passengers will transfer at the airport in the third country.

In addition, the home airport will handle less traffic than under a free trade regime because the higher price for air travel on the direct route as well as the inconveniences of travelling on the connecting route will induce some passengers to abstain from travelling at all. In contrast, the airport in the third country benefits from strategic regulation of the home country, because it gets more (connecting) traffic to handle than under the conditions of free trade on the b-link.

The OD-market between the home and the third country The strategic regulation of the direct route between the home and the foreign country spills over to the market between the home and the third country as traffic density increases on the c-link. The costs of service provision decrease, and residents who demand air transport services between the home and the third country benefit by lower prices. Thus, traffic in this market increases.

The OD-market between the foreign and the third country The OD-market between the foreign and the third country is also indirectly affected by regulation: Traffic diversion from the regulated b-link to connecting flights on the combined a-c-link leads to a higher traffic density on the a-link. As a result, air transport users from the foreign country as well as those from the third country benefit from lower prices for air transport services in this market, as unrestricted designation guarantees that prices are held down to long run marginal costs.[61] The third airport clearly gains from more traffic to handle.

The OD-markets between the foreign and the fourth country The OD-market between the foreign and the fourth country is served by two different connecting routes, from which one passes through the home country, while the other passes through the third country. As regulation generates a higher traffic density on the a-link, while reducing traffic density on the b-link, it is cheaper to connect in the third country than in the home country. As a result, the home airport suffers from decreasing volumes of connecting traffic. In contrast, the airport of the third country again benefits from this spillover effect.

The OD-market between the third and the fourth country The last discussed effect increases traffic density on the e-link. As a result, prices for transport services between the third and the fourth country fall, thus inducing further traffic increases on the e-link. As a consequence, also passengers travelling between these two countries benefit from regulation of the b-link.

The OD-market between the home and the fourth country In the long run, also traffic flows between the home and the fourth country will be affected by spillover-effects of strategic regulation of the b-link, because diversion of connecting traffic between the fourth and the foreign country leads to increased traffic density on the e-link at the expense of the d-link, which translates into lower costs for providing services on the former, higher costs on the latter and, hence, into lower prices for flights to the third country compared to flights to the home country. As a consequence, direct traffic contracts between the home and the fourth country, which negatively affects the not only the home airport, but also the flag carrier, and (via higher air fares) the residents as well as other branches of the economy that demand direct services in this market. In contrast and again, the airport of the third country will benefit by this spillover effect.

Repercussions of traffic diversion to the OD-market between the home and the foreign country The various traffic diversion effects discussed so far will generate repercussions to the OD-market between the home and the foreign country: As all these effects lead to a further decrease of traffic density on the b-spoke, also air fares in this market raise further, thus leading to a further decrease of demand, and concurrent reducing the prospects of generating rents for the flag carrier by regulation. In an extreme case, the repercussions from the other markets might make the direct traffic flow between the foreign and the home country too thin for direct services to break even. If such a case should materialize, operations on that route would have to be ceased, which would clearly negatively affect the flag carrier as well as the home airport. The home country's airport might even lose all of its hub-functions as a result of regulation and degenerate to a pure feeder-destination, representing just one spoke of the network of routes that centers around the third country.

Overall assessment of regulation The extensive analysis has demonstrated that regulation of a single international route generates non-negligible spillover-effects to other markets which are governed by free trade. Already liberalized competing links will attract traffic volumes from the link that is subject to strategic regulation. These spillover effects yield repercussions that harm the home airport in all markets. Also the prospects of generating any rent for the flag carrier are reduced the stronger the threat of traffic diversion and the concurrent spillover-effects are. In contrast, the airport of the third country benefits by the spillovers, not only directly by traffic diversion from the regulated to the liberalized route, but also indirectly because traffic diversion yields cost advantages for the third country's airport, which translates into a competitive advantage in all other markets. Furthermore, other sectors located in the third country get a competitive advantage on world's goods and service markets vis-à-vis the home country as they benefit from superior location because of better accessibility.

In performing the role of the prime competitor from outside, the third country can reap the gains of a 'free rider' of the restrictive market regime governing the air transport link between the home and the foreign country. In an extreme case, the various spillovers might impair the competitiveness of the domestic hub in international inter-hub competition, which clearly has negative effects on the accessibility of the home country, and hence for the national economy as a whole. To avoid these adverse results, the best strategy for the home country is to liberalize all markets between all countries which may be affected by spillover-effects of traffic diversion.

Market Access The welfare effects of regulating market access will be discussed first with reference to fifth freedom rights. Later on, the regulation of multiple landing points and cabotage rights will be discussed.

Fifth Freedom Rights In order to analyze the effects of regulating fifth freedom rights the same four countries, four airlines and five air transport links as in the last sub-section will be considered (Figure 2.13). A restrictive ASA is defined here as one that prevents the foreign and the fourth airline to exercise fifth freedom rights via the home country, while the markets for OD-traffic between the home country and the foreign as well as the fourth country are fully liberalized. [62] It is assumed, that the third country has liberalized all of its air transport links.

To analyze the effects of regulation, first have a look at the direct effect of 5th freedom-regulation on the b- and d-links: For the reasons described above regulation of fifth freedom traffic via the home country (i.e. via the combined b-d-link) spills over to the 3rd/4th freedom markets between the home country and the foreign as well as the fourth country, making the flag carrier dominant in these two markets. However, the more fifth freedom traffic will be diverted by regulation to use the third country as a transfer point instead of using the home country, the smaller is the cost advantage which the flag carrier can leverage into the other two markets. In addition, the home airport handles less traffic the more traffic volume is diverted as a result of regulation. Because less traffic handled by the airport means higher average costs of providing infrastructure facilities, airport charges have to raise, which exerts pressure on the flag carrier's profit, thus partly deteriorating its regulatory gain. Obviously, also residents and other sectors of the home economy suffer the more traffic is diverted as a response to the restrictions on fifth freedom traffic.

To the contrary, the third country clearly benefits by the restrictive air transport policy of the home country: First, regulation diverts some traffic between the foreign and the fourth country to pass through the third airport, thus lowering costs of infrastructure provision in that country. Second, as traffic diversion increases traffic density on the a- and e-links, travelling on these links becomes cheaper than travelling on the b- and d-links. Therefore, the third country becomes more attractive as a destination for passengers originating in the foreign and fourth countries, while the home country looses attractiveness. This leads to a further decrease of traffic volume to and from the home country. Again, as in the last sub-section, in an extreme case traffic flows on the b- and d-links might become too thin for making the operation of these links remunerative, and the home airport looses all of its hub functions. To the contrary, the third country benefits by a positive externality effect which results from the regulatory action of the home country, yielding superior accessibility to the third, and deteriorating accessibility to the home country. Moreover, as traffic density increases at the third airport, while it decreases at the home airport, the former will attract additional new links, while the competitiveness of the later will be reduced. This may generate a cumulative process, and, in an extreme case, all international air transport links will center around the third country's airport, while the home country degenerates to a pure spoke within the world wide network of air transport routes.

Multiple Landing Points and Cabotage Rights In this sub-section the same four countries as in the last section will be considered, albeit that now two airports are located in the home country, one of which is called the 'hub airport', while the other is called the 'secondary airport'. Figure 2.14 gives an overview on transport links which constitute the relevant markets.

Figure 2.14: Endogenous Market Structures and Multiple Landing Points

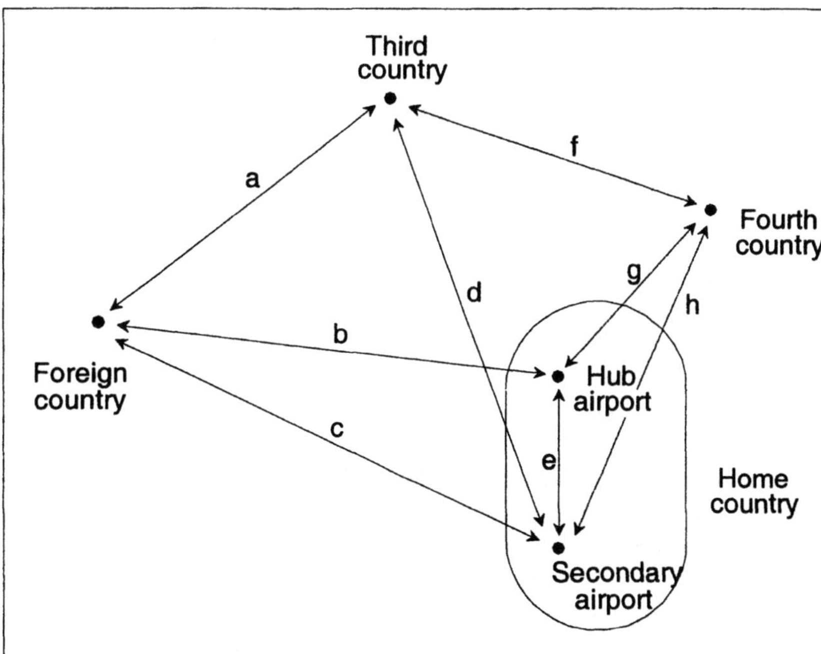

The restrictive ASA under consideration is that between the home and the foreign country: It prevents direct services between the foreign country and the secondary airport. All other transport links are considered as being fully liberalized here.[63] In addition, it is assumed that traffic flows between the fourth country and all other airports are too thin to make the operation of any air transport links originating in the fourth country remunerative on a stand alone basis.

In this case, not only the third country, but also the hub airport within the home country benefit by regulation, because all traffic between the foreign country and the secondary airport has either to pass through the hub airport, of through the third country.[64] This increases traffic density on the combined a-d- as well as on the combined b-e-link. Furthermore, also both airports benefit by higher traffic densities. Moreover, the increase in traffic handled at both airports might enable the airlines to consolidate traffic in order to introduce new routes to the fourth country (i.e. to operate the f- and g-link). Accordingly, the respective regions benefit by better accessibility than under free trade on all links. Note however, that all of the costs of regulation are borne by the secondary airport and its region, while part of the benefits go to the third country.

In contrast, liberalizing the c-link would benefit the secondary airport not only at the costs of the hub airport and its region, but also at the costs of the third country. Hence, all benefits of liberalization go to the home country, while only part of the costs are born by the hub airport, making liberalization a positive sum game for the home economy.

The net effect of regulation in terms of social welfare of the home country cannot be deduced in general, but depends on the magnitude of economies of traffic density that affect the flag carrier and the domestic airports, as well as the price elasticities of passengers from all countries, as was already analyzed in the preceding sections. However, what is clear in any case, is that the design of the home country's air transport policy generates externalities on other countries, which compete for international traffic flows: While the costs of regulation will be largely borne domestic airports and residents, whereas the benefits are shared by other countries as well, in the case of liberalization only part of the costs will be borne by the home country, whereas it receives the full benefits of liberalization. Hence, the stronger the spillover-effect of air transport policy with regard to traffic flows, the more favorable is liberalization.

Overall Assessment of Regulation The preceding analysis of strategic regulation structures has shown that the prospects of generating rents for the national economy by means of a restrictive air transport policy are even lower if market structures are endogenous than if they are exogenous. Not only does regulation of international air transport markets hamper competition in an already liberalized domestic market, but regulation generates spillovers that affect interconnected markets, particularly those markets, that are already governed by a fully liberalized market regime. As an effect, third countries which have already liberalized their ASAs benefit by regulation to the detriment of the home country.

Although the possibility of generating any positive rents by a restrictive air transport policy cannot be fully ruled out on the basis of the preceding analysis, it should have become clear anyway, that liberalization is a superior strategy in the presence of interconnected markets. That country which is a frontrunner in liberalization benefits from a first mover advantage. Furthermore, if interconnected markets are already liberalized, a country that still executes regulation runs the risk that it air transport links degenerate to merely spokes of comprehensive hub-operations which are located in other countries, thus experiencing a deterioration of the quality of its air transport links, which transforms into a poor accessibility of the country. This clearly affects the national economy negatively.

Furthermore, the prospects of generating rents by a restrictive air transport policy, which were already assessed to be unlikely to emerge, must even be regarded to be overestimated by the preceding analysis, because the reasoning until now has abstracted from some important features of air transport markets and also the transaction costs of managing the bilateral system of regulation. The next chapter will turn to these up to now neglected aspects.

The Case of Germany

In the preceding sections, it has been demonstrated that the prospects for a strategic air transport policy to be successful in terms of the nation's social welfare crucially depend on

- That policy's effects on the costs of providing airline and airport services;
- The effects on air fares; and, in particular,
- The probability of compensating spillover-effects to and from interconnected markets that are induced by the market regime governing competing routes.

In this section, we will apply the results of the preceding sections concerning cost- and price-effects as well spillover-effects of regulation to the specific German case.

Regulation and the Costs of Airlines' and Airports' Services

Although regulation might support resident airlines and domestic airports in their endeavor to save costs (by enabling them to exploit additional economies of scope and traffic density), in reality regulation tends to raise the costs of the air transport system. Cost inefficiencies may arise from a variety of sources, notably from

- Administrative restrictions on market growth;
- Restrictions preventing the emergence of efficient air transport networks; and
- Reduced competitive pressures as a consequence of regulation.

In the following, each of these obstacles to achieving a better air transport system by regulation will be considered in detail.

Administrative Restrictions for Market Growth Most ASAs explicitly designate specific carriers and identify certain city pairs which the airlines are allowed to serve within the limits of predetermined capacities. Once negotiated, they are difficult to change. Usually, a country which is unhappy with the arrangements laid down in an already existing air service agreement can terminate it unilaterally within twelve months after announcement. However, renegotiating is often cumbersome and time-consuming, because the partners often need to solve dissents on matters in principle as well as in detail. As a result, a two-year wait for a new agreement is not unusual, and many of the larger countries have a large backlog of bilateral negotiations, with many countries each waiting for their turn.[65] In effect, once implemented, most bilaterals endure for long periods which means that the arrangements cannot be adjusted sufficiently to rapidly changing circumstances under which airlines operate (Doganis 1993: 59; Findlay et.al. 1996: 24). For instance, the proposed cross-border alliance between British Airways and American Airlines has been a matter of dispute between the United States, the United Kingdom, and the Commission of the EC for several years and still has not yet reached antitrust immunity, which would be a prerequisite for the joint operations to start effectively.

Additional administrative regulations which impede market growth result from ownership rules: These rules normally call for a majority stake of a designated airline to be held by residents of the country of that carrier's registration. Within the logic of the bilateral system, ownership rules are a necessary requirement to prevent third countries from circumventing the negotiated principles. This which would exert a threat of deterioration to bilateral regulations. However, they also prevent carriers from consolidating with foreign airlines through equity transfers and limit their access to the capital market.[66] Hence, today it is far from clear that the growing number of cross-border alliances between airlines reflects an efficient industry structure. Alliances may have several advantages over mergers, but they also create an element of instability for the industry's configuration. As recent experience has shown, not only may alliances between independent carriers involve huge costs for administering the partnerships and for controlling the partners' behavior. But even with extensive control mechanisms it may be hard for an airline in a specific partnership to protect itself against opportunism by its partners (and especially against the loss of its core partners), which makes sunk investments at the network level risky. In contrast, partial or even full mergers limit the costs of instability, but are vulnerable to X-inefficiency within the consolidated firm, because mergers mean the substitution of the control mechanisms of the market by hierarchical government structures. Hence, the decision between alliance and merger is a delicate one. The liberalization of ownership rules would give the airlines option to decide on the most efficient form of consolidating their operations, i.e. they would have freedom to choose between joining an already existing or creating a new alliance or, as an alternative, to consolidate by acquiring majority stakes in their partners or even by full merger.

With respect to the access to the capital market, restrictions on ownership may raise the costs and availability of capital and also distort the airlines' choices between equity and debt capital given that access to debt is not constrained by regulation. This may be a serious impediment to the growth of airlines, especially because air transport is a relatively capital-intensive business, combined with the fact that airlines are generally regarded as being inherently risky investments (Productivity Commission 1998: 105).

Apart from the high costs to administer the system of bilateral air service agreements, ASAs are prone to regulatory capture, because arrangements once agreed upon by governments tend to create vested interests which may prove to be insurmountable obstacles to future renegotiations. In addition, the task of negotiating bilaterals normally lies with the national ministries of transport and thus with specialized agencies, which may be prone to pursue the interests of the national flag carrier, thereby neglecting the needs of the carriers' and airports' customers as well as the transport needs of the economy as a whole. Thus, instead of being focussed to overall welfare effects of specific arrangements, renegotiations are often biased by vested interests of resident airlines, which hampers the abolishment of regulations which have become obsolete from the perspective of economic efficiency.

As a result, provisions for permitted routes and capacities cannot be quickly enough adjusted to changing needs of the national economies. The industry is thereby prevented from taking full advantages of new opportunities that emerge from changing market conditions, and hence its growth will be limited. Furthermore, restrictions to the designation of airlines prevent the substitution of high cost carriers by more cost-efficient ones, thus contributing to higher costs of air transport.

For the case of Germany, the encouraging experience with the liberalization of intra-EU air transport has clearly demonstrated how much the former bilateral air service agreements among member countries hampered the introduction of efficient cross-border air transport links. Not only has the number of scheduled air transport links between Germany and its EU partners increased significantly since the implementation of the third liberalization package in 1993, but also many of the new transport links were established by independent airlines who did not possess the status of a flag carrier (Table 2-10).

Often, former charter airlines used their new freedom to enter international scheduled markets by providing scheduled services to destinations for which tickets could only be bought as part of complete tour packages prior to liberalization. In addition, the number of direct links between German regional airports and other EU countries has increased significantly.[67] Most of these new air transport links were provided by competitors to traditional flag carriers, either by already existing domestic independents or by newly certified air carriers. Although some routes to foreign secondary airports have been abandoned, regional airports have gained by new routes to foreign hubs and thereby reached better access to the worldwide air transport system.

Restrictions Preventing the Formation of Efficient Air Transport Networks

Air transport and airport market performance is crucially influenced by the existence of economies of scope and traffic density in both industries. Regulation-induced failures in realizing cost advantages from efficient route networks contribute to high costs of air transport and thus may prove to be an impediment to growth of the national economy as a whole. Obstacles to the formation of efficient route networks do not only emerge from ownership restrictions (as was already stated). Instead, the restrictive allocation of traffic rights is probably a far more important impediment. Although unilateral restrictions on foreign airlines' market access may, under certain limited circumstances, enhance social welfare, the usual practice in air transport regulation is the bilateral exchange of traffic rights between signatory countries on the basis of reciprocity; i.e. denying a foreign airline 5th freedom rights, for instance, will result in a retaliate denial of comparable rights to the own carrier by the partner government. In effect, regulation of market access constrains the ability of all airlines which fly on a regulated route to increase the size of their networks, to develop efficient hub and spoke-systems, and hence to generate economies of scope and traffic density. Although such restrictions to network design can partially be overcome by codesharing between airlines, such strategies do not come without costs as has already been discussed.

Table 2-10: Cross-border Air Transport Links from German Airports to Destinations in the European Union [a], 1983-1998[b]

	From all airports in Germany	From secondary airports in West Germany	From secondary airports in West Germany to main hubs in the EC[c]	From airports in East Germany
all routes				
1983	155	101	54	.
1986	192	132	55	.
1989	255	190	68	.
1991	282	216	71	4
1993	348	266	79	14
1994	380	294	82	18
1998	593	463	83	53
routes which are only served by independent airlines[d]				
1983	7	6	6	.
1986	16	12	11	.
1989	33	31	10	.
1991	40	36	6	0
1993	117	97	17	6
1994	142	121	17	10
1998	292	236	16	40

[a] Austria, Belgium, Denmark, Eire, Finland, France, Greece, Italy, Luxembourg, Netherlands, Portugal, Spain, Sweden, and the United Kingdom were counted as members of the EU throughout the entire period 1983-1998. _ [b] Air transport links that were served directly in July. _ [c] Amsterdam, Brussels, Copenhagen, London, Madrid, Paris, Rome, Vienna, Zurich. _ [d] Independent airlines: Western European airlines which hold no flag carrier status prior to 1989. Crossair, DLT, and NLM were not regarded as independent because they were wholly owned by a traditional flag carrier.

Source: ABC World Airways Guide (various issues). - Statistisches Bundesamt, Fachserie 8, Serie 6 (various issues). - Own calculations.

In addition, being barred from acquiring traffic rights prevents airlines from including other new routes in their networks which lack the traffic potential to make stand-alone operations economically viable, but which could be profitable if they could be operated as a (5th freedom) sequel of international 3rd/4th freedom routes. Likewise, still unserved thin routes could sometimes be operated profitably if airlines would be allowed to establish own hubs within the national borders of the partner country using seventh freedom rights. Furthermore, restrictions on flying 5th freedom routes may prevent airlines from operating 3rd/4th freedom markets with greater frequency compared to stand-alone operations. Finally, capacity restrictions and denying traffic rights impede the airlines' operational flexibility with respect to freely switching aircraft between routes, thus raising the airlines' risk of operating certain routes. For instance, when the Asia/Pacific air transport markets collapsed in 1997, most airlines had no opportunity to re-deploy idle large aircraft on other routes but on the North Atlantic, which lead to severe overcapacity on these routes. The switching of aircraft to other long haul markets, such as between Europe and South Africa, South America and the Middle East, was largely hampered by restrictive bilateral air service agreements.

Moreover, denying traffic rights reinforces the overconcentration of international routes centering around national hubs, thus contributing to airport congestion. But even if the national hub is actually uncongested, and thus may benefit from more traffic by lower average operational costs, secondary airports will in any case suffer from a regulation-induced loss of traffic and negative economies of traffic density. Furthermore, the limited volume of international feeder traffic available at secondary airports, and charges that may be higher because of higher average costs, sets limits to these airports' ability to attract additional domestic routes. This holds especially for thin routes between secondary airports, which are primarily served by small aircraft, because an increase in airport charges may seriously affect the profitability of such operations.

In the case of Germany, the airport of Frankfurt/Main, which serves as the main national hub, is already congested and operates at its physical capacity limits for most of its daily operational hours all over the week. Furthermore environmental considerations severely constrain its ability to expand capacity. Thus, economies of traffic density seem to be exploited almost completely for this airport. Instead, the large volume of traffic that has to pass through the bottleneck of Frankfurt/Main airport has generated considerable diseconomies of traffic density for the part of the airlines, which suffer increasingly from delayed flights. For example, in September 1999 about 30% of all flights were delayed, an increase of 30% compared with September 1998 (Flughafen Frankfurt AG/Marktforschung 1999). Institutional shortcomings prevent congestion to be tackled effectively: The airport is denied the right to decide on the allocation of slots to airlines, while airlines have no incentives to give up inefficiently used slots they actually hold because they are not compensated for relinquishing these slots. This hampers an efficient use of existing runway capacity, and it also impedes flexible adjustment of flight schedules to the needs of airlines' customers. At the same time, the nearby airport of Cologne, which is located less than 100 miles to the north of Frankfurt/M. still is underutilized, although it serves a hinterland that has an economic potential comparable to that of Frankfurt. If foreign airlines could get traffic rights that would allow them to serve still underutilized airports directly, and if they could freely move from Frankfurt to these airports, then slots at Frankfurt might be reallocated and, hence, that airport's capacity would be used more efficiently, which would lower aggregate costs of air transport. Hence, given almost full saturation of the airport Frankfurt/M. for most of its daily operational hours, it is unlikely that the regulatory burden of the secondary airports in Germany may be outweighed by regulation induced cost advantages of Frankfurt airport.

Implications of Restrictive Regulation for Airline and Airport Competition

Increased competition renders a variety of favorable effects on market performance: notably, it puts a downward pressure on output prices, it gives incentives for improving productivity and, it leads to the development of new markets. Regulation tends to restrain competitive pressures. In air transport, restrictive regulation hampers competition between airlines by a restrictive designation of airlines, by capacity and frequency controls, by administrative controls of output prices, and by withholding of traffic rights. Barriers to entry and capacity/frequency constraints protect incumbents and allow them to earn higher-than-normal returns, which may be enjoyed by shareholders or absorbed in higher-than-normal costs.[68] Regulatory restrictions are likely to increase factor costs. Such increases most probably outweigh possible economies of scope and traffic density that may be gained by regulation. This suggests that competition may be a necessary precondition for making use of economies of density. Oum and Yu (1998) provide evidence in support of the beneficial effects of competition on prices and costs in air transport. They investigated productivity, price recovery ratios and profitability for large European, North American and Asian airlines in the period 1985-1995. Their results indicate that the second and third EU liberalization packages of 1990 and 1993 had a significant impact on the performance of European flag carriers. Although these airlines experienced a decline of output prices throughout 1990-1995, they managed to improve productivity substantially and, as a result, also improved profitability. In contrast, North American and Asian airlines experienced lower productivity growth than European carriers. As for the North American carriers, the observed productivity record is not inconsistent with the beneficial effects of competitive pressures. It may just be explained by the fact that the US airlines achieved tremendous productivity growth immediately following the deregulation of the US domestic market in 1978. Thus they had already reached a higher productivity level before 1985 (Oum and Yu 1998: 237).

As regards Germany, the liberalization of EU air transport has forced Lufthansa to undergone a deep restructuring in order to improve its productivity. Lufthansa successfully reorganized its business and was able to earn higher profits throughout the second half of the 1990s than before.

Regulation also impedes competition between airports, as the withholding of traffic rights influences traffic flows. Actually, the airport of Frankfurt/M. has a strong dominant position within the German airport sector, although the airports of Cologne (less than 100 miles to the north of Frankfurt), Düsseldorf (about 120 miles to the north of Frankfurt) and Stuttgart (less than 100 miles to the south of Frankfurt) are located nearby and all serve hinterlands with great economical potential.[69] In order to prevent abuse of market power in the airport sector, airport charges are subject to economic regulation by the Länder. However, regulation is based on the principle of cost recovery, and on constraints for regulators who can only act on request of airport authorities. Both measures serve as safeguards against regulatory risks of airports (Wolf 1996b). Thus, on the one hand regulators have to approve an upward adjustment of airport charges to higher airport costs, thereby severely limiting incentives for airport authorities to improve productivity. On the other hand, even if strategically motivated interventions into air transport markets might lead to improved productivity of airports because of the realization of airports' economies of traffic density, the procedural fact that regulators can only act on request of the airports would hamper the passing on of cost reductions to the airports' customers. In contrast, liberalization of air transport markets would enhance the prospects of competition between airports and therefore limit the need for airport regulation and its adverse consequences.

Strategic Regulation and the Level of Air Fares

Strategic regulation of international air transport might render benefits even to air transport users as well as to the economy as a whole if it would allow for an improved exploitation of economies of scope and traffic density that would outweigh the effect of reduced competition on prices for air transport services. However, the preceding discussion of the effects of regulation on airlines' and airports' costs has demonstrated that costs of the air transport system tend to increase by far more than marginal costs might decline in practice. On balance, prices under restrictive regulation are likely to be higher than under a liberal market regime.

As regards Germany, supporting empirical evidence can be provided. Boss et. al. (1996) have investigated the effects of regulation on air fares for scheduled flights originating in Germany by comparing the development of prices in markets that were directly subject to the EU liberalization packages with prices in markets which were not affected, either because they link Germany with European non-member countries of the EU, or because the routes had already been almost liberalized prior to 1989.[70] They controlled for route distance as well as for currency exchange effects, which both may affect the costs of serving the routes under consideration. Furthermore they controlled for market entry by independent airlines that did not hold flag carrier status prior to 1989, and for the number of competitors actually serving a route. Although the results did not indicate any direct regulatory effect on prices for fully flexible fares, on routes where independent air carriers entered the market, as they would have not been able to do under the old regulatory regime, prices in this fare class significantly declined. In contrast to fully flexible fares, the results show a considerable direct effect of liberalization on discount fares, with prices on routes that were directly affected by liberalization significantly dropping between 1986 and 1996, while discounted air fares for routes linking Germany to non-EU members declined to a much lesser extent than fares for liberalized routes. In addition, the entry of a third competitor on a route led to further decline of discounted airfares. Hence, it may be concluded that price competition is effective in the Single European Air Transport Market, while passengers on still regulated routes under bilateral agreements could not enjoy the same benefits of reduced prices. This indicates that lower prices as a result of restrictive regulation of air transport markets are unlikely.

Spillover Effects of Regulation on Third Markets

We have argued that a strategic air transport policy approach will prove counterproductive for the national economy if market structure and traffic flows are no longer under full regulatory control of national authorities, thus making bilateral agreements a blunt sword for strategic action. The threat of traffic diversion clearly limits the prospects of generating rents for the flag carrier on the regulated routes; moreover, any attempt of restrictive regulatory action might, via spillover of effects to interconnected markets, induce a redirection of traffic flows in favor of other countries. This might easily translate into a location disadvantage not only for the airports of the regulating country, but for the national economy as a whole.

As regards Germany, the threat of traffic diversion is particularly a serious one because of

- Germany's central location in Europe;
- The polycentric nature of the German economy (which is reflected in the location of airports being rather evenly scattered throughout the country);

- The strong dependency of the viability of the German air transport system on international traffic flows; and
- The strong export orientation of the German economy as a whole which depends on efficient international transport services.

Central location in this case does not mean any privilege but, on the contrary, being surrounded by a large number of potent competitors.

Almost all larger secondary airports in Germany are closely located to at least one major foreign hub in Europe. For seven out of twelve of these airports the distance to the nearest foreign hub is below that to Frankfurt/Main. Among the foreign hubs, Amsterdam enjoys a favorable location with respect to Northern and Western German airports, with route distances for non-stop flights from Amsterdam to Bremen, Düsseldorf, Hamburg and Münster being shorter than that from Frankfurt/Main. The same holds for Berlin and Hamburg with respect to Copenhagen, and for Munich and Stuttgart with respect to Zurich. Taking also into account that the route distance between Dresden and Vienna is almost the same as between Dresden and Frankfurt/Main, that the distance between Cologne and Amsterdam (less than 150 miles) is only about 60 miles longer than that between Cologne and Frankfurt/Main, and is in the range where even ground transportation modes are strong competitors to air feeders, and finally, that route distances on another twelve routes between German secondary airports and foreign EU-hubs are less than 100 miles longer than that between the former and Frankfurt/Main, it is clear that almost any of the secondary airports in Germany lies in the hinterlands of at least two hubs. At least one of these is a foreign airport which is engaged in locational competition with Frankfurt/Main for hub services and, hence, exerts a threat of traffic diversion if restrictive regulation should lead to higher prices and/or lower quality of service on intercontinental routes under bilateral agreements. In particular Amsterdam, London, Paris and Zürich are very favorably linked to German secondary airports, with each of the four holding air services links to any one of the larger secondary airports in Germany in 1998.

Table 2-11 allows to assess the relative geographical location of the airport of Frankfurt/Main with respect to intercontinental traffic that originates in Hamburg as an exemplary secondary airport, and which has to connect at a European hub.[71] Included are high-density routes (in terms of passengers carried) to/from the global regions for the year 1998.

As can be seen from the selected routes from Hamburg, the German hub Frankfurt/Main is very well located at the center of intercontinental route networks compared with other EU hubs. However, Frankfurt/Main can claim to be the prime location in Europe (in terms of shortest distance) only with respect to destinations in Sub-Saharan Africa. In contrast, Copenhagen and Vienna are more favorably located than Frankfurt/M. with regard to intercontinental traffic flows between Hamburg and the Far East/Australia, which represents the region with the highest growth rates in intercontinental air transport to and from Germany. The same location advantage holds for Amsterdam, Brussels, London and Paris for several routes to North America, and for Amsterdam, Madrid, London and Paris for most of the selected routes to Middle/South America. In North Africa and the Middle East, most of the destinations can better be reached (in terms of route distance) when connecting at a foreign EU hub instead of Frankfurt/Main.

Since the third EU package for air transport liberalization has been implemented, all air carriers registered in the EU have unlimited access to all German airports.[72] As can be seen in Table 2-12, EU carriers used their new freedoms to link more secondary airports in Germany to foreign hubs and to increase flight frequencies on feeder routes. Between 1991 and 1998 seventeen new feeder routes were established, from which five link Amsterdam to Cologne, Dortmund, Dresden. Leipzig and Münster, one Brussels to Dresden, one Copenhagen to Bremen and three Vienna to Bremen, Dresden and Leipzig. With regard to flight frequencies, 42 out of those 95 feeder routes already established in 1991 were served by higher frequencies in 1998 compared to 1991, while only 12 experienced a reduction of the number of daily flights or ceased to be operated any more at all. Hence, service quality has increased on many feeder routes, which translates into an easier access than before for passengers living near secondary airports to flight connections on foreign EU hubs.

Table 2-11: Ticketed Point Mileage for Intercontinental Flight Connections from Hamburg

Destinations	European hubs					
	AMS	CPH	FRA	LHR	CDG	ZHR
Far East						
Bangkok	5939	5523	5832	6368	6323	6041
Beijing		4645	5097	5502	5562	5386
Hong Kong	6008	5559	5955	6428	6441	6210
Seoul	5686	n.a.	5628	6112	6022	6099
Singapore	6768	6387	6644	7197	7132	6836
Tokyo	6243	5809	6185	6669	6669	6456
Middle East/North Africa						
Amman	2350	n.a.	2149	2729	2565	n.a.
Bahrein	3203	n.a.	3016	3603	3461	3134
Cairo	2278	2161	2072	2636	2456	2137
Casablanca	1683	1992	1672	1762	1653	1719
Dehli	4190	3803	4061	4618	4549	4253
Tel Aviv	2289	2124	2088	2665	2499	2174
Sub Saharan Africa						
Harrare	5357	n.a.	5096	5609	5480	5197
Johannisburg	5839	n.a.	5657	6089	5885	5663
Nairobi	4384	4339	4181	4695	4493	4211
Middle/South America						
Buenos Aires	7351	n.a.	7396	7378	7343	7030
Bogota	5732	n.a.	5904	5743	5830	n.a.
Caracas	5108	n.a.	5276	5106	5200	5438
Mexico City	5957	n.a.	6192	5992	6179	n.a.
Santiago	7900	n.a.	7924	7942	7881	7986
Sao Paulo	6314	6644	6350	6345	6302	6408
North America						
Boston	3685	3860	3917	3716	3903	4167
Chicago	4345	4434	4589	4399	4605	4862
Los Angeles	5795	n.a.	6043	5891	6117	6350
Miami	4862	n.a.	5081	4879	5042	5308
New York	3875	4023	4108	3907	4093	4358
San Francisco	5696	n.a.	5942	5807	6037	6267
Toronto	3956	n.a.	4196	4002	4202	4462
Washington	4088	n.a.	4322	4121	4308	4572

Source:ABC World Airways Guide (July 1998).

Table 2-12: Air Transport Links between German Secondary Airports and EU Hubs, 1991 and 1998

	Amster-dam	Copen-hagen	London	Paris	Zurich	Total
Berlin	5 (3)	4 (3)	7 (9)	8 (4)	0 (5)	30 (33)
Bremen	5 (4)	1 (0)	5 (2)	2 (3)	2 (3)	19 (14)
Cologne	4 (0)	3 (1)	8 (5)	9 (7)	5 (4)	34 (20)
Dortmund	8 (0)	0 (0)	0 (1)	5 (0)	2 (0)	15 (1)
Dresden	3 (0)	0 (0)	2 (0)	2 (2)	2 (2)	11 (2)
Dusseldorf	6 (4)	4 (4)	21 (10)	9 (7)	9 (6)	62 (41)
Friedrichs-hafen	0 (0)	0 (0)	0 (0)	0 (1)	0 (2)	4 (3)
Hamburg	5 (7)	4 (4)	11 (8)	8 (6)	7 (3)	47 (41)
Hannover	5 (4)	4 (2)	4 (5)	6 (5)	5 (3)	31 (24)
Leipzig	2 (0)	0 (0)	2 (0)	0 (0)	2 (2)	7 (2)
Munich	8 (5)	5 (3)	14 (8)	11 (10)	9 (5)	68 (42)
Munster	3 (0)	0 (0)	1 (0)	3 (0)	2 (2)	9 (2)
Nuremberg	5 (4)	0 (0)	3 (2)	4 (3)	5 (3)	21 (16)
Stuttgart	6 (4)	3 (1)	5 (5)	8 (6)	6 (4)	40 (29)

Source: ABC World Airways Guide (July 1991 and July 1998).

Moreover, the market entry of independent airlines has made access to foreign EU hubs easier for customers of secondary airports. As the already mentioned study by Boss et. al. (1996) has demonstrated, the presence of independent airlines tends to lower airfares for passengers who demand a high flexibility for planning their journey and generate above-average yields for the airlines. As Table 2-13 shows, 37 feeder routes out of a total of 80 are served by independent airlines. Another 5 are served by Crossair, which is a regional carrier legally affiliated with Swissair, and a further 5 routes are served by airlines using 5th freedom rights. Among the independents, especially Eurowings is very active in feeding foreign EU hubs, linking almost any of the German secondary airports to Amsterdam. This airline and also Tyrolean Air operate code-share flights with Air France.[73] Only 23 feeder routes are exclusively served by EU flag carriers. Hence, also with regard to pricing it might be expected that any approach to regulate intercontinental routes to and from Germany has to face a strong threat of traffic diversion.

Table 2-13: Air Carriers Operating between German Secondary Airports and EU-hubs, 1998

	Amsterdam	Copenhagen	London	Paris	Zürich
Berlin	KL	LH, SK	BA, 7L[a]	LH, AF, CO[c]	SR, LH, DL[c]
Bremen	KL, WA[a]	ZR[a]	—	LH	LX[b]
Cologne	EW[a], KL	—	BA, BD[a], LH	LH, AF, CO[c]	LH
Dortmund	EW[a], KL	—	—	AF, EW[a]	EW[a]
Dresden	EW[a], KL	—	BD[a], EW[a], LH, UK[a]	LH	LX[b]
Dusseldorf	EW[a], KL	LH, SK	BA, LH, UK[a], VG[a], 2G[a]	AF, LH	DL[c], LH, SR
Hamburg	KL	FI[c], LH, SK	BA, LH, UA[c], UK[a]	AF, LH	LH, SR
Hannover	—	LH, SK	BA, LH	AF, EW[a], LH	LH, SR
Leipzig	EW[a], KL	—	LH	—	LX[b]
Munich	KL, LH	LH, SK	BA, LH, UA[c], 2G[a]	AF, CO[c], LH	DL[c], LH, SR, TG[c]
Munster	EW[a], KL	—	5E[a]	AF, EW[a]	LX[b]
Nuremberg	EW[a], KL	—	EW[a], LH, UK	EW[a], HF	LX[b]
Stuttgart	EW[a], KL	LH, SK	BA, LH	AF, CO[c], LH	DL[c], SR

Source: ABC World Airways Guide (July 1998).

Spillover effects of market regimes might also be determined by frequent-flyer programs. As has already been discussed, these programs are designed to lure passengers into dedicated networks, thus protecting the airline that has introduced a frequent flyer program from vigorous competition. The effectiveness of frequent-flyer programs depends not at least on the number and geographical variety of destinations offered within the respective network. The domestic hub would be in a superior position only insofar as the frequent-flyer program of the resident carrier would provide passengers with more, and more attractive, travel options (and opportunities to 'collect miles') than the bonus schemes of the carriers operating from competing foreign hubs. However, as meanwhile every major airline operates its own frequent-flyer program, and often is linked to the bonus programs of attractive alliance partners, the number and attractiveness of routes offered to connecting passengers at foreign hubs may well equalize any competitive advantage of the resident carrier's program in binding travelers to the domestic hub.

Table 2-14: International Routes[1] Offered at European Hubs 1998

	Intra-EU	Rest of Europe	North Atlantic	Rest of America	Middle East	Sub-Saharan Africa	Far East
Amsterdam	48	17	11	3	20	2	8
Brüssel	54	12	11	1	6	6	4
Copenhagen	50	26	4	3	4	0	5
Frankfurt	51	30	24	5	28	5	13
Istanbul							
London	78	27	32	14	26	9	15
Madrid							
Paris CDG[2)]	73	21	21	7	20	12	12
Rome							
Vienna	30	33	2	0	4	2	4
Zurich							

[1)]Number of Destinations at Wednesday, 1st week of July — [2)]CDG = Charles de Gaulle

Source: ABC World Airways Guide (July 1998).

Table 2-14 shows the number of routes offered at major EU hubs in July 1998. As can be seen, the airport of Frankfurt/Main is among the top three European hubs with regard to the number of international connections offered. Only London and Paris offer more international routes. Hence, Frankfurt/M. holds a strong position among European hubs. However, while the German hub offers travelers more routes to North Africa/Middle East than any other EU hub, London and Paris offer more routes to Middle/South America and also to Sub-Saharan Africa. Frankfurt/M. is also only second with regard to routes to Far East/Australia, closely followed by Paris. Hence, it may be concluded that, although the German hub is a major player in the European interhub market, the frequent-flyer program of Lufthansa, the dominant carrier in Frankfurt/Main, is insufficient to shield this airport from competition.

Finally, another determinant of interhub competition and hence of the threat of traffic diversion is airport capacity. Frankfurt/Main already operates at its declared maximum capacity and is prevented by environmental reasons from building additional capacity. Hence, its potential of attracting new traffic is limited. Even if environmental concerns could be overcome, it could be expected that it will last a very long time until new runway capacity will come into operation.[74] In contrast, a number of competing EU hubs either have not yet reached their declared capacities, or are planning new terminals and runways in the mid future (Button et. al. 1998: 82):

- Amsterdam intends to double its capacity (in terms of passenger throughput) until 2003, including the construction of new runways and taxiways;
- Brussels is going to triple its capacity in the following two decades;
- Paris (Charles de Gaulle) increased its capacity in recent years stepwise for an additional throughput of no less than 10 million passengers annually; moreover, an entirely new airport for Paris is planned at Charters;
- The runway capacity of Rome is thought to be sufficient until 2005.
- The provision of new runways is also part of the master plans of Athens (in the course of replacing the old airport of Hellenikon), Helsinki, Madrid, Manchester, Oslo, Rotterdam (also a replacement project) and Stockholm.

Hence, major competitors to Frankfurt/Main. will ease their existing capacity constraints in the medium-term future. It can be expected that these airports will benefit from congested capacities at Frankfurt/Main in any case, given the serious impediments for increasing capacities there. Accordingly, they would benefit from any traffic diversion that might be induced by restrictive regulation of German intercontinental air traffic under the still existing bilateral agreements.

In contrast, granting foreign air carriers from non-EU countries new traffic rights to directly serve additional German secondary airports can be expected to challenge the market position of Frankfurt/Main compared to foreign hubs only to a minor extent, although it might be expected that it would lose traffic to German secondary airports. However, also foreign hubs such as Amsterdam, London and Zurich can be expected to lose traffic as liberalization redirects diverted traffic from foreign hubs to secondary airports in Germany. New direct links would not only take away traffic flows from Frankfurt/Main but to a large extent also from its close European competitors, given the dense European feeder network. Moreover, in view of the expected overall air traffic growth, doubts may be raised whether Frankfurt/Main will be able to maintain its privileged position among German airports, unless the limitations to increase its capacity would be eased at rather short notice. Taking these limitations for granted, not only German secondary airports would benefit from granting additional traffic rights, but also the German air transport system as a whole.

Conclusions

This chapter started with two kinds of arguments, which are usually, put forward in favor of regulation of international air transport markets by means of bilateral air service agreements. The first kind of these arguments refers to conjectured failures of deregulated air transport markets. However, the experiences with such markets in the United States as well as with intra-EU air transport reveal that liberalized air transport markets perform better than regulated ones, because competition forces the airlines to improve productivity and to supply services that better match the preferences of passengers and freight forwarders. Although deregulated air transport markets do not mirror perfect contestability, competition between airlines is workable. In contrast, regulation not only proves to be inflexible and thus hampers dynamic responses of the air transport system to changing patterns of transport demand, but is also prone to regulatory capture. Thus, regulation clearly tends to raise the costs of air transport to the detriment of air transport users. Empirical evidence also shows that deregulation does not affect the airlines' safety records negatively. Putting both results together, it may be concluded that deregulated air transport markets show no tendency to produce systematic market failures. A need for sector-specific regulation does therefore not exist.

The second kind of arguments in favor of regulation by bilateral air service agreements refers to the prospects of generating rents for the national air transport system or even for the national economy as a whole. The discussion in previous sections has, however, shown that the prospects of success depend on a number of strong preconditions, which must be fulfilled to render a strategic policy approach successful. The prospects of generating rents by restricting foreign airlines' ability to compete with the national airline(s) are limited by

- The threat of retaliation;
- Reduced incentives for the airlines and airports to improve their productivity; as well as

- The emergence of spillover effects of regulation to third markets.

All of these factors have a negative impact on the national economy. As has been demonstrated, the threat of regulation-induced traffic diversion is a serious one particularly for Germany: Since all EU air carriers have unrestricted access to all German airports, while the national centers of economic activity are geographically dispersed throughout the country and linked by high-quality feeder services to foreign EU hubs which offer passengers and freight forwarders a dense network of routes, any negative effect of regulation on air fares and service quality might induce a redirection of some traffic flows via foreign hubs to the detriment of the German airport system as well as to the detriment of the German economy as a whole. This redirection would result in regulation-induced positive externalities on airlines and airports in foreign EU countries, which compete with the German air transport system but have already liberalized their air transport relationships with countries outside the EU. Such externalities might be particularly important if non-EU airlines are disallowed to serve German secondary airports directly. They would not only affect traffic flows to German secondary airports that are denied direct access to world air transport, but also yield repercussions to other yet liberalized markets. In effect, national passengers and freight forwarders who prefer using direct air services from secondary airports instead of connecting at a hub, will suffer immediately from regulation, whereas foreign EU airlines and airports will benefit from increased economies of scope and density. As a result, competitiveness of the German air transport system will deteriorate. At the same time, with respect to other sectors of business, the foreign economies' access to worldwide air transport would improve if their air transport relationships to non-EU countries should be liberalized while Germany would still prefer a restrictive policy approach. Their transport costs would be reduced, and their presence on world markets could be strengthened. As just the reverse would be true for the German economy, it would suffer from a locational disadvantage vis-à-vis its rivals in other countries.

Clearly, the threat of traffic diversion in the wake of the liberalization of intra-EU air transport also limits the prospects of using bilaterals as a means to enhance the bargaining power of Germany vis-à-vis its trading partners. Hence, this argument has also lost much of its appeal with regard to supporting the still existing system of bilateral air service agreements.

The point that is to be made here, is that since the complete liberalization of intra-EU air transport all EU countries compete with each other for international air traffic flows by means of the institutional design of their bilateral agreements with non-EU countries: Those EU members will be successful in attracting international traffic flows, and hence will reap the greatest benefits from the liberalized EU air transport markets, that manage to attract international air traffic to their own national air transport system by means of liberalizing still existing restrictive bilaterals, and thus enable the exploitation of economies of scope and traffic density by their own airlines and airports. Hence, it may be concluded, liberalization of international air transport will be a chance rather than an impediment for enhancing social welfare of the German economy as a whole, because early liberalization might generate a first-mover advantage for the German air transport system vis-à-vis its EU rivals, while a delay of liberalization might work in favor of other EU countries.

---

[1] For a comprehensive overview on intra-regional air services agreements see Lyle (2000).

[2] See Sichelschmidt (1991) on the conseqences of the Gulf war for international aviation.

[3] Information on the IATA's and ACI's growth forecasts can be found in Airline Business (February 1998: 65 and November 1998: 86).

[4] Of course, also specialized freight carriers can be found in the marketplace. For instance, Federal Express which operates a fleet of all-freight aircrafts was in terms of revenue generated the third largest airline of the world in 1997 (Productivity Commission 1998: 9).

[5] 1 work load unit = 1 WLU = 1 passenger or 0,1 tonnes freight.

[6] Own calculations according to Statistisches Bundesamt (various years).

[7] More recent data is currently not available. Calculation is based on Institut der Deutschen Wirtschaft (1992); Deutsches Institut für Wirtschaftsforschung (1996).

[8] Calculation is based on Institut der Deutschen Wirtschaft (1998).

[9] In 1991 more jobs than on the site of Frankfurt airport were only offered at the sites of Volkswagen in Wolfsburg and of BASF in Ludwigshafen (Meier 1991: 48).

[10] Calculation is based on Deutsches Institut für Wirtschaftsforschung (1996).

[11] See Bremmiker et. al (1982); Gresser/Kessel (1983); Sorgenfrei (1989); Hübl et. al. (1990); Atzkern (1992); Pagnia (1992).

[12] Another necessary prerequisite for air carriers' operations is the provision of air traffic control (ATC) services. However, as ATC services will not be relevant to this report they are not considered here.

[13] As a result of the liberalization of air transport markets, discount tickets at substantially lower fares, which are attractive in particular to leisure travelers, are offered by the carriers since the beginning of the 1990s. This may have reduced the share of business travelers in terms of passengers carried. However, as air fares for flexible business travel remained high, business travelers' share in terms of airlines' revenue may even have increased.

[14] Gillen, Harris and Oum (1997: 45) report an upper range of price elasticity of leisure travelers to be -1,65; i.e. a 10percent price rise will lead demand for leisure travel to drop to up to 16.5percent.

[15] The existence of economies of traffic density in the airline industry means that the volume of traffic throughput within a given route network consisting of a given number of points served is negatively correlated with the airlines' average costs. For an empirical study on the existence of economies of density in the airline industry see Caves, Christensen and Tretheway (1984). Economies of scope in the airline industry means that the consolidation of various traffic flows on a given number of routes by the use of hub-and-spoke systems leads to a decline of the airlines' average costs.

[16] Economies of scale refer to the cost effect of mere firm size. Positive economies of scale would exist if a large airline could provide its services at lower costs than a smaller one, with size measured either in revenue, in technical parameters, such as aircraft fleet, or in size of the network (but, in the latter case, without reference to network externalities). For surveys on empirical studies on the existence of economies of scale in the airline industry see Laaser (1991: 75 ff.) and Oum and Tretheway (1992: 7 ff.).

[17] For empirical studies see Doganis and Thompson (1973), Doganis and Graham (1987) and Doganis et. al. (1995).

[18] Economies of scale in the airport sector would exist if unit costs decrease as an airport's capacity increases. The existence of economies of traffic density in this industry means that unit costs fall as more traffic is handled with a given airport capacity.

[19] With the liberalization of the EU Single Air Transport Market intra EU-air travel is legally treated in the same way as purely domestic travel. Therefore a higher proportion of intra-EU passengers does not mean automatically higher costs of airport operation any more. Only handling of non-EU traffic by EU-airports will induce extra costs compared with the handling of domestic traffic due to the reasons mentioned above.

[20] This holds especially for Europe, because distances within this region are rather low (compared with, for example, the U. S.), which limits prospects to build en-route hubs without a sound base of direct flying passengers (Behder 1995). For empirical studies on the geographical determinants of hub location in the United States and Europe see Bauer (1987); and Butler and Huston (1991 and 1993).

[21] For details on the design and the effects of the regulatory framework which may affect the airports's ability to attract traffic see chapters C and D.

[22] A later attempt to reach agreement on a multilateral market order for international air transport at the Geneva Conference of 1947 also failed.

[23] The transit agreement was signed by 100 states (Nuutinen 1992: 14). A noticeable exception was the former Soviet Union which for military reasons denied to grant first and second freedom rights on a multilateral basis.

[24] The institutional framework for the operation of air transport services to and from the geographical area of the former GDR and Berlin (West) did not change until German reunification in 1990. Therefore it will not be mentioned in the following expositions.

[25] Some US airlines used their extensive fifth freedom rights they have gained to build own hub operations in Europe (Levine 1989: 4).

[26] Because of the small geographical size of the former GDR domestic scheduled air traffic was nonexistent in Eastern Germany until reunification of Germany in 1990. Therefore the following expositions are limited to the air transport policy of the FRG.

[27] Exceptions were some very low density routes between the mainland of Germany and some islands in the North Sea which were operated by small turboprops on a regular basis ('Seebäderverkehr'). A special case held for Berlin (West). As a result of the legal status Berlin had gained in foreign politics after World War II no German airline was allowed to serve the city's airports. Instead, traffic to and from Berlin was reserved for airlines of the U.S., the United Kingdom and France.

[28] In Germany, this procedure stands on the legal grounds of the 10th amendment of the national Air Transport Law of June 1990.

[29] The problem of "double monopolization" refers to the pricing decisions of independent firms, which provide services at subsequent stages of a vertically industry structure (Spengler 1950). For the case of airlines it may be explained as follows: If one airline provides a service which feeds traffic into the network of another air carrier, and if both airlines price their services to customers independently, not taking into account the effect of the own price setting behaviour on the profit of the other airline, then the aggregate profit of both airlines will be lower than if they would co-ordinate their pricing in order to maximize joint profit. If instead both air carriers co-ordinate prices of their services by offering through fares, then they would gain additional aggregate profit, which they can distribute among themselves. Furthermore, price co-ordination leads to more output in the market, because the optimal through price is lower than the aggregate of two prices which emerge by independent pricing for both interconnected services. Hence, also consumers benefit.

[30] The airport of Dusseldorf does not directly suffer from inadequate physical runway capacity, but is prohibited to use that capacity to its technical limit because of a cap on the number of allowed air transport movements, which is due to environmental policy reasons.

[31] Apart from the economic arguments of market failures in liberalized air transport markets, a somewhat related argument is derived from a national security perspective (e.g. Doganis (1993: 61 f.). According to this argument, a country which operates its own airlines is prevented from becoming subject to the whims of periodic international economic or political crises. As the scope of this study is limited to the effects of regulation on productive and allocative efficiency of the national air transport system, we will not analyze the significance of this argument (although several counterarguments can be raised, cf. Knorr (1998a: 384) on this topic). However, even if it is felt that this kind of security reasoning had to be considered when deciding on the design of national air transport policy, the results of this study will reveal the economic costs of such a policy approach and, hence, will allow for a comprehensive assessment of this argument against economic efficiency criteria.

[32] Although the European Commssion has labeled the implementation of the liberalization packages for intra-EU air transport 'liberalization' as opposed to 'deregulation (US-style)', the main difference between the EU- and the US-move to free market regimes seems to be that the former had introduced a phased process which lasted for more than a decade, while the US-government choose a 'big-bang'-approach. A comparison of the EU- and the US-policy approaches can be found in Button et. al (1998: 54 ff.).

[33] For older assessments cf. e.g. Laaser (1991: Sect. VII.2.g) and Keeler (1992), for a more recent one Knorr (1998b: 440 ff.).

[34] With regard to increased concentration at hub airports and spatial price differentials the term 'fortress hubs' has emerged.

[35] However, at the network level sunk costs might be non-neglible.

[36] A 'Ramsey-price pattern' describes a social welfare-maximizing price structure set by a multiproduct firm for its products. Social welfare is maximized if relative prices for different goods/services are set accordingly to short run marginal costs plus mark-ups that ensure break even. The relative mark-ups are inversely related to the relative price elasticities for these goods/services. Hence, goods/services offered on price sensitive markets are sold at a lower price-mark up than goods/services that are sold on price insensitive ones.

[37] In this respect, the emergence of 'fortress hubs' might be an essential feature ensuring the stability of the airlines' networks. Interestingly, Borenstein and Rose (1994) report price differentials between different fare classes to be positively correlated to the number of competitors on a route, and hence to the degree of competition that might be expected on (imperfect contestable) OD-markets, thus supporting the above stated argument. For problems of sustainability of efficient airline networks which are perfectly contestable see Bittlingmayer (1990).

[38] Incumbent carriers at several US hubs have acquired the exclusive right of disposal for the majority of gates on the base of long-term leasing contracts, which often last for more than twenty years. By this they can easiliy discriminate against competitors in a variety of ways (Langner 1996).

[39] For the effects of liberalisation of EU air transport markets in general c.f. Button et. al. (1998: 47 ff.). With particular regards to Germany c.f. Sichelschmidt and Wolf (1993) and also Boss et. al. (1996: 150 ff.).

[40] Terminal gate scarcity and dominance is not a problem at European airports.

[41] The topic of ASA-induced transaction costs will be discussed at length in a later section.

[42] A survey of the theory of strategic trade policy is given by Bletschacher and Klodt (1992). Main contributions to this theory were delivered, for example, by Brander and Spencer (1983), Dixit (1984), and Krugman (1984).

[43] Air transport services provided by air carriers on the same routes are not perfect substitutes if passengers and freight forwarders have distinct preferences other than price when choosing a carrier for their flight. Empirical studies have shown that passengers often prefer to fly with airlines registered in their own countries even if the price is higher

than that charged by competing foreign air carriers. For example, an empirical study by Ghobrial (1989) who attempted to assess the effects of some quality-of-service variables on the competition situation of U.S. and foreign carriers, could demonstrate that Europeans usually prefer to take their national carriers. One of the reasons for this observation might be, for instance, frequent flyer programs.

[44] The assumption of single designation assures exogenous market structures within this context.

[45] Formally, economies of traffic density are expressed by a cost function C(Q) satisfying $C'(Q) > 0$ and $C''(Q) < 0$, whereby C represents the cost function and Q the volume of traffic (Caves, Christensen and Tretheway 1984; Brueckner, Dyer and Spiller 1994; Zhang 1996).

[46] In order not to overcharge Figure 2.9 it is assumed that both carriers operate with identical cost functions C.

[47] The less price elastic residents react the steeper is the respective demand curve. The same holds for the demand of foreigners. Thus, the less price elastic both groups react, the more will the price for air transport increase as an effect of a given output contraction in the market.

[48] For this reason OD-markets which are heavily frequented by business travellers and forwarders which demand short delivery times may be prime candidates for unilateral regulation. This reasoning is consistent with the historical fact that European charter air services were excluded from regulation of international air transport markets from the 1950s on, while scheduled services had been subject to tight regulation up to the 1980s. A formal analysis in which way the price elasticity of air transport users affects the optimal design of unilateral regulation of third/fourth freedom traffic within an (implicit) analytical framework of exogenous market structures is presented by Clarke (1995).

[49] However, distributional consequences might be high.

[50] Both countries face a 'prisoner's dilemma': Independent profit seeking by both countries will leave both worse off than coordinated action.

[51] Cost reductions of the flag carrier might, for example, stem from deploying larger aircrafts with lower unit costs to serve the route whereby the additional traffic volume would allow for sufficient load factors of the larger aircraft.

[52] With regard to the graphical illustration presented by figure 2.9 an increase in X-inefficiency of the flag carrier as a result of regulation would increase that carrier's marginal costs and hence would induce a downward shift of its reaction function. The function's shift was ommitted in figure 2.9 in order not to overcharge the drawing.

[53] However, when reading the following sub-sections, the likelyhood and the effects of retaliation and regulation induced X-inefficiency as discussed above should always been kept in mind.

[54] Both assumptions together guarantee an exogenous market structure.

[55] As was already described, a 6th freedom right represents a combination of two third/fourth freedom rights.

[56] As was already discussed many passengers and freight forwarders prefer online connections. Furthermore, by offering through fares, the flag carrier can avoid the problem of double monopolization.

[57] Because of regulation, traffic consolidation is not contestable by the c-link.

[58] However, the prospects of generating rents for the flag carrier will be reduced or even vanish if also the foreign country ceases to represent a dimensionless spot place, but if instead multiple airports are located in this country. Then, the foreign country may retaliate by restricting access to its domestic market in a similar way for the flag carrier, thus reserving feeder traffic which originates or terminates in the foreign country for its own airline. In general, retaliation will harm the flag carrier the more, the higher the share of connecting traffic in the foreign country is, and the more negligible the role of connecting traffic is within the home country. Hence, the smaller the traffic potential of a country compared to its trading partner, the less effective will be the foreclosure of secondary airports in the home country to the foreign airline.

[59] However, when reading the following sub-sections, the likelyhood and the effects of retaliation as discussed above should always been kept in mind.

[60] However, a highly significant danger of retaliation exists, unless the existing air service agreement would provide the opportunity for multiple designation. It could be expected that the foreign country would try to receive compensation for being restricted twice: by restricting its airline's output in the first place and by additional competition from the home country in the second. Hence, making use of the competitive countervailing powers of the independent carriers may not be feasible without granting the same rights to the foreign country, i.e. to resign from strategic restrictions altogether.

[61] Accordingly, the foreign airport may partly offset its loss with regards to traffic on the b-link.

[62] The results of the analysis will not be fundamentally affected by the assumption of free trade in air transport services between the home and the foreign as well as the fourth country. The alternative assumption (regulation of the b-link as in the last section) would alter the general results of this section only quantitatively, not qualitatively. We assume free trade in air transport services between the home and the foreign country here only for the sake of concentrating on the problem of 5th freedom rights.

[63] This case (for instance) air transport relationships between Germany and EU-countries (i.e. the third and fourth country) and a Non-EU-country (i.e. the foreign country).

[64] Off course connecting traffic in the market between the foreign country and the secondary airport may prncipally also connect in the fourth country. However, as passengers would have to make two connections in two different countries, and moreover, trip distance would increase significantly, this option will not be considered here.

[65] Once an agreement is terminated and no follow-up is negotiated, transaction costs may increase substantially because each single flight has to be approved by both national

authorities, a case to be found between the USA and France for more than three years (Knorr 1998a: 385, footnote 4).

[66] For a critical assessment of ownership rules see also Findlay et. al. (1996: 21) and Productivity Commission (1998: 105 f.).

[67] In July 1983, only 3 direct air transport links between regional airports in Western Germany and foreign EU-countries. In July 1993 their number has increased to 12 and even to 27 in July 1998 (ABC World Airways Guide (various years).

[68] See also Productivity Commission (1998: 104).

[69] The distances between the airports were extracted from the ABC World Airways Guide (July 1998), which shows 'ticketed pont mileages', i.e. airport to airport and non-stop by the shortest operated route, measured in statute miles.

[70] Routes that were exclusively served by charter airlines before 1989 and routes between Germany and the UK were already liberalized prior to 1989.

[71] Geographical distances are used here as a proxy for measuring the potential for traffic diversion. Of course, there is no direct strict relationship between distance and costs or fares, at least on deregulated markets (former, i.e. pre-deregulation, US domestic air fares were indeed regulated by the Civil Aeronautics Board according to a distance scale; the same was true for pre-deregulation charges in German trucking). But using distances in our analysis is justified by their relevance for airport authorities' and carriers' decisions on adequate reactions to competitive pressure.

[72] Although legally all EU-air carriers have unlimited access to all German airports, in practice airport congestion will hamper access especially to the airports of Frankfurt/M. and Düsseldorf.

[73] Accordingly, the label 'independent airline' may be somewhat ambiguous. The formation of strategic alliances can also contribute to this ambiguity if former independents become allied partners of flag carriers. But as long as there is sufficient competition between such alliances, the effect of traffic diversion to foreign hubs is likely to occur.

[74] For example, the planning and building of the new Munich airport which went into operation in 1992 took more than 20 years.

3. Analytical Framework

Introduction

A change in the bilateral agreements governing access to the German market as well as access by German and other European carriers to other markets will have a number of outcomes. These include changes to the frequency of flights, the gauge of aircraft flown and the number of passengers carried. These changes will be distributed among the various airports in Germany according to the competitive circumstances and the comparative advantage of each airport. Our interest is Hamburg Airport and the region surrounding the Hamburg Airport. How will the changes brought about by changes to the bilateral influence the fortunes of Hamburg Airport and environs?

The economic impacts resulting from changes to the ASA can be represented in four separate components. First, with changes in the number of flights, size of aircraft and numbers of passengers in total and per flight, the airport revenue will be affected. Second, the economy of the airport region will be affected due to changes in access to external markets. This can be modeled in two ways, as a conventional input-output (IO) model using economic multipliers or as a regional econometric model that links aviation activity, employment and income. Third, the linkage between aviation activity and investment can be modeled using a single or multi-equation regional economic model. Finally, using the most recent measures of tourist response to changes in access and applying the elasticity to the representative countries in our investigation can assess tourism impacts.

Overview of the Air Liberalization Model

This section describes the methodology behind the Air Liberalization Model (ALM). This model generates representative and policy relevant measures of the magnitude and distribution of benefits and costs from liberalizing international air services agreements. Supporting the need for policy oriented results, the model provides policy makers with an approximation of the [welfare] impacts of bilateral air transport liberalization on domestic and foreign consumers, airlines, and airports. One of the main features of the model is that it is adaptable to a full range of liberalization scenarios, regardless of specific national circumstances.

The need for general, policy relevant results drives the model's structure. The model strikes a balance between the complexity of modeling, the minute detail of a bilateral relationship, and the need to maintain a model structure that is applicable to a broad range of regulatory and market circumstances. The demand model takes full advantage of the available demand data for international OD routes by incorporating price, demand, and qualitative factors. The supply model utilizes airline data as the basis for constructing costs and adjusts these costs to reflect international carrier circumstances.

Policy orientation demands that ALM be capable of modeling 'real world' changes in the bilateral conditions. For this reason, the policy instruments or levers most commonly encountered in international aviation markets have driven the modeling effort. The result is an equilibrium model which is fully capable of capturing the effects of modifications in frequency, number or type of carriers, connection, travel time, and national preferences as well as the impacts of fare changes.

This model combines elements of many previous studies in international aviation to provide quantitative evidence of the magnitude and distribution of benefits and costs from liberalization. This 'Core Model' is modified to account for the effects of non-competitive markets and third country effects.[1]

The prescribed model is best characterized as a competitive analysis set in a bilateral negotiating framework. The principal assumption of this case is that markets are [highly] competitive because it is assumed that there are no economies of firm size or economies of traffic density in air transportation. The implication of this assumption is that changes in bilateral regulatory conditions, which reduce airline costs, will translate into an equal reduction in fares paid by consumers.

To operationalize this framework, the study team developed the ALM. The model has three principal components:

1. *Demand Module*—The behavioral module is used to simulate the changes in demand, which result from either a change in price or a change in service quality. Underlying methodology taken from trade economics to estimate the change in an airlines market share resulting from a change in price or product quality.[2]
2. *Carrier Cost Module*—This module develops component airline costs (direct and indirect) for each airline segment and carrier by comparing the relative productivity of carriers in a competitive market setting.
3. *Policy Module*—This module contains the rules that define the process of market transition from a more to less restrictive regulatory regime. These rules, or transition scenarios, reflect actual airline operations in alternative market circumstances and are related to frequency of service, load factors and carrier entry and exit.

These model components are then used to simulate liberalization scenarios estimate the potential gains (losses) from liberalization, for consumers and producers. Consumer benefits are measured in terms of the value travelers' place on reduced fares and changes in service quality as measured by flight frequency. Producer effects are measured in terms of changes in flight segment profits. The model also distributes benefits and costs by stakeholder group (consumers and producers of each nation).

Model Overview

The modeling approach is represented by the stylized demand and supply (cost) functions illustrated in Figure 3.1. Underlying each of these functions is a well specified relationship and a collection of behavioral assumptions set in a particular market structure.

The status quo, defined for the existing set of bilateral and market characteristics, provides the current number of passengers traveling, by carrier and route between the countries at issue at the current fares, service quality, product offerings, number of carriers and seats supplied. This can be used to define the level of consumer welfare (A), producer profit (B) and factor employment and payments. When bilateral reform takes place, this provides the basis from which benefits and costs are measured and their distribution identified.

Figure 3.1: Welfare Analysis Framework for Bilateral Reforms

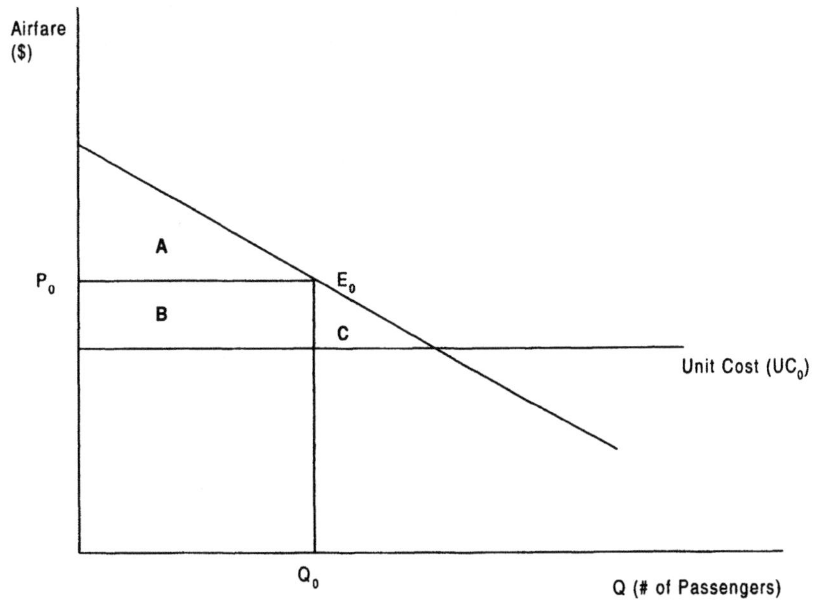

Under the existing bilateral regimes, the airlines may receive profit as a result of fares that exceed average unit costs, Area B in Figure 3.1, for example. If we move to a competitive equilibrium fares will equate with [constant] average costs. Therefore, consumers receive all of the gains, measured in terms of consumer-surplus.

The model must be sufficiently rich to capture the effects of changes on the level and distribution of benefits which occur in terms of both demand and supply side. Considering a change in a bilateral, how would the effects manifest themselves in the model? There are three changes: (i) a change in relative fares which generates a movement along the demand function; (ii) a change in service quality which results in a shift of the demand function; and (iii) a change in passenger or flight costs which cause a shift of the supply function. These outcomes are illustrated in Figure 3.2. The model links these changes with the [particular] bilateral reforms.

The equilibrium prior to the reforms is at P_1Q_1, or E_1. After reforms the new equilibrium is at P_2Q_2, or E_2. An important point to be made is that we observe E_1 as our base case. The gains from liberalization are calculated by estimating what the equilibrium would be in the event that a policy lever or combination of levers change. In Figure 3.2 this is identified by the point E_2. In a perfect competition model, point E_2 is identified by assuming: (i) price should equal average cost; (ii) industry costs will be reduced to UC_2 with these costs reflecting the degree of liberalization and best practice technology; and (iii) demand will shift to D_2 reflecting the change in key quality of service variables which are regulated by a bilateral agreement. The shaded area in Figure 3.2 represents net benefits.

Figure 3.2: Welfare Analysis for Change to Base Case

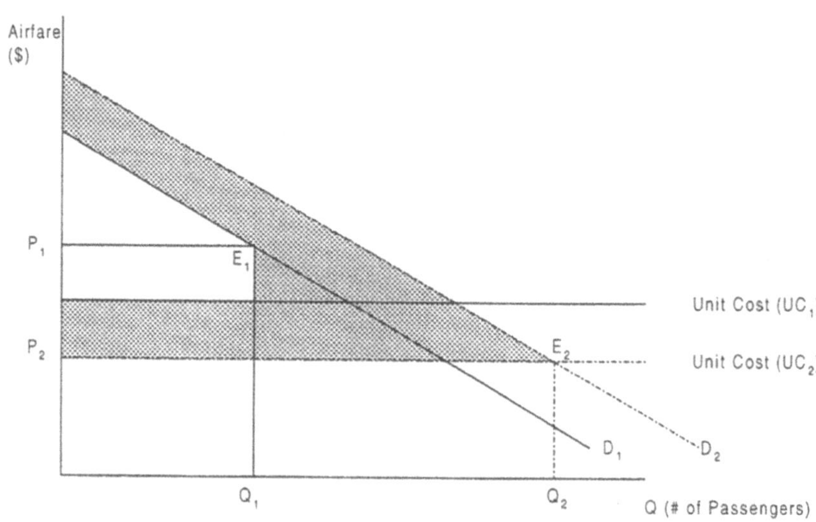

Trade Policy Analysis

Trade policy analysis uses the analytical framework of the neoclassical model of international trade developed extensively over the last fifty years. Three assumptions are common to traditional trade theory: (i) at least one factor is internationally immobile, or the technologies for producing the traded goods are fixed (i.e., could not move between countries); (ii) countries differ in either their endowments of the primary factors of production or in terms of relative levels of productivity; and (iii) the various commodities being traded are produced with no economies of scale at the national level. In the last decade, trade policy analysis has developed to the point where it now allows for more realistic assumptions on market structure (economies of scale, differentiated products), but it otherwise uses the same micro-economic tools found in traditional trade theory.[3]

Trade policy examines the magnitude and distribution of gains and losses among countries, owing to changes in factors that affect trade, including policy changes. The policy instruments are usually in the form of changes in the level of either tariff or non-tariff barriers, expressed either as price distortions or quantitative constraints on exports or imports. These gains or losses have two sources: (i) a country's specialization in industries where it enjoys a comparative advantage, and (ii) relative price changes which favor one country at the expense of another. A distinguishing feature of trade policy analysis is its concern with how the burden of adjustment is distributed among factors of production and trading partners as a consequence of policy changes.

Trade policy analysis is often conducted with a strategic view in mind, in that it evaluates the trade-off between one industry versus another at the domestic level. This multi-industry focus is quite different from the single-industry regulatory approach that has characterized the analysis of the air transport industry to date.

The above discussion identifies the requirements for our modeling approach, namely, a level of disaggregation to distinguish demand by nationality, traveler type, carrier and route. Furthermore, the demand specification needs to have both price and non-price factors [service quality, numbers of carriers] and the cost function must be specified in such a way as to be sensitive to flight and non-flight costs [direct and indirect costs] as liberalization takes place. This combination of features distinguishes this model from others in that it blends the standard benefit cost framework with the advantages of a product differentiated trade policy model.

Model Specification

Cost-benefit analysis is used to measure the costs and benefits accruing to consumers and producers of a commodity when the price of that commodity, its quality or its production costs change. These changes usually result in new output levels and a corresponding, economy-wide, re-allocation of productive resources.[4]

In the case of air travel (assumed here to be produced at constant long-run average costs), a decrease in the price of travel over a city-pair will have two effects: (i) travelers who are already flying will benefit from paying less (area A in Figure 3.3), and (ii) travelers who previously would not travel by air between the two cities will buy flights at the new affordable rates (area C in Figure 3.3). New consumers could either be those who previously did not travel by air or at all, or individuals who previously could only afford one flight but can now purchase more at the lower fare.

For the same commodity, an improvement in quality represented perhaps by an increase in flight frequency from one level to another will shift the demand curve. The benefits will go to current travelers who enjoy the higher quality for the same price (area B in Figure 3.3), or to new travelers who find that the improvements justify the price, or to some combination of the two (area C' in Figure 3.3).

Figure 3.3: Welfare Analysis for Air Transport Liberalization

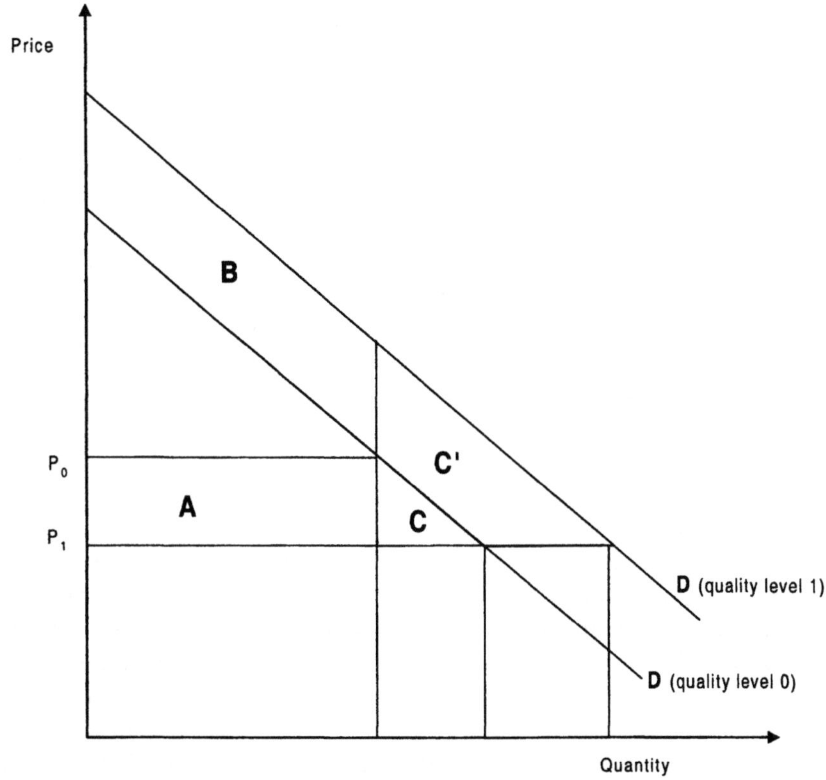

For a reduction in price consumer benefits can be expressed mathematically by the following equation:

$$\int_{p_1}^{\infty} q(p)dp - \int_{p_0}^{\infty} q(p)dp \qquad \textit{Equation 1}$$

Where $q(p)$ is the quantity q (of flights) demanded as a function of price p. The variable p_0 is the current price of the commodity and p_1 is its changed price. (Here, costs are constant and do not enter into the equation directly.)

With an increase in product quality, the demand curve shifts to $q'(p)$ so that the benefits to consumers assuming price remains constant at p_1 are given by:

$$\int_{p_1}^{\infty} (q'(p) - q(p))dp \qquad \textit{Equation 2}$$

For a change in both cost and quality, the benefits to consumers are given by:

$$\int_{p_1}^{\infty} q'(p)dp \; - \int_{p_0}^{\infty} q(p)dp \qquad \textit{Equation 3}$$

One of the assumptions underlying cost-benefit analysis, apart from the specification of supply and demand equations, is that savings from a drop in the price of a commodity will not be large enough to significantly change people's spending patterns. Therefore, the bundle of goods and services consumed remains unchanged as air travel is liberalized.

Demand Model Specification The model provides estimates of the impact on consumers and producers from a change in one or a combination of four policy levers: (i) a change in flight frequency, (ii) a change in the number of carriers allowed to enter a market, (iii) fare regulation, and (iv) the designation of particular carriers to serve a market. The objectives and the complexities associated with international air travel command a comprehensive yet flexible approach to modeling. On the demand side, the model must accurately represent the wide range of factors that influence an individual's decision to travel on a particular route and choose a certain carrier. This requires that both price and non-price factors such as flight frequency be included in carrier and aggregate demand functions. In addition, the demand model needs to be capable of distinguishing travel demands by nationality, carrier and route in order to allocate welfare changes.[5] The incidence and distribution of the changes in benefits are an important component of this study and, indeed, in any trade negotiation.

Model Development and Estimation The modeling approach captures the behavior of consumers and producers of international air services under a wide range of market conditions. This differs from the alternative, bottom up approach, which models and estimates the interrelationship of demand and supply under specific market circumstances.[6] The model developed here represents a theoretically preferred approach to modeling international trade in aviation services.

ALM combines analytic and simulation techniques to approximate market outcomes under alternative forms of bilateral agreements. The modeling approach is based on an integration of the economic cost-benefit model with the conventions from trade policy analysis to account for issues that arise when analyzing the structure of international trade in services.

To provide credible and policy relevant results, the model was developed around a two-tiered approach. The first tier builds the analytic foundations based on the first principles of microeconomics, including; conditions for demand derived from utility maximization, conditions for supply derived from cost minimization and, market clearing equilibrium quantities and prices.

The second tier utilizes numerical methods (simulation techniques) to solve for market equilibrium in a multidimensional airline market i.e., composed of multiple-carriers for multiple-routes in an origin destination pair. The approach adopts an Armington-type demand model for differentiated products, to develop individual demand relationships for each route carrier combination that serves a particular OD market.[7] This modeling technique provides a theoretically consistent means of distributing market shares among carriers for policy analysis and forecasting.

Past studies suggest the following relationships with respect to non-price factors and their impact on traveler demand:

- *Frequency* – With more frequent flights, passengers are more likely to find a convenient flight departure or arrival time. This improvement in service quality results in an increase in demand stemming from both current travelers taking more trips and new air travelers entering the market.
- *Travel Time* – The shorter and more reliable the travel time between OD pairs the more likely people are to travel on a particular route. Improved travel times could arise with better routing or better aircraft. Both of these factors are within the purview of bilateral agreements.
- *Nationality/Carrier Preference* – International travelers often prefer their national carriers over all others and may be willing to sacrifice price and non-price advantages of non-national carriers. In some cases this preference may be related to language or specific services which are offered and in others it is simply because of long-standing loyalty. This is even more likely in areas supporting a publicly owned or subsidized airline with a long history or in cases when carriers have aggressive frequent flier programs. Frequent flyer programs are more valuable to residents than to non-residents because the latter group have less access to the foreign carrier network.

The Demand Model The relevant market for analysis is the OD pair where the product that is demanded is a trip from origin to destination. Carriers (suppliers) offer this trip over different routes and with different levels of quality. The quality variation includes frequency of service, number of connections and certain in-flight and airport services. The demand model must therefore be capable of representing the value which passengers place on the product and the differences in levels of quality in which the product is offered.

The demand model follows the conventions of the Armington model specification that uses index number/consumer theory to derive demands for substitutable but 'differentiated' goods. The Armington model was chosen because it allows both market size and carrier shares to change in response to regulatory changes. At the same time, it prevents a 'winner take all' scenario where prices between carriers differ, it uses existing parameter estimates, reflecting evaluation of price, quality and service substitution, from secondary sources, and it readily allows for the entry of new firms. In the model the consumer distinguishes between alternative route/carrier choices over a given OD pair. The competitive model is augmented to incorporate quality or non-price factors that can vary across route-carrier alternatives.

The demand model distinguishes between total market OD demand, and the demand for individual routes connecting an OD pair.[8] It starts with a definition of quality adjusted units of service, where a quality coefficient adjusts the actual quality of service according to the level of service attributes. When service is adjusted for differences in quality, it is expressed as 'real service'. As the quality level rises, the model interprets this change as a reduction in the real price per unit paid and in graphical terms this change is represented by an [outward] shift in the demand curve (See Figure 3.3). While consumers actually buy the physical or nominal quantities at observed prices, from a utility perspective they purchase the quality-adjusted quantity at the quality adjusted price.

The quality adjusted prices and quantities are used in the calculation of consumer surplus, which in this model is the measure of benefits. To implement such a procedure it is necessary to have information on the quality coefficients so that the real quality adjusted prices can be calculated and substituted into the price index and demand function. 'Unadjusted demand' or physical demand; corresponds to the number of passengers on a route in the relevant OD market. Higher valued coefficients correspond to higher quality and thus higher consumer welfare in the event that one or more of the quality variables improves following liberalization.

A benefit of this particular demand specification is that it explicitly allows for the calculation of changes in consumer welfare and demand as a consequence of adding or reducing route choices in a given OD market. The demand is structured to account for inter-route substitution in a network context. For example, liberalization of routes between Germany and Canada is likely to induce substitution from alternative routes connecting the two countries, but passing through a third country. The extent of inter-route substitution in response to liberalization and its welfare consequences for consumers will depend on key parameters such as the route substitution elasticity and the relevant quality characteristics of competing routes.

The Armington Model The demand model follows from the Armington model specification, which uses index number/consumer theory to drive demands for substitutable but 'differentiated' goods. The Armington model was chosen over similar alternatives primarily because it allows for both market size and shares to change. At the same time it prevents a 'winner take all' scenario when prices between carriers differ, it accommodates existing parameter estimates from secondary sources, and it readily allows for the entry of new firms under non-competitive conditions. In the air travel liberalization model the goods are alternative route/carrier over a given OD pair.[9] The basic model is amended to incorporate quality or non-price factors that can vary across route-carrier alternatives. The demand model distinguishes between total market OD demand, and demand for individual routes connecting an OD pair.

The basic model starts with a definition of quality adjusted units of real service, interpreted as units of the particular good measured in quality units with the quality function $a_r(.)$.

$$q_r^* = a_r(x_r)q_r \qquad \textit{Equation 4}$$

Where,

$$a_r(x_r) = cF^{\varepsilon_f}T^{\varepsilon_t}N^{\varepsilon_n} \qquad \textit{Equation 5}$$

The number q_r is referred to as the 'unadjusted demand' or physical demand; in measurement terms it corresponds to the observable quantity of good r purchased by the consumer. In this case it corresponds to the number of passengers on a route in the relevant OD market. Higher a_r coefficients correspond to higher quality. Corresponding to the quality adjusted demand q^* in quality units is a price p^*; i.e., the price per unit of q^*.

Given the linearity of q_r^* in q_r it follows that:

$$p_r^* = \left(\frac{1}{a_r(x_r)}\right)p_r \qquad \textit{Equation 6}$$

The quality units are chosen such that for a good with quality level $a_r=1$, $p_r=p_r^*$. As the quality level rises for given p_r, the real price per unit of quality, p_r^* falls. Consumers actually buy the physical quantity q_r at price p_r, but from a utility point of view purchase q_r^* at price p_r^* per unit of quality-adjusted demand. This is the value that affects the calculation of consumer surplus, our measure of benefits. Depending on the nature of the supply side of the model, consumers take either p_r or p_r^* as given and choose q_r^* and thus q_r.

The approach in the previous section to deriving individual unadjusted route demand curves is applied in exactly the same manner with quality adjustments except that all prices and quantities are expressed in quality adjusted units.

$$Q^* = f(P^*) \qquad \textit{Equation 7}$$

$$P^* = \left[\sum_{r=1}^{R} \delta_r p_r^{*-\sigma}\right]^{-1/\sigma} \qquad \textit{Equation 8}$$

$$q_r^* = \delta_r \left(\frac{p_r^*}{P^*}\right)^{-\sigma} Q^* \qquad \textit{Equation 9}$$

To empirically implement such a procedure it is necessary to have information on the quality coefficients a_r so that the real quality adjusted prices p_r^* can be calculated and substituted into the price index and demand function. Having derived a quality-adjusted individual route demand via the same process outlined in the previous section, demand in observable units (passenger volumes) is given by:

$$q_r = \frac{\delta_r}{a_r(x_r)} \left(\frac{p_r^*}{P^*}\right)^{-\sigma} Q^* \qquad \textit{Equation 10}$$

One of the benefits of this particular demand specification is that it allows explicitly for calculating consumers welfare and demand consequences of adding new routes or reducing route choices in a given OD market. As a simple illustration, suppose there is a market where there are only two routes, so $R = 2$ and both quality adjusted prices are equal to 1.0; thus demand on both routes is equal. Under these market conditions, the aggregate price index is given by:

$$P^*(2) = (\delta(1)^{-\sigma} + \delta(1)^{-\sigma})^{-1/\sigma} = (2\delta)^{-1/\sigma} \qquad \textit{Equation 11}$$

Now suppose a new route is introduced that offers the same characteristics (price and non-price characteristics) as the previous routes so that its hedonic price is also unity, but now R = 3. In this case the new aggregate price index is given by:

$$P^*(3) = (\delta(1)^{-\sigma} + \delta(1)^{-\sigma} + \delta(1)^{-\sigma})^{-1/\sigma} = (3\delta)^{-1/\sigma} \qquad \textit{Equation 12}$$

We see in comparing these two equations that the real price index falls if $\sigma > 1$; i.e. the elasticity of substitution between route/carriers exceeds unity. If $\sigma = 2$, $P^*(3)/P^*(2) = 0.81$; an increase from 2 to 3 routes is equivalent to a 19% reduction in the real price of aggregate travel. When substituted into the demand function the increase in real quality adjusted demand is approximately $\eta^d \bullet \Delta P^*$ where η^d is the elasticity of demand (see Equation 13). Note that in the case of exit the adjustment would be in the opposite direction.

$$\eta^d = \frac{\partial q_r^*}{\partial P^*} \frac{P^*}{q_r^*}$$ *Equation 13*

This demand structure is also explicitly planned to deal with the issue of inter-route substitution in a network context such as that outlined previously. For example, liberalization of FRG – YVR is likely to induce substitution between alternative routes connecting Germany and Canada, but passing through third countries. The extent of inter-route substitution in response to liberalization and its welfare consequences for consumers will depend on key parameters such as the route substitution elasticity and the relevant quality characteristics of competing routes.

Benchmarking Carrier Costs The specification of the cost function plays a key role in the model by defining the floor, below which, fares will not fall. It is the lower limit of price and the upper limit on consumer surplus. The specification of the cost model can, therefore, affect the magnitude and distribution of surplus from changes in market conditions. Notwithstanding the competitive model's assumption of constant average cost, the model is capable of representing the realities associated with the provision of international air services; namely, the direct and indirect costs of serving an OD market as well as the variability in factor prices across international markets.

An airline's ability to achieve cost savings through more effective utilization of their network has a clear influence on the range and prices of services they can provide. The cost specification in ALM is rich enough to react to changes in the rules governing the provision of air services in an international setting. As relaxation of the rules governing gauge of aircraft, frequencies and fare setting take place, the consequences of those changes on costs are considered.

The final results of the model are developed in the standard cost-benefit analysis framework. The common metrics of cost-benefit analysis used to measure the impacts of regulatory change are changes in consumer and producer surplus. This study is also concerned with the distribution of these impacts, both positive and negative, between consumers and producers, between nations, and among the factors of production.

Carrier Costs and the Supply Model As with the demand model, the supply model was constructed to represent the competitive model assumptions while remaining flexible to consider alternative assumptions. The supply model captures changes in the cost of air carrier services that may be influenced by a change in a bilateral. Airlines may respond to changes in the rules of international air travel (e.g., flight frequency) by expanding current output, supplying new services or extending the markets served. To the extent that airlines experience cost economies, these supply responses are represented by a shift in the cost function.

The supply model must be consistent with the demand side. Costs are therefore measured on the basis of a flight segment; a flight joining two airports. The costs must also distinguish flight (direct) costs and indirect costs. The model treats these two costs as constant unit costs; analogous to the concept of constant marginal cost in the usual competitive model. Total flight costs increase as flight frequency increases. Total passenger costs increase with the number of passengers carried. Air carrier load factors (utilization rates) are calculated by assuming an aircraft capacity on a given flight segment and comparing that to the actual passengers carried.

Average per-passenger segment costs are computed by dividing the total segment cost by the number of passengers. Total segment costs include direct and indirect costs. The approximate average cost per passenger can be obtained by dividing the total block hour costs (flight costs) for the segment plus the total indirect costs by the number of segment passengers. In the event of two segment routes, unit cost is defined as the sum of segment unit cost using load factors on each segment. We then define profits on a route basis: (i.e., fare on the route minus route unit cost multiplied by route demand). Load factors, as specified in the model, gauge the results to ensure reasonable results.

Estimation of Average Cost Per Passenger on a Given Route For this study, it is necessary to estimate the per-passenger costs of all carriers and future entrants in a particular market. This section describes the methodology for establishing such per-passenger costs for each airline. The main objectives of this cost analysis are as follows:

- Develop a method to assess the relative cost efficiencies of international airlines;
- Construct airline cost estimates which are consistent with the demand model specification (i.e., segment costs);
- Provide accessible airline specific databases for continued use by model users; and
- Develop a methodology that allows model users to apply it for other OD markets of interest.

The average cost per passenger for a flight segment consists of two components: the cost of aircraft and flying operations (direct cost) and all other airline costs (indirect costs). In order to compute the average cost per passenger for a given flight segment, it is necessary to estimate each carrier's total direct and indirect costs for that segment. Then, the average cost per passenger on that segment is computed by dividing the total segment cost by the number of passengers. This step-by-step procedure is described below.

(A) Computation of Direct Cost Per Passenger

Step 1: Estimate U.S. Carrier Costs per Block Hour (Direct Costs) Because of the detailed cost data available for the US carriers, it is possible to establish average cost per block-hour of flight operation for each aircraft type. The Form 41 Data that the U.S. carriers routinely file with the US Department of Transportation contains the direct cost per block-hour by aircraft type. For the same aircraft type, each U.S. carrier has different direct costs per block-hour. Therefore, the average cost of the three largest international carriers (United, American and Delta) was used as the reference point.

Step 2: Estimate Non-U.S. and Other U.S. Carrier's Direct Costs The cost per block-hour for a particular aircraft type (say, B747-400) was estimated by adjusting the block-hour cost for the US reference carriers (average of United, American and Delta) for the productivity and input price differentials between the reference carriers and the carrier. For example, if the US reference carriers' block-hour cost for a B747-400 was $5,000, and Air Canada has 20% lower productivity and 12% lower input price than those of the U.S. reference carriers, then the cost per block-hour for Air Canada is computed as follows:

$5,000 divided by 0.8 (20% lower productivity)multiplied by 0.88 (12% lower input price) = $5,500 per block-hour.

Step 3: Estimate Direct Cost Per Passenger For each route segment, a representative aircraft type (e.g., Boeing 747) was chosen, and the number of block hours required to serve that route is estimated (say, 10 hours for an average one-way flight). The total direct cost for the flight segment is computed by multiplying the number of flights per year, the estimated block-hours per flight and cost per block-hour. Then, the direct flight cost per passenger is then computed simply by dividing the segment total direct cost by the number of passengers carried.

The calculations for the block-hour costs for Air Canada and other carriers described in Step 2 are adjusted to reflect the relative productivity of the carriers serving a market. In order to do this the model incorporates data provided by Oum and Yu (1995) who computed and compared the (residual) productivity index and aggregate input price index for twenty three major airlines. Oum and Yu compute the productivity indices using the total factor productivity computation method proposed by Caves, Christensen and Diewert (1982) using 1986-1993 panel data for the world's 23 major airlines. These total factor productivity (TFP) estimates are unique in their incorporation of the most recent data. One of the useful features of the residual TFP index reported in Oum and Yu is that it compares the true productive efficiency after removing the factors beyond managerial control, such as, differences in average stage length and mix of outputs (scheduled passengers, non-scheduled services, scheduled freight services, and non-core airline outputs).

The effects of output, load factor and capital stock remain and are used to gauge the relative net productive efficiency of each airline in the sample. Productivity indexes are normalized to an individual carrier and year to provide the basis for comparison among carriers and over time. The airline and year are not fixed but may be chosen at any time in the future and normalized again. This choice has no effect on the final results of the analysis. Oum and Yu also provide the aggregate input price index which allows for the comparison of input prices across all major carriers. A value of the price index less than 1.00 means that carriers enjoy an input price advantage relative to American Airlines while a value greater than 1.00 means that there is an input price disadvantage.

Table 3-1 reports the residual TFP index and input price index for selected carriers in 1993. This table shows that when allowances are made for uncontrollable factors (stage length and output mix), Northwest Airlines emerges as the most productively efficient carrier among US carriers. The other four major US carriers (Delta, United, American and Continental) are closely grouped together slightly behind the productive efficiency of Northwest. US Air, Canadian, and Air Canada are close rivals but are as much as 31% less efficient than Northwest. Major Asian carriers (Singapore, Korean Air and Cathay) are somewhat less productively efficient than the large U.S. carriers.

(B) Computation of Indirect Cost Per Passenger

Step 1: Estimate Total Indirect Cost An airline's total indirect cost is the difference between its total cost (which is readily available from ICAO publications) and the total direct cost for the that airline's route system. From Step 1 of (A) above, the cost per-block-hour is established for each carrier and each aircraft type. Then, the total direct cost for that airline is computed by summing the total direct cost for each aircraft type (i.e., the total block hours operated for the aircraft type multiplied by the cost per block-hour) across all types of aircraft the airline operates.

Step 2: Compute Indirect Cost per Passenger for Each Flight Segment The total indirect cost for a flight segment is estimated by allocating the carrier's total indirect costs in proportion to the revenue generated from a particular route. For example, if Air Canada generated one percent of its total revenue from the YVR-FRA route in 1994, and its total indirect cost for the system is $1 billion, then the portion allocated to YVR-FRA route is

$10 million (one percent of $1 billion). The indirect cost per passenger on a route is computed by dividing the total indirect cost for the segment by the number of passengers carried. This is an approximation given data limitations. Ideally, indirect costs would be assumed proportional to direct costs.

Table 3-1: Productivity and Prices Indices (American = 1.00)

Airline	TFP	Price Index
American	1.000	1.000
United	1.045	1.035
Delta	1.069	1.075
Northwest	1.124	1.036
Air Canada	0.807	0.881
Japan Air Lines	0.851	1.421
All Nippon	0.777	1.432
Singapore Airlines	0.958	0.813
Korean Air	0.988	0.781
Cathay	0.969	0.926
Qantas	0.875	0.897
Thai	0.647	0.520
Lufthansa	0.965	1.190
British Air	0.893	0.974
Air France	0.875	1.089
Alitalia	0.840	1.250
SAS	0.838	1.289
KLM	0.946	1.098
Swissair	0.950	1.360
Iberia	*0.800*	*1.200*
Canada 3000	*1.200*	*0.800*
Lan Chile	*0.800*	*0.900*
Ghana Airways	*0.800*	*0.900*
LTU	*1.200*	*0.800*
Gulf Air	*0.800*	*0.900*
Emirates Air	*0.800*	*0.900*
Aeroflot	*0.800*	*0.900*
Ukraine Air	*0.800*	*0.900*

Source: Oum, T. And Yu, C, 'A Productivity Comparison of the World's Major Airlines,' Journal of Air Transport Management, vol., No.4 (1995), pp. 181-195.

The Supply Model The above cost calculation methodology uses existing and readily available data to calculate segment costs. In what follows, we describe an approach that would, given additional data and econometric estimation, provide a dynamic supply model. The study team attempted to estimate such a model, but found current data did not allow successful estimation of these supply functions. The preceding approach does, however, provide a reasonable solution to the data limitations and produces an appropriate basis upon which to estimate order of magnitude effects from liberalization.

In the demand model, any OD market may be served by a number of routes and each route is composed of one or more segments. A segment is a flight between any two airports. In a network of multiple OD's, it is probable that changes in one OD will affect passenger demands over the other OD's. For example, if higher frequencies are allowed between Germany and Canada not only will this OD market expand, but additional traffic may be garnered from passengers who are traveling to Germany via France. The flight segment FRA–YVR will carry more than simply the OD traffic and this will affect costs through economies of traffic density. The base unit for the cost function will therefore be the flight segment. Once the segment costs are calculated it is possible to construct a route cost by aggregating the relevant segment costs. The total carrier costs are calculated as the sum of all passenger costs and segment costs.

In describing a carrier's costs we distinguish costs which vary by segment and those which vary by route. In many cases the source of cost differences will be in the airline system or station costs. For example, if carrier *i* were to extend its operation from point B to point C, when it was already in an AB market, the additional costs would include the increase in flight operating costs and passenger costs. However, since it is already serving airport B, the cost of adding an operation will be quite low. This is quite different from a circumstance of entering an entirely new market. Clearly, both passengers and flight frequency are important.

Total cost for a flight segment is equal to passenger costs plus flight cost. Passenger costs on a segment are obtained from Form 41 data by subtracting flight-related costs from total costs. These calculated total indirect costs are allocated to each segment by multiplying system-wide total indirect costs by the ratio of segment revenue to system-wide total revenue. Flight cost can be measured by adding the cost per block hour multiplied by the number of block hours required for the flight segment and a measure of the opportunity costs of flight capital.[10]

These two costs which are treated as constant unit costs to the airline is analogous to the concept of constant marginal cost in the usual competitive model. These are unit flight costs and unit passenger costs, *w* and *v* respectively. Unit costs will change (UC will shift down) as the volume of passengers changes and as flight frequency and load factors change. Total costs are then defined as:

$$TC = vQ + wF$$ *Equation 14*

Where:

F = segment frequency; and

Q = segment passenger demand.

Carrier load factors are calculated from our data as follows:

$$z = \frac{Q}{F} \Big/ G$$ *Equation 15*

Where:

G = is gauge (available seats or plane capacity).

Average per-passenger segment cost, *u*, can be computed by dividing the total segment cost by the number of passengers. The approximate average cost per passenger is obtained by dividing the total block hour costs (flight costs) for the segment plus the total passenger costs by the number of segment passengers. Unit cost on a per passenger basis are expressed as follows:

$$u = \frac{TC}{Q} = \frac{wF}{Q} + v = \left(\frac{w}{Gz}\right) + v$$ *Equation 16*

In the event of two segment routes unit cost is defined as the sum of segment unit cost using load factors on each segment. We then define profits on a route basis (i.e., fare on route minus route unit cost multiplied by route demand). In this way, load factors are endogenized in the model and used as a feasibility check on the results of the model.

Using the Air Liberalization Model to Produce Results The ALM is an interactive model that allows users to alter model inputs, develop policy scenarios, and estimate consumer and producer impacts resulting form changes in bilateral aviation agreements. The model simulates market conditions resulting from changes in air transport policy levers in a bilateral context. Consumer impacts are calculated in the traditional manner using consumer surplus. Impacts on producers are calculated in terms of market share and revenue changes, and as producer surplus (profits).

The model provides possible market outcomes of liberalization scenarios. The models can be described generally as Price Competition, Frequency Regulation Model

The competitive price is found by iteratively solving for a price that clears the market for a given frequency. The model can also used solving with a range of frequencies and choosing the frequency which provides the highest level of net benefits while maintaining profitability for each carrier.

Constructing the Base Case

The initial phase of an analysis using ALM describes the market situation in the base OD market. Since ALM is a route and segment based model, the market conditions for an international city pair are required. The key variables used to describe the base case OD route are:

- Airlines serving market;
- Type of aircraft;
- Passenger volume by airline;
- Fares by airline;
- Frequency by airline;
- Travel time by airline; and
- Carrier specific preference (nationality) factor.

These variables are entered into the model to describe the initial market conditions for the market segment under consideration. All variables that describe the base case are observable in the marketplace and published in a variety of sources such as ICAO, Official Airline Guide (OAG), the German Database (ADV, Flughafen Hamburg), travel agents, and the airlines themselves.

The carrier specific preference variable is found by calibrating the model to the base case data. The base case data is entered into the model. The model is then run, estimating an intermediate result which corresponds to the initial model iteration on the base case route characteristics which should replicate the base case demand data. If it does not, consumers display a preference for some carriers that cannot be explained by the route characteristics. The carrier specific preference factors are then adjusted and the model re-run. This procedure is replicated until the base case data is approximated with the modeling inputs.

Constructing Scenarios

The scenarios are based on an analysis and simulation of the market response to changes in the bilateral relationship. These changes will be reflected in changes in fares, changes in frequency, and entry of new carriers. As described earlier in this chapter, these variables are impacted by changes in policy levers. The policy lever changes are created by entering data into the model defining an alternative scenario in terms of new carriers and any changes in the frequency (or other characteristics) of the route carrier choice.

The model calculates the market clearing prices based on the supplied capacity. Prices are adjusted such that each carrier's aircraft are filled according to their supplied capacity and their optimal load factor. The fare adjustment mechanism allows the model to iterate on price until demand equals supply. This approach allows for each carrier to either make or lose money depending upon their ability to fill capacity at fares above marginal cost.

Carrier Costs

In ALM, the user defines the aircraft type of each carrier. ALM then calculates direct and indirect costs per passenger using the planes capacity, demand and resulting load factor. ALM uses a database of block hour costs and aircraft purchase prices to derive the direct costs and the opportunity cost of flight capital (see Table 3-2). Indirect costs (estimated as described previously) are added to these to calculate the total carrier costs for the flight segment. In modeling scenarios where a benchmark carrier paces all other carriers' costs, the user may enter the index number of the benchmark carrier that is chosen. The model then adjusts all carriers' costs according to the benchmark accounting for productivity and factor price differences. In performing these iterations the users are effectively constructing an aggregate downward sloping cost curve.

After all inputs are entered in the database simulations are run to estimate consumer impacts, carrier market shares, carrier revenues, and profits. All inputs can be varied according to the users preference.

Estimation of Average Cost Per Passenger on a Given Route

For this study, it is necessary to estimate the per-passenger costs of all carriers and future entrants in a particular market. This section describes the methodology for establishing such per-passenger costs for each airline. The main objectives of this cost analysis are as follows:

- Develop a method to assess the relative cost efficiencies of international airlines;
- Construct airline cost estimates which are consistent with the demand model specification (i.e., segment costs);
- Provide accessible airline specific databases for continued use; and
- Develop a methodology that allows model users to apply it for other OD markets of interest.

The average cost per passenger for a flight segment consists of two components: the cost of aircraft and flying operations (direct cost) and all other airline costs (indirect costs). In order to compute the average cost per passenger for a given flight segment, it is necessary to estimate each carrier's total direct and indirect costs for that segment. Then, the average cost per passenger on that segment is computed by dividing the total segment cost by the number of passengers. This step-by-step procedure is described in the supply modeling section earlier in this Chapter. ALM contains a block hour cost database to allow calculation of direct costs based on inputs for flight time and aircraft type. Indirect costs are based on a calculation of indirect costs as described earlier.

Table 3-2: Aircraft Operations Data Inputs

Plane Type	Block Hour Costs [a]	Plane Capacity [b]
A300-600	$4066	300
A300-B4	$3059	250
A310-300	$3674	245
A320-100/200	$1825	150
A330	NA	335
A340-300	NA	300
B 747-400	$6249	374
B727-200	$2457	148
B737-300	$1857	131
B747-100	$6790	450
B747-200	$6711	369
B757-200	$1880	186
B767-200	$2060	230
B767-300	$2695	250
B777	$3863	282
DC-10-10	$4282	276
DC10-30	$4918	281
MD-11	$3682	350

Sources: a. US Department of Transportation, Form 41 database.

b. Aviation Daily.

Model Parameters and Data

All the model inputs are presented in this section. The inputs fall under the following categories:

- Demand model inputs (demand parameters and elasticity of substitution); and
- Carrier cost inputs (productivity and price indices).

  Each category is discussed in turn.

Demand Parameters

There are two types of data required to estimate the demand model under alternative regulatory regimes. The first is 'baseline' data which establishes the current demand profile (e.g., quantities and prices) for the routes under study, and the operating characteristics for given routes in OD pairs (e.g., travel times, flight frequencies). The second type of data is related to the parameters in the model (e.g., elasticity of substitution between carrier route combinations).

Baseline data has been gathered primarily from the German Database (ADV, Flughafen Hamburg) and the OAG database. Baseline data for the three markets under consideration are presented in Chapter 5 of this report. The second type of data required to operationalize the model relates to parameter estimates and elasticities. The study team, to the greatest extent possible, has drawn from secondary sources for these estimates. There are numerous econometric studies which have generated estimates for a number of the key parameters.[11]

The model uses demand elasticities through the hedonic quality equation. Elasticity estimates are interpreted in ALM as elasticities of quality with respect to a series of quality variables. These quality variables include travel time and frequency. In the demand model, travel time is defined as flight time from point A to point B for each carrier route combination. Frequency refers to average weekly frequency from point A to point B for each carrier route combination. These elasticities are related to the traditional demand elasticity. To allow the straightforward interpretation of the elasticities entered into the model, the user enters the traditional demand elasticity that is converted in the model to the elasticity of quality with respect to the particular variable.

This approach allows the user to enter elasticity estimates as estimated in the economics literature. Demand elasticities are widely published for most of the inputs needed to run ALM. Table 3-3 presents the ranges of elasticity estimates available in the economics literature. Sources are provided as references for the reader.

Table 3-3: Demand Elasticities and Sources

	Range	*Sources*
Price	-0.51 to -1.65	Abrahams, M. 1983. Trans. Res.: 385-393; Cheung, H.-K. 1995. Transport Canada; Oum, T.H., D.W. Gillen and S.E. Noble. 1986. Logistics and Transportation Review: 195-222.; Oum, T.H., A. Zhang & Y. Zhang. 1993. JTEP: 171-192.; Maillebiau, E. & M. Hansen. 1995. JTEP: 115-136
Flight-Frequency	0.05 to 0.20	Street, Et. al. 'An Analysis of the Trade Off's in International Aviation Rights,' Australasian Transport Research Forum, 1994. Agarwal, V. and W. Talley. 1985, Int. J. of Transport Economics: 63-70.; Ippolito, R.A. 1981. JTEP: 7-15; Talley, W.K. and A. Schwarz-Miller. 1988. Int. J. of Transport Economics: 159-168.
Travel-Time	0.15	Agarwal, V. and W. Talley. 1985, Int. J. of Transport Economics: 63-70.

Several key demand assumptions are needed to operationalize the model. Table 3-4 provides the demand parameter estimates that are used in each of the markets.[12]

Table 3-4: Demand Parameter Estimates

Demand Parameters	*Median Value*
Elasticity of Substitution	1.75
Elasticity of Demand with Respect to Frequency	0.10
Elasticity of Demand with Respect to Price	-1.35

*This probability range corresponds to an 80% confidence interval.

Elasticity of Substitution

The elasticity of substitution has a positive sign. Although in theory it can vary from 0 to infinity we expect it to have a value between 0.5 and 3. A low (high) value implies a low (high) degree of substitutability between a carrier-route combination. It shows the percentage by which a carrier's relative market share (i.e., the ratio of market shares) increases (decreases), given a one percent decrease (increase, respectively) in that carrier's fare (quality adjusted) relative to all other carriers serving the market. For example, for an elasticity of substitution equal to 2, a 10% decrease in carrier A's fare, relative to all other carriers serving the market would lead to a 20% increase in A's *relative* share of that same market.

Based on previous research on the trade in goods and services, the elasticity of substitution has been shown to be greater than 1, yet less than 3. Preliminary testing of the model was conducted and it was estimated that the elasticity of substitution was approximately 1.75 by calibrating the model with historical data.

Carrier Cost Inputs

U.S. carriers are required to report costs per block hour for aircraft operations by type of aircraft. These data are contained in Form 41 and are available from the U.S. Department of Transportation. Block hour costs refer to total direct operating and maintenance cost per hour of aircraft operation. This figure multiplied by the flying time over a given segment provides a precise estimate of the direct costs incurred flying that segment. These data include detailed information regarding the components of operating and maintenance costs including:

- Crew costs;
- Fuel and oil;
- Rental expenses;
- Insurance;
- Taxes;
- Airframe maintenance;
- Engine maintenance;
- Maintenance burden; and
- Depreciation.

The Form 41 data provide detailed cost accounting by expense type and detailed information regarding the sources of revenues by airline.

Productivity and Price Indices

Productivity and factor price indices are used to generate the segment costs for all relevant international airlines. Total factor productivity (TFP) has been measured by Caves et al (1982),[13] Windle (1991),[14] Windle, et al (1992)[15] and Oum et al. (1996).[16] Based on panel data, Oum and Yu, 1995, adopted the total factor productivity computation methods of Caves, Christensen and Diewert (1982), to compare the TFP for 23 airlines. The Oum and Yu productivity figures are the only estimates available using recent data. This is important since a great deal of industry restructuring occurred between the late 1970's and 1980's. Oum and Yu's use of data from the period 1986 to 1993 provides the most accurate set of productivity indices available at present.

Total factor productivity is the amount of aggregate output produced by a unit of input. To estimate the index, a translog multilateral index procedure is used to construct the output and input indices and the amount of aggregate output generated by a unit of aggregate input. This multilateral TFP index procedure is applied to the panel of airline data for the 23 airlines over the 1986-93 time period to construct and compare the 'gross' TFP levels across airlines and over time (Oum, et al., p. 5).

The input categories included in the TFP estimation procedure are: labor, fuel, materials, flight equipment, and ground property and equipment. The measurement of productivity requires detailed information regarding outputs, inputs, and network and output attributes. Most of Oum and Yu's data is derived from ICAO publications, Statistics Canada and the annual reports of airlines.

Oum and Yu (1995) report both gross TFP and residual TFP indices. The 'gross' TFP index is influenced by factors beyond managerial control, including, variations in network, operating and market conditions. 'Residual' TFP indices remove the impacts outside the purview of airline managers. 'Gross' TFP estimates shows how efficiently the airlines outputs are produced without accounting for items such as stage length of the carrier's flights, or whether the government helps the airline achieve high load factors by restraining competition. Therefore the 'gross' TFP index is not a measure of pure competitive advantage and should not be used to compare the productive operating efficiencies between airlines but, rather, the residual index should be used.

The productivity adjustment also plays an important role in adjusting carrier costs should liberalization lead to changes in factors that affect productivity. These factors were described in the second step of the benchmarking analysis.

Residual TFP indices are estimated using regression analysis to compare pure productive efficiencies over time and across airlines. These estimates remove the effects of the following 'uncontrollable' variables:

- Average stage length which is largely determined by geographic location; and
- Composition of airline outputs (freight vs. passenger) is influenced strongly by geographic location and government regulation.

The effects of output, load factor and capital stock remain and are used to gauge the relative net productive efficiency of each airline in the sample. Productivity indexes are normalized to an individual carrier and year to provide basis for comparison between carriers and over time. The airline and year are not fixed but may be chosen at any time in the future and normalized again. This choice will have no affect on the final results of the analysis.

Productivity indices provide a credible approach to managing data limitations for foreign carriers. The residual TFP estimates in Table 3-1 were used in the calculations. By comparing the residual TFP estimates from the foreign carriers to a US carrier for which detailed cost information is known, we are able to provide estimates of the cost structures of all international airlines for which residual TFP indices are available. Potential entrant carriers need not be the initial US benchmark airline, but can be any international airline whose costs are adjusted using residual index calculations for a given segment in a given OD market.

Introduction into the Airport Choice Problem

Within this project major changes of the air transport supply side will occur due to the assumed 'Open Sky' strategy in transport policy which directly will effect the individual consumer. Therefore the reason for modeling airport choice is based on analyzing the consumer behavior due to the increasing competition of airports and airlines who will inaugurate new services in context to the new liberalization, bottlenecks at airports and the competing environment of the land based modes. In addition changes in the fee structure at airports due to the internalization of external costs and the ongoing privatization of airports as well as the changes in the tariff structure due to the competition of airlines are of interest in a liberalized market as long as they become relevant to the consumer. The idea was to provide private investors, airlines, airports and political decision makers with supply and demand sensitive information to make the market more transparent to actions planned.

On the more political side the system can be used in the area of environmental policy (e.g. regulations), regional development and spatial planning. The latter encloses questions about the accessibility of single regions and its enhancement when improving the infrastructure (e.g. location of a new regional airport, build a new road link towards an airport or to equip an airport with a railway station).

For airlines the focus may be on the introduction of a new OD service, the decrease or increase of tariffs, the market analysis of the existing air network or a future one considering new hubs, changes in the frequency of a service offered or the co-operation with other modes in the sense of rail and fly.

And for the airports it is of interest to analyze the effects of new OD services, capacity constraints, changes in the structure of aircraft fees and passenger charges, investments in infrastructure (new airport location, high-speed train station, terminal or runway) and the co-operation or competition of airports. Of course any of these analysis of actions stated can be used as input for an economic analysis.

Before starting to discuss the theoretical background and the model itself, let us focus on some basic examples to explain the necessity of this modeling step for the 'Open Sky' project at all.

Basic example: Principle problem of consumers choice. Coming back to the roots of the original question why airport choice should be considered within this project a small example (basic year 1991) will demonstrate the decision problem a consumer faces and which even become more difficult in a wide liberalized air market with capacity constraints at different airports.

Comparing two German business travelers - e.g. one living in famous Heidelberg (county) and the other one in the neighboring county of Karlsruhe - their decisions concerning the chosen airport for a trip will vary. If we neglect possible individual preferences a set of external factors influences their choice between possible starting points for a flight. If we study trips destination in e.g. North America (Figure 3.4) we will find that the probability to travel via Frankfurt-Main Airport for both travelers is close to ninety percent. This is not very surprising due to the fact that Frankfurt dominates the German market as the largest hub and being the homebase of the national carrier Lufthansa.

Figure 3.4: Airport Choice, Destination: North America, Trip Purpose: Business

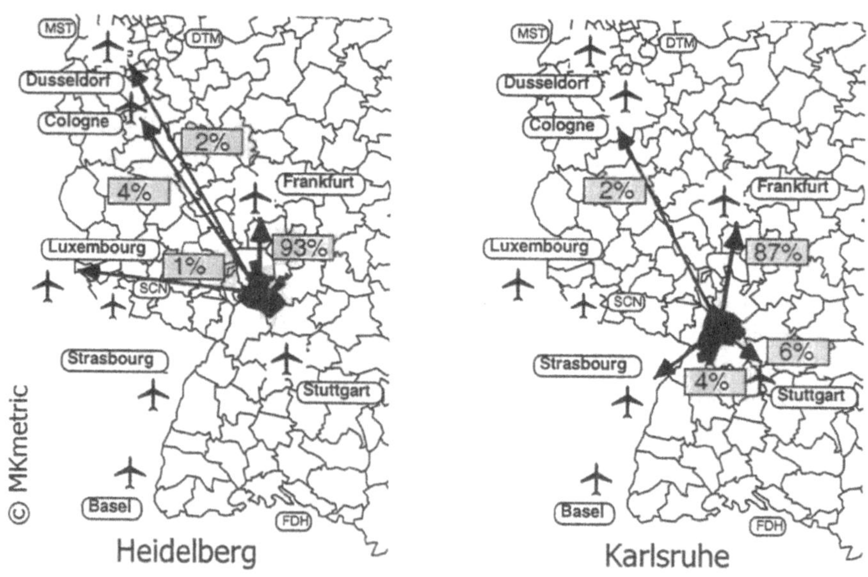

Much more interesting are the remaining probabilities to choose alternative airport for business trips crossing the Atlantic. As described in the following sections the choice of airports is determined by a set of factors including accessibility, offered frequencies and destinations. Figure 3.4 shows how the combination of these factors influences the probability to choose one of the remaining alternatives for such a trip. While the airport characteristics are equal in both cases the accessibility by private and public transport differs. In general it was found that business travelers prefer strongly the airport, which offers the highest flight frequencies and the shortest duration of the whole trip, including access and egress.

When analyzing vacation trips one observes a completely different choice structure for the travelers in the example above. Due to less restrictions in time but higher price sensitivity holiday-makers prefer the most convenient kiss&fly access to possible airports offering non-stop or via flights to start their journeys but are open enough to choose other alternatives as long as the price differs significantly. Figure 3.5. depicts the choice probabilities for vacation travelers from Karlsruhe and Heidelberg, respectively, to an Italian destination.

Major differences rise from other characteristics, namely the distance between the origin and the airport or the availability of a non-stop flight (even if only once a week) or the accessibility by public transport. So travelers from Karlsruhe prefer strongly Stuttgart Airport. Frankfurt, which is situated additional 50 km away, can only attract a market share of 13%, although much more flights are offered than in Stuttgart. Due to a missing non-stop-flight to Rome, only eight percent remain for Strasbourg Airport, despite the fact is it is the nearest one to the area of Karlsruhe county.

When starting a holiday trip from Heidelberg, Frankfurt is certainly the best choice for two third of all vacation travelers. But the second best alternative via Stuttgart gets still 30%, while choosing other airports as e.g. Strasbourg or Basel will be an exception.

Figure 3.5: Airport Choice, Destination: Rome (Italy), Trip Purpose: Vacation

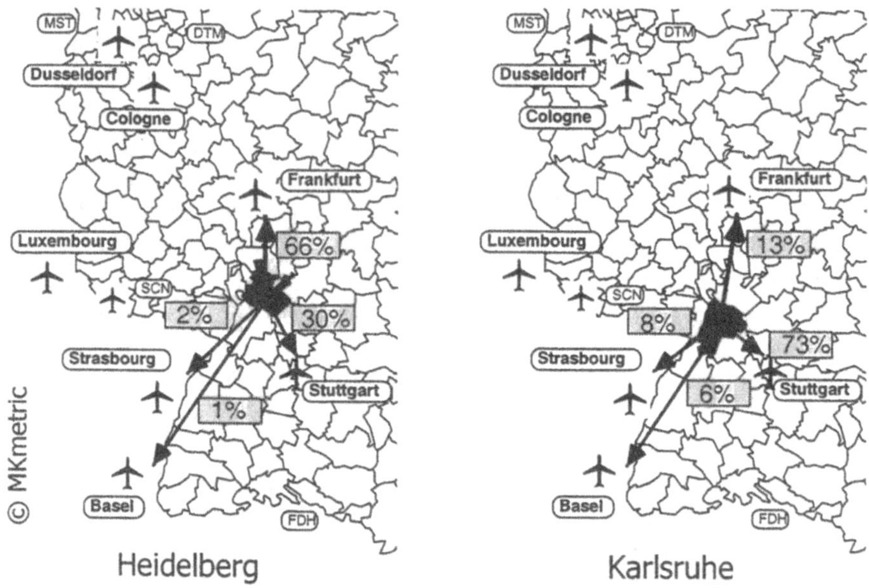

For the sake of understanding only this small example of Heidelberg and Karlsruhe was presented. By the way, in the meantime (1997) in the area of Karlsruhe a regional airport (Baden-Airport) opened and already offers interesting services to tourist centers which unfortunately could not be taken into account for these examples based on 1991. Of course such examples can be extended when one moves to areas where a lot of services and airports are competing, like in the Rhein-Ruhr, Berlin, Paris or London area, and one analyses all possible destinations and alternatives. Some analyzes follow below

Basic example: Regional point of view After we saw, how people from two different counties chose their airport, we now depict on a single area and compare differences in airport choice depending on the passengers destination. Figure 3.6 shows the market shares for some destinations, different airports can realize in the Hanover area. Here consumers airport choice is shown for the trip purpose 'vacation'. Analysis can be done as well for other trip purposes, destinations or regions.

Figure 3.6: Airport Choice from the County of Hanover to Different Destinations 1991

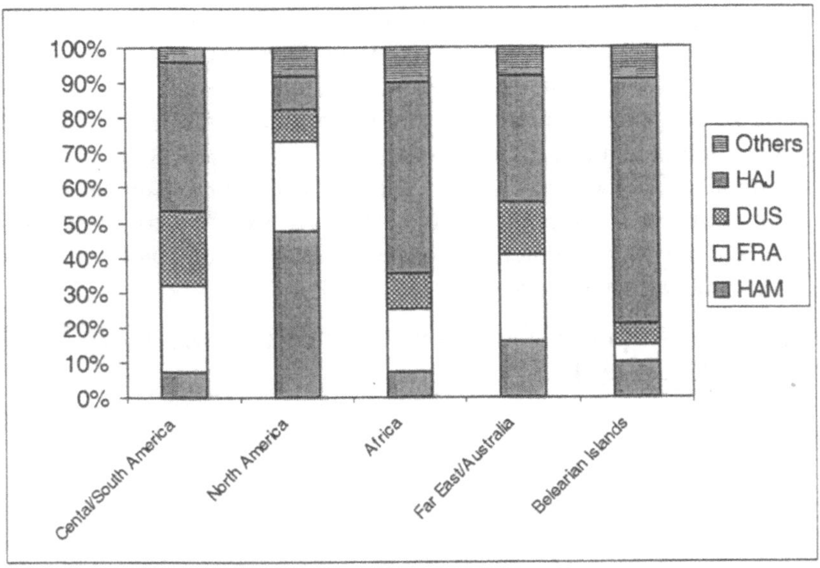

Others are: BRE, FMO, CGN, PAD.

This airport choice differs, strictly depending on

- Availability of non-stop-flights to the specific destination at the airports,
- Distance (travel-time) between the county and the different airports,
- Price for the flight to the specific destination from the airport and the costs of access/egress,
- Total travel-time (access/egress, check-in/out, flight-time)
- Frequency offered on the specific routes offered at the airports.

So as an example people from the area of Hanover chose Hanover Airport for holiday-trips to the Balearian Islands with a probability of more than 70%, due to access/egress plays a major role on such a short-haul flight. In addition non-stop-flights to that destination are offered at Hanover Airport with high frequency.

On the other hand passengers from that area travelling towards North America prefer the Frankfurt Airport (48%), as the prices offered there to that destination in average bet the costs from starting at Hanover, including the railway fare when using the available high-speed trains Hanover – Frankfurt. Additionally in this case the consumers more accept an exceed of time for access/egress to Frankfurt, due to the longer total travel-time on such long-haul trips. The stated situation will change if based on the 'Open Sky' scenario new services will enter the market and increase competition between airports as well as airlines.

Basic example: Demand distribution on routes. The next possibility to analyze the regional/consumers' point of view concerns the competing alternatives considering the different transfer locations. This analyses is based on the principle idea shown in the beginning but allows in addition to show hub-potentials, if an aggregation over all regions to one destination is computed. Anyhow to understand the principle one example is selected which shows the competitive situation from Bielefeld to Hong Kong in 1994. By the way Bielefeld is located south-west of Hanover where the EXPO 2000 will take place.

Figure 3.7: Airport Choice from Bielefeld to Hong Kong, Full Fare Business Class, 1994

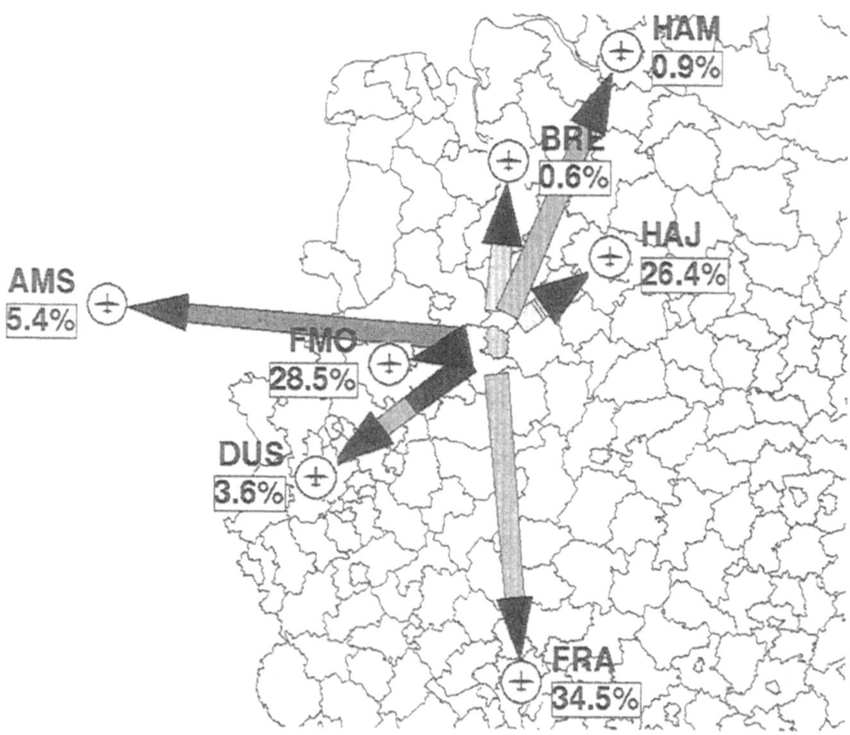

From Bielefeld towards the destination of Hong Kong, full fare business class (NTP)-passengers in majority prefer flights from the two nearest available airports (Hanover-HAJ and Munster/Osnabrück-FMO) although no non-stop or direct flights are offered there. Another third of all those passengers take the route via Frankfurt (FRA), as it is equipped with non-stop flights to Hong Kong and Frankfurt can be reached in almost adequate time by rail or road. Amsterdam (AMS) can still realize a market share of more than five percent, although it is quite far away, but can be reached by rail in a good way and offers non-stop-flights as well as Frankfurt. The rest of the shown alternatives are only rarely chosen, as they neither offer non-stop flights nor those airports are situated very close to Bielefeld.

Table 3-5: Airport Choice from Bielefeld to Hong Kong

Alternatives	Origin from	via 1	via 2	Destination	Share for full fare business
1	FRAU	----	----	HKG	34.5
2	AMS	----	----	HKG	5.4
3	HAJ	CPH	----	HKG	3.3
4	BRE	CPH	----	HKG	0.6
5	FMO	FRA	----	HKG	28.5
6	HAM	CPH	----	HKG	0.9
7	DUS	CPH	----	HKG	1.2
8	HAJ	ZRH	----	HKG	3.0
9	DUS	ZRH	----	HKG	2.4
10	HAJ	FRA	----	HKG	20.1

In Table 3-5, we can focus on the stop-over connections and the hubs people change plains. Here the consumer prefers flights via Frankfurt, offering good connecting times, due to the high frequency of the feeder flights from FMO and HAJ to that hub. This two alternatives already form 48.6% of the 54.9% passengers using FMO and HAJ at all. Other hubs chosen are Zurich (ZRH) and Copenhagen (CPH). As we regard the full fare market sector, other big European hubs like London or Paris do not play any role, due to their geographic situation according to the Germany – Hong Kong routes. It has to be remarked that no alternative with two stopovers has been selected and we just display ten alternatives which summed up to 100% although there are plenty more possibilities. It has to be noted that the same analyses for economy class will show another preference of alternatives, e.g. share distribution.

Based on this analysis the influence of an 'Open Sky' and/or pricing strategy upon the demand distribution on routes and in consequence the hub potential is obvious.

All three basic examples show that consumer reactions on changes of the supply side are very inhomogen and therefor have to be analyzed on the disaggregate level to face the specific market situations for each trip.

Otherwise transport policy decisions like the 'Open Sky' strategy are based on insufficient conclusions about consumer behavior down to synergetic effects of the air network and follow up analysis like economic matters can not be handled appropriately.

It should be noted that the complexity of the problem was simplified at this point but the approach applied in this project considers of course the access/egress problem of the airports as well as capacity restrictions and competing land based modes.

Theoretical Background and Data

On most flight journeys consumer have the opportunity to start their trip from more than just one single airport. Just in Germany there are 16 international airports and several regional airports which are all accessible by a good or even very good land based infrastructure so that often the situation appears where the consumer can choose out of a whole bunch of alternatives all serving his needs in nearly the same way. So it often happens that there are more than four airports offering the same destination and in addition at each airport non-stop as well as via services are available. At least once the consumer evaluated the different opportunities he selects only one out of the available set of alternatives. This is a classical discrete choice problem. For details see the suggested literature about mode choice and discrete choice modeling stated in the references so that there is no need to go through the whole theory again.

Here the focus is on the differences of the chosen to the standard approach and the resulting advantages. To understand the issues in an easy way it will be referred to examples taken from the field of mode choice alternatives).

Properties of the linear standard model. The 'classical' linear Logit model specification normally assumes (Gaudry 1992):

(i)linearity in variables;

(ii)the exclusion of characteristics of other alternatives $j \in Cn$ from the representative utility of the i-th one ($i \in Cn$, $i \neq j$);

equal 'abstract' or 'generic' coefficients for the network characteristics, a constraint that is not necessary but is frequently imposed.

These assumptions lead to unrealistic properties. Because of (ii), the standard model implies:

- Equal cross elasticities of demand: this means that setting up a bicycle path between two cities will draw the same percentage of travelers from the plane, car and train or in the sense of airport choice the same percentage of travelers will be drawn from all considered air services. Furthermore (iii) implies identical values of time across the alternatives: this means that representative train and plane users (mode choice) or non-stop and via flight passengers (airport choice) value time identically;

- The exclusion of complementarity among alternatives;
- That only differences in the level of characteristics matter, or that the function is not homogenous of degree 0: in consequence doubling all fares and income will change the market shares.

Because of (i) the standard model further implies that:

- The effect of a given difference in transport conditions is independent of the service level characteristics so that the response curve to changes in service characteristics is symmetric with respect to its inflection point (Figure 3.8). For instance, a 30 min train service improvement has the same impact on choice probabilities for the Hamburg-Hanover OD pair as for the Hamburg-Munich pair. Similarly increasing the air tariffs by 50 DM has the same impact on choice probabilities for the Hamburg-Frankfurt OD pair as for the Hamburg-Paris pair. Further on adding an amount of 20 DM to the price of travelling by plane will have the same impact as adding 20 DM to the price of travelling by train. Generally speaking, symmetry, with respect to the inflection point, implies that potential asymmetry of behavior, where consumers/travelers suddenly start to react and then change their behavior, cannot be detected;
- Coefficients for the constants and for the variables common to all alternatives are underidentified, which means that, for these variables, only differences with respect to an arbitrarily chosen reference can be identified.

We also note in passing that the logit form requires that

- The choice probabilities go to zero (one) when the representative utility V_i goes to $-\infty$ ($+\infty$) so that (Figure 3.8) one cannot model thick tails due to specification error, modeler ignorance, compulsive consumption or captivity to alternatives. The latter case includes the situation of business travelers which have to do a one day return trip and are therefore not elastic to price.

Figure 3.8: Linear Logit versus Box-Cox Logit

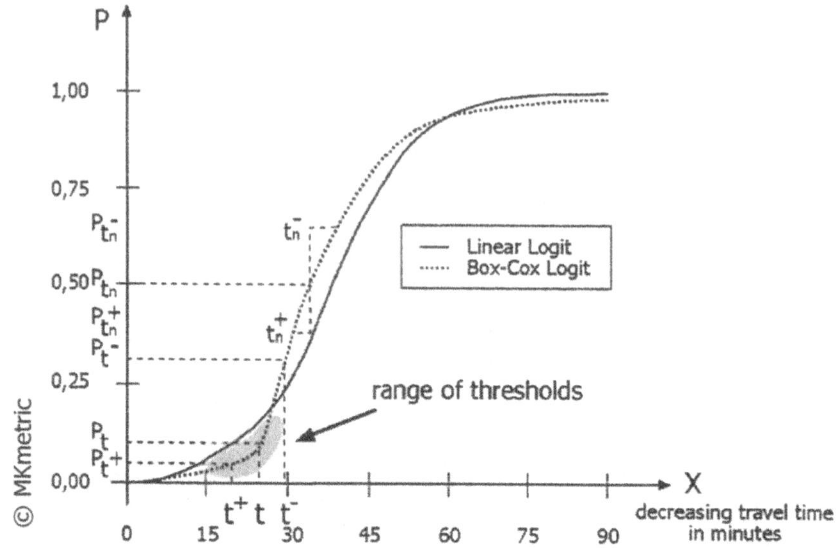

The Box-Cox device To bypass most of these constraints (generally speaking, only (c) and (f) will remain), the Box-Cox transformation is used:

$$X_{kjn}^{(\lambda_{kj})} = \begin{cases} \dfrac{(X_{kjn}^{\lambda_{kj}} - 1)}{\lambda_{kj}} & \text{if } \lambda_{kj} \neq 0, \\ \ln X_{kjn} & \text{if } \lambda_{kj} = 0. \end{cases} \tag{1}$$

Hence, the choice model can be written as:

$$P(i)_n = \frac{\exp\left(\beta_i X_i + \sum_{k=1}^{K} \beta_{ki} X_{kin}^{(\lambda_{kj})}\right)}{\sum_{j \in C_n} \exp\left(\beta_j X_j + \sum_{k=1}^{K} \beta_{kj} X_{kjn}^{(\lambda_{kj})}\right)}, \tag{2}$$

where Xi = Xj = 1 are regression constants.

If λ_{kj} is equal to 1 (or zero), then the variable is entered in its linear (or logarithmic) form. Since the transformation is continuous for all possible values of the λ-parameter, but defined only for a positive variable, it is clearly understood that in above formulas some of the X_{kjn}'s cannot be transformed: the constant, the dummies and the ordinary variables that contain negative observations. Variables that contain positive and null values can be transformed as long as a compensating dummy variable is created (Gaudry et al. 1993).

Visual and economic significance. Figure 3.8 clearly shows the difference between the linearity and nonlinearity of a variable. The asymmetric curve (in respect to its inflexion point) given by Box-Cox transformation (Box et al. 1964) of the strictly positive variable X_t illustrates the error which will occur when a non-linear variable is forced to be linear. For example, assume X_t denotes total travel time: in the linear case, the value X_t equal to 30 is associated to the probability P equal to 0.25; in the non-linear case, the probability is higher if $\lambda < 1$ and smaller if $\lambda > 1$. Hence, if one forces a non-linear variable or in equality the utility function to be linear, this will result in an over- or underestimation of the probability related to this variable. In addition to asymmetry of the response function ($\lambda \neq 1$), reaction thresholds, defined in terms of acceleration of the rate of change of the probability, can be identified.

The Box-Cox transformation of the strictly positive variables of the linear Logit model leads to the Box-Cox Logit model with an asymmetry of response, as shown in Figure 3.8, because the effect of a unit change in the service will depend on the levels of the variables X_{kj} for all values of λ_{kj} not equal 1. This can be seen by examining the partial derivatives of the representative utility function V_j of the j-th mode. It is obvious that the effect of additional service will be smaller at higher service levels than at lower ones if λ_{kj} is smaller than 1. These diminishing returns mean that given absolute reductions in total travel time have more impact when total travel times are low than high: a gain in travel time of 15 minutes means less on a long trip than on a short one. The same effects appear in the case of an increase of air tariffs. Conversely, increasing returns exist if λ_{kj} is larger than 1.

Clearly, if one is considering very small changes in the service levels of a mode, the mathematical form used does not matter very much because one is forecasting in the immediate neighborhood of current sample values. However, if one is considering significant changes in service levels, such as increasing aircraft fees or decreasing air tariffs by a third or reducing train travel time by one half with high-speed trains, then curvature is decisive.

Asymmetry To illustrate the asymmetry of the response functions due to the inflexion point of the curve and the threshold effect mentioned before, Figure 3.8 shows a general example of a response curve for an alternative with respect to the variable travel time while all other conditions (characteristics and alternatives) remain unchanged. On the x-axis the change in travel time is displayed (t minutes decrease in travel time on the air service alternative) and on the y-axis the change of the probability choosing this alternative is given. Hence the interdependency of airport choice and travel demand is obvious when the probability is multiplied with the total demand of the OD pair which will show you the demand for the alternative.

To describe asymmetry more formally one first has to define the inflexion point of the curve. At this point the curvature changes its functional shape from convex to concave and one can compute the value of the inflexion point (P_{t_n}, t_n) by equating to zero the second derivative of the alternative share in respect to the travel time. The response curve can be called asymmetric with respect to its reflection point if equidistant reductions and increments of travel time t_n by: Δt [that is, $t_n^+ = t_n - \Delta t$ and $t_n^- = t_n - \Delta t$] will give different absolute values, namely $\Delta P^+ = | P_{t_n} - P_{t_n}{}^+ |$ and $\Delta P^- = | P_{t_n} - P_{t_n}{}^- |$: otherwise the curve has to be called symmetric. More formally, one can define asymmetry, as in Laferrière and Gaudry (1993) in terms of the partial correlation ξ of $P_{t_n}{}^+$ and (1- $P_{t_n}{}^-$): this yields an indicator that is necessarily between 0 and 1.

Threshold A threshold effect occurs when the travel time reaches a critical value of t beyond which any further reduction of t to $t^- = t + \Delta t$ provokes a more substantial growth of the mode share P_t than an equidistant increment of t to $t^+ = t - \Delta t$, so that the absolute difference of the mode shares $| P_t - P_{t^-} |$ is higher than $| P_t - P_{t^+} |$.

The word threshold implicitly involves an individual evaluation of the perception of change; hence it is up to decision maker to define his threshold by exploring the percentage of alternative share increment which he will consider as a threshold i. e. which will satisfy his opinion about a threshold. More formally a critical value η has to be defined so that the absolute difference of $| P_t - P_{t^-} | = (1+\eta) | P_t - P_{t^+} |$. Alternatively, $\Delta P_{t^-} = (1+\eta) \Delta P_{t^+}$ and hence $\eta = (\Delta P_{t_-} / \Delta P_{t_+}) - 1$. From a visual point of view, one would intuitively expect to find the thresholds to be in the range given by the gray zone in Figure 3.8, where a reduction of one unit would increase the probability of choosing the alternative by an additional 20% (η = 0.3), so that ΔP_{t^-} would be equal to 6 times ΔP_{t^+}.

It is obvious that the given results in Figure 3.8 are based on a ceteris paribus assumption: consequently a variation of other mode specific characteristics like frequency and travel cost would imply a change of the location of the response curve so that the threshold would have to be relocated.

It has to be mentioned that in general by interpreting the results shown in Figure 3.8 one has to take into account that the travel time represents the time of a door to door trip. Therefore a change of the access/egress services can have an important impact on the choice of an alternative.

Other considerations. The purpose of the latter example is to visualize the asymmetry of the response functions, the existence of the thresholds and the impact of travel distance on consumer behavior: it is clear that for a detailed analysis of an investment or planned action it would of course be necessary to consider in addition the impact of travel cost, frequency, access/egress characteristics, etc.

The examination shown in Figure 3.8 also can be done in reverse direction where one first defines the probability of choosing the mode and then computes the necessary characteristics which satisfy this condition. Different kinds of services, which are related to different actions can be represented by changes in the underlying characteristics. Implicitly there is the possibility to verify the optimal investment by relating it to the alternative specific characteristics that maximize revenue.

System approach In general it has to be stated that the model discussed has to be embedded into a more complex system to catch all the effects mentioned in a consistent way. Therefore it is referred to Mandel 1999 where this issue is shown by describing the system approach as well as the interdependency of the different models.

Data The major source for the airport choice model presented in this paper is a disaggregate database based on air passenger surveys of all international airports of Germany. These data were checked and corrected by the DLR (German Aerospace Center - Cologne) and enriched by the access/egress mode characteristics based on the road and rail networks provided by MKmetric. To define the air alternatives the publicly available schedule information of some tourist offices, the OAG (Reed) and airport publications were implemented as air network.

How the network is implemented and which sources were used in detail you'll find in Mandel 1992 and Last et al. 1997. For further details of the survey all international airports of Germany or their association ADV have to be approached because unfortunately there is no public availability of these data.

The illustrative examples are based on raw data withdrawn for several years from public available statistics (Statistisches Bundesamt – Wiesbaden) as well as from other national statistical offices and the statistic department of Hamburg airport. These data were combined and enriched by MKmetric GmbH to one consistent database. The same holds for the 1997 database which was used in context of this 'Open Sky' project. In addition specific fare and schedule information was provided by SAIC as well as the induced demand rates by Prof. Dr. David Gillen.

Model Specification and Parameters

The specification of the airport choice model touches two issues. First variables have to be defined which explain the decision process of the consumers and in this context one has to take care of the functional form which is decisive to represent the behavior in a realistic manner. Second the definition of alternatives is essential because they restrict the set of possibilities a consumer has, e.g. they reflect the possible alternatives the consumer is aware of when taking the decision.

To define the alternatives of the choice set an air network was created which reflects the existing services at this time. To do this world airways guides, airport, airline and tourist office information were used. Flights of different airlines were considered as equal services as long as they did not differ in travel time significantly and type of connection. The survey did not allow to extract information on the real ticket price spend by the consumer so that average prices based on the published information have been used. Therefore it was not necessary to distinguish services at the level of tariffs, but it has to be stated that this would increase the quality of the models.

Analyzing the network database by applying the route choice algorithms in different ways and comparing the results with the available ca. 238.000 observations it was found that there is a necessity to split the database by trip purpose. The reason for this was the high difference in the number of alternatives taken into account by the consumers. While holiday-makers consider up to eight alternatives the business travelers just take note of four. Within the choice sets it is clear that the highest preference is on the alternative which is closest to the starting point of the trip and offering a non-stop service. The preferences of the following alternatives are rapidly falling for business and slowly for vacation trips. Non-business trips with a total duration of four days are defined as trips with private purpose and they are somewhere within between the two other purposes due to their sensitivity to the price and their restricted time limit of four days. Anyhow out of the economic point of view the segmentation by trip purpose is sensitive due to the quite different priorities and elasticities on price and time. To be sure to capture all possibilities the set of alternatives was defined for all trip purposes by the maximum of eight alternatives for each OD trip. But due to the very time consuming computational burden and the requested interactivity of a simulation tool one can restrict the set of choice to six alternatives in the case of vacation, to three for business and to four for private trips without a big loss of precision in the result.

Characteristics The analysis of the available disaggregate information of the survey resulted in a set of characteristics which are determining the airport choice, namely:

- Access/egress to the airport - weighted travel time and travel costs of individual and public transport to/from an airport - and distance from origin to the airport.
- Further attributes of public transportation to/from an airport - summarized in the denominator of the access/egress choice model
- Total travel times between origin and destination of passengers trip via several airports and/or air services, transfer and check in/out time inclusive.
- Travel costs of each trip, including access and egress (average costs are used because the survey did not contain the real ticket price).
- Service attributes of the flight - e.g. frequency and type of connection (non-stop, via).
- Attractiveness indicator of an airport, e.g. number of destinations and non-stop flights offered in total.

Further socio-economic variables and characteristics of the land based modes were not considered because the generation-distribution and mode choice part of the system approach are already taking care of them. In addition the use of nonlinearity reduces the need for certain kinds of segmentation - e.g. by fare or distance classes - typically done in order to obtain adequate representation or fit in domains other than that of the sample mean. Of course it would be very useful to study the extent to which market segmentation is a partial substitute for nonlinearity, as it is clear that nonlinearity—whether applied to network variables or to socio-economic variables like income or age—is distinct from market heterogeneity.

Based on the listed characteristics for each trip purpose a model was developed to explain the airport choice. The specification of each model is shown in Table 3-6.

Table 3-6: Model Specification

Variable	Business	Private	Vacation
Travel cost	Generic, λ-1	Generic, λ-1	Generic, λ-1
Travel time	Generic, λ-1	Generic	Generic, λ-2
OD frequency	Generic	Generic	Generic
Non-stop connection*	---	Specific	Generic
Airport attractivity	Generic	Generic	Generic
Distance to airport	---	Generic	----
Access/egress utility index	Generic	Generic	Generic

*for the last three alternatives

As already indicated in Table 3-6, the most variables are used in a generic way so that the β of this variable is common to all alternatives. Only the type of connection used in the private model is defined specific so that each alternative has its individual β. In general the specification focuses on robustness so that all variables have a t-student of at least 2.81 and sign conversions do not show up when setting variables to specific or adding other variables or exponents. Variables are only used as specific if the gain in likelihood justifies this. Of course the specifications were checked to avoid correlation and multicolinearity.

For example business travelers have a high time sensitivity and therefore prefer fast non-stop connections which are offered as close to the starting point of their trip (e.g., origin) as possible. This behavior is already reflected in the number of alternatives considered as stated above. Therefore the variables non-stop and distance to the airport are indirectly captured by the travel time variable.

For the vacation model the travel price is the dominant variable and the distance to an airport is just a matter of time which is already captured in the travel time variable. Another variable which could be of redundancy to travel time is the type of connection. Clearly a non-stop flight is usually faster than a via flight and therefore this information should already be covered by the time variable. But the type of connection also mirrors the service quality, e.g. vacation travelers with a lot of luggage prefer to check in close to their home even if it is a via flight. In addition they often use as access/egress mode the kiss&fly service offered by relatives or friends. The alternatives four to eight seem only to be taken into account if this is a non-stop flight.

The latter argumentation concerning non-stop flights also holds for the consumers travelling on private purpose. Here it was even more interesting to find out that private travelers are so sensitive to this non-stop service that the variable could be set to specific. The variable distance to the airport is only taken into account by the model for trip purpose private. Due to the fact that no correlation to other variables of the specification was detected this information could be interpreted as a kind of familiarity to the air mode if an airport is close to the home. May be the offers for short trips are much more intensive in high populated areas where airports are located than elsewhere. Further analysis of the survey showed in addition that there is a correlation to the age classes 20 to 40 years. Therefore this variable might also capture socio-economic effects and is no redundant information to travel time.

Functional form The next step to develop the models was the check on functional form, e.g. are the variables linear or non-linear. As stated in earlier forcing variables to be linear is equal to accepting errors of mis-specification. Therefore it has to be analyzed whether there is an asymmetry in the consumers behavior or not and whether there are there thresholds where consumer start to change their behavior more rapidly.

Concerning the functional form several tests have been made. The sign of λ identifies in Table 3-7 the variable as non-linear, where in the case of the same number the variables have a common transformation and elsewhere a different one. A λ in specific or generic form was only justified if there was a gain in the likelihood value and the t-student was at least 2.33. If there was more than one λ then a test was made to check whether one found a local or global maximum whereby only the latter was accepted.

Table 3-7: Selected Results for the Linear and Non-Linear Analysis

Model	Business		Private		Vacation	
Characteristics	linear	non-linear	linear	non-linear	linear	non-linear
Final loglikelihood value	-45100070	-43334113	-8030071	-7663015	-73800195	-72697398
λ-1	1.000	0.399	1.000	0.694	1.000	0.010
λ-2	1.000	0.399	1.000	1.000	1.000	0.637
Rho-squared	0.251	0.281	0.301	0.333	0.147	0.160

In the case of the business model it was decided to use a common λ because in the specific case they were not quite different and the gain in likelihood was small. For the vacation model the contrary was the case. Here two different λ were necessary because λ-1 on travel cost indicated a logarithmic form which was quite different from λ-2 indicating a strong non-linearity of travel time. For private trips the λ on travel time was not significant so that only one on travel cost was used. In all cases where the Box-Cox transformation was applied the gain in the final log-likelihood value was large and the rho-squared values improved.

Table 3-8: Weighted Aggregate Elasticity of Choice Probability of the Non-Linear Airport Choice Models

Model	Alternative	Business	Private	Vacation
Own elasticity travel cost	1	-0.233	-0.879	-1.219
	2	-1.696	-4.955	-3.846
	3	-2.464	-5.503	-4.879
	4	-2.881	-6.263	-4.928
	5	-3.156	-6.369	-5.043
	6	-3.292	-6.529	-5.162
Own elasticity travel time	1	-0.932	-0.480	-1.948
	2	-7.081	-3.195	-6.569
	3	-10.109	-5.649	-8.812
	4	-11.696	-5.727	-9.408
	5	-12.659	-6.312	-9.738
	6	-13.281	-6.312	-10.597

Elasticity and value of time. Of practical importance are the elasticities of demand. In Table 3-8. the elasticities of the Box-Cox estimates for the first six alternatives are given for the most interesting variables travel time and travel cost. A comparison of the linear and the Box-Cox estimates showed that there were strong differences to the linear ones. Generally in the linear case of the models the elasticities differed strongly; the ones for the cost variable were lower and the ones of time were higher. Of course if one computes the values of time they will differ for each alternative in the non-linear case while they are equal for the linear models. It is important to note that values of time are, technically speaking, marginal rates of substitution between two variables - cost and time - holding the level of utility constant. As these marginal rates are simply ratios of partial derivatives, the Box-Cox logit results will have a significant built-in advantage over the linear logit results because they will vary not only with each mode (as the derivatives will not be evaluated at the same point for each alternative on average) but will also depend on how much time is saved, as the value of the marginal minute depends on trip length, e.g. trip time (Mandel et al. 1997). Therefore non-linear models imply that consumers using the first alternative (e.g. the fastest) are evaluating their time differently from the ones choosing the last alternative (e.g. slowest).

The computed elasticity of demand reflects a one percent change of the variable so that the values given in Table 3-8 indicate a percentage. For the interpretation it has to be clear that the elasticities have to be evaluated only in context to the market share of the alternative. Therefore the low value of the elasticity of alternative one has a much higher impact on the market share of alternative one - which is big - than a high elasticity of alternative six - which has a small market share (Mandel 1992).

To demonstrate the practical relevance of the consumers elasticities the change of the market shares and travel demand of an alternative is computed in condition to an absolute change of the travel costs of this alternative whereby all other conditions remain *ceteris paribus* equal. As example the alternatives at the Hamburg airport in the year 1991 are used and displayed for three different market segments, namely domestic, European and intercontinental. The computed probabilities of the models will differ for each OD pair as well as they depend on the specific trip purpose. The curvatures of elasticity are aggregated for each market segment based on the specific OD results.

Figure 3.9 displays the change of passenger demand (y-axis) based on the year 1991 when tariffs change (x-axis). The zero-zero co-ordinates display the status quo at Hamburg in 1991. It can clearly be seen that the elasticity of business travelers is the smallest because changes of the tariffs have the smallest effect on their behavior. Although increasing the tariff of domestic flights by 100 DM only 28% will skip the alternatives offered at Hamburg. At the same price change the share of holiday-makers will decrease by 37% and the private travelers by 51%. On the domestic market segment the air services have to face a strong competition to the land based modes and in addition there are a lot of other air alternatives around so that easily instead of Hamburg the airports Hanover or Bremen can be used.

The results at a 100 DM change of the tariff for European destinations give roughly the same picture just the losses of market shares are smaller (business 7%, vacation 25%, private 38%). Surprisingly the results for intercontinental destinations are different. While the holiday-makers react strongly (24%) followed by the business travelers (19%) the private travelers show the smallest effect (12%).

The strong reaction of private travelers has to be seen out of the point of view that the total length of the trip does not exceed four days and therefore the ticket takes over a major part of the total trip expenditures. This argumentation even holds if one has a look on their behavior if the price decreases by 100 DM. The gain varies from 100% on domestic and 64% on European to 25% on intercontinental destinations.

Figure 3.9: Share of Travel Demand Depending on Cost Changes

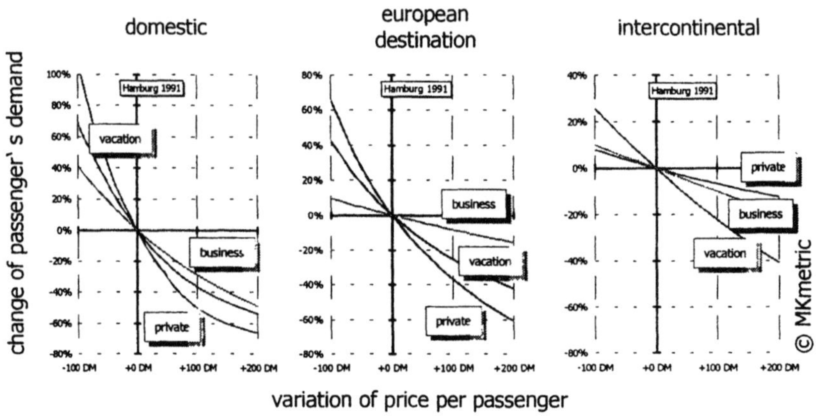

The small reaction of business travelers is consistent with the idea of the high time sensitivity of these consumers and the fact that the ticket is usually paid by the company or the visited client.

The idea of price sensitivity of vacation travelers is reflected at least in the domestic and European cases while on intercontinental trips the change of the ticket price does only slightly increase the total expenditures of the trip, so that this is of minor relevance. Anyhow the high competition on the intercontinental market is ensuring a low price level.

By the way in an air demand forecast study for Hamburg (1996) it was found that holiday trips to the same destination, same hotel etc. in the same time period offered by Hamburg tourist offices differed in price by up to 1.000 DM to those offered in other German cities. The major difference was just the originating airport: instead of Hamburg airport the journeys started from Frankfurt or Düsseldorf Airport.

To see the effects of consumer behavior on travel demand Figure 3.10 displays the results already explained on the market share level. The absolute passenger values (y-axis) refer directly to the market shares stated above so that the interpretation of the results is obvious. One remark should be made. Some changes of the travel shares seemed to be high or low but looking at the absolute number of travelers will adjust this objective.

Figure 3.10: Travel Demand Depending on Cost Changes

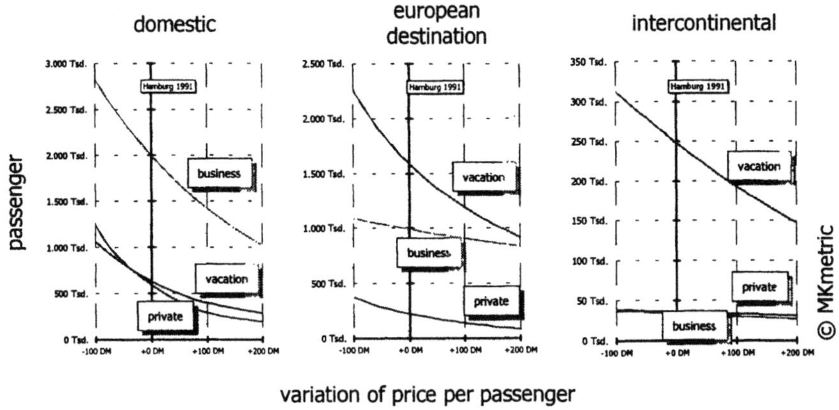

Generally it has to be stated that changes of tariffs higher than 150 DM are not covered by the database and therefore the precision of the results is decreasing. The models have to be updated when new observations are available which catch consumer behavior due to such large changes.

But despite this fact to the real example of an unrestricted return business trip between Hamburg and Frankfurt should be referred to because the comparison of model results and the true observations was encouraging in the sense that nor large changes of air tariffs are unusual neither the elasticities found by the models can be neglected.

For example an increase of the tariff of about 50 DM within a year (9.96 to 8.97) or a drop of the price by 30% and more as soon as another airline offers their service (e.g. Frankfurt – Berlin, Hamburg - Munich or Munich - Ruhr area in 1997) or the anti trust office claims monopolistic behavior of an airline are normal if one observes the market in detail. In the light of the ongoing liberalization, deregulation and privatization process and the very elastic pricing strategies of airlines the question is: How can airports participate at market procedures like airlines already do for some time? Due to the enlarging capacity constraints the growing air market is facing and the huge infrastructure investments airports have to undertake the airlines and respectively the consumers have to face higher charges and/or fees. It will be a matter of time that airports will be forced to turn to a more market oriented pricing strategy like peak & off peak pricing or the more general approach of slot trading to handle the spare capacity resources more efficient or say on the level of a real market price.

Concerning the elasticities it is referred to the example of the Frankfurt - Hamburg OD passenger market which decreased by 4.8% from 1996 to

1997 stated by airport statistics Hamburg. Within this time period not only the air tariff increased also the service frequency on this OD was reduced. Taking into account the average growth rate of about 7.4% in 1997 on the domestic German market the imaginable losses on this leg were 12.2% for the OD traffic. Obviously the growth rates were induced by the additional competition of airlines on several markets in 1997 where the prices dropped significantly. Therefore considering all effects the elasticities of the models tend to be conservative. In this context the question rises: Who can benefit of consumer elasticity by applying a market oriented pricing strategy, exclusively airlines? More and more the airports view the travelers directly as clients and apply aggressive marketing strategies to increase their attractivity (free or cheap parking and overnight stay, shops, play grounds, restaurants, high-speed rail access, etc.) to enlarge their catchment area. A new pricing strategy for the aviation side would be a natural enrichment of the existing marketing tools. In addition one could use a market oriented pricing as instrument to impose a price structure to meet political constraints like environmental benchmarks.

By the way by increasing tariffs on an OD the total demand on this leg need not necessarily decrease if one takes into account the transfer passengers, who usually pay different prices. In the case of the Hamburg - Frankfurt leg which is dominated by the OD passenger market the losses on total demand were 1.8% to the demand in 1996 because the share of transfer passengers increased by ca. 2.3%.

At the end of this elasticity analysis it has to be stated that the also sensitivity curves can be obtained for all alternative characteristics of the model. Specially travel time and service frequency play another major role in context of the 'Open Sky' strategy as the acceptance of new services is not only determined by the travel price. An inaugurated non-stop service at Hamburg Airport which reduces travel time in respect to transfer flights can only gain a significant market share if the service frequency is appropriate. But in reverse airlines will only establish a new connection with high frequencies if they expect a profitable mixture of passengers and their network in total does not suffer due to passengers withdrawn from existing routes. Anyhow the airlines are permanently optimizing their network and will serve the existing demand (once detected) within the existing competitive environment.

Therefore to compute the effects on the leg level all itineraries on the total network have to be considered. Obviously it is wrong to concentrate on one airport and single services without considering the synergetic effects of a network and the competitive situation around. To face such and other complex problems the airport choice models have been embedded in the system approach (see Mandel 1999).

Economic Impact Models

Economic impact models fit into three classifications. First, is a methodology called economic base multiplier (EBM). This approach divides the economy into two sectors, basic and non-basic and uses multipliers to measure the impact of changes in the basic sector on the non-basic sector. The basic sector includes the total value of sales from all goods and services that are exported from the region. The non-basic sector includes the value of output for meeting all local demand and supports the basic sector. If the basic sector expands it will have spillover effects into the non-basic sector because income flows in and the demand for goods and services increases. This leads to increases in income, employment and output. The measure of this change is the multiplier. The simplicity of this approach is attractive but it also is highly aggregated and generally has multipliers that overestimate the impacts of changes in demands.

A second approach is to develop an econometric model that relates inputs and outputs and estimates the multipliers. Regional econometric models have been used in some cases but this is not necessary. The parameter estimates from even a relatively simple model estimated on a current set of time series data can provide timely estimates of the impacts of changes in the demands for an output on output, employment and income. A set of econometric models is developed below for different airport sectors. The attractive feature of this methodology is the timeliness of the estimates and ability to identify microeconomic relationships. The cost is one of complexity and significant data requirements.

A third methodology is an IO model. These are commonly used in economic impact studies. They are based on production theory. Economic impact metrics require a census of the factors of production measured in terms of employment, income, labor, business expenditures and taxes. Subsequently, general IO coefficients from a macro model are used to measure the direct and indirect impacts. While this is a common methodology used in many countries, it requires up to date multiplier values and, the measures assume linear production relationships. This generally results in overestimates of direct and induced impacts.

Airport Impacts

Airport impacts from added flights and passengers can include increases in employment, airside and terminal investment, aviation revenues and non-aviation revenues. Our data only permitted us to examine the changes to airside and non-airside revenues.

A change in the bilateral leads to a change in the demand for airport service. A change in aircraft operations affects aviation revenues and non-aviation revenues. We wish to distinguish a change in the frequency of flights depending on the origin of the flight; Germany, Europe or International.[17] There is also a change in the numbers of passengers of different origins and trip purpose that would impact the non-aviation revenues.

Aviation Revenue

A number of models were examined to understand how aviation revenue would change as a result of a change in the number of different types of flights. The data distinguished three types of flights; within Germany, intra-European and international flights. We might also expect the aircraft gauge would change as well and this will have an impact on aviation revenues.

The data for estimating this model were gathered from the National Airports Council. This council collects information on revenues from different sources from each airport in Germany. Unfortunately, the council serves only as a collection agency and the airports providing the data do not follow a common format. Hence, some airports offered detailed information on revenue from each source while others only provided aggregate information.

The first model was estimated to investigate the impact of flights and aircraft gauge on aviation revenue. The results of the estimates are contained in Table 3-9.[18] Aviation revenue increases with increases in both German and European flights and International flights but in a very different way. The elasticity of revenue with respect to changes in German and European flights is 0.15, meaning a 10% increase in this type of flight would increase aviation revenue by 1.5%. The elasticity of revenue with respect to international flights is .69, a 10% increase in International flights would increase aviation revenue by 6.9%, *a difference of a factor of over four.*

The model also shows that revenue is higher at Frankfurt Airport because it is a hub for Lufthansa and much larger than other German airports. Revenue is also increasing over time. The time elasticity is .07 and reflects change to rates and charges.

An interesting outcome is the influence of aircraft size on revenue. Many charges are based on aircraft weight. German and European flights have about the same size of aircraft on their flights (130-150 seats) while International flights have larger aircraft (220-380). The lack of variation in the intra-European market aircraft size indicates a marginal change has no statistical impact on revenues.[19] However, there is considerable variation in the international aircraft size and increases in size have a non-trivial impact on revenues. Airports may realize increased revenue from international flights both because of the increase in flights and because of the increase in aircraft gauge.

Table 3-9: Estimates of Aviation Revenue Related to Flights and Aircraft Gauge

Variable Name	Estimated Coefficient	Standard Error	T-Ratio	Elasticity at Mean
Constant	-72629	42420	-1.712	NA
German & European Flights	0.99696	0.501	1.990	0.15
International Flights	42.894	3.164	13.557	0.69
Time	7018.1	1850	3.794	0.07
European Aircraft Size	-1019.6	938.9	-1.086	-0.25
International Aircraft Size	1190.4	557.7	2.134	0.54
Frankfurt Dummy	149550	68870	2.171	NA
Adjusted R-Square = 0.996				

In the course of the modeling, the impact of passengers on aviation revenue was explored. As one would expect, no statistical relationship could be found. This is not surprising since aviation revenue derives from landing, gate and parking fees for the most part. The amount would not vary with the number of passengers, beyond the impact of changes in aircraft gauge.

The essential information from Table 3-10, is the responsiveness of aviation revenue with respect to changes in flight frequency and type as well as gauge. These values are required to calculate the impact of changes in flights, aircraft size and passengers resulting from changes to any bilateral on airport revenue. The changes to the sum landing, parking and gate fees depend on aircraft size, where they arrive from and whether there I substitution between flight frequency and aircraft size.

Table 3-10: Elasticity Values for German and International Flights and Aircraft Size

Variable	Elasticity Value
German and European Flights	0.15
International Flights	0.69
European Aircraft Size	-0.25
International Aircraft Size	0.54

For intra-German or European flights, a 1% increase in these flights will increase aviation revenue by 0.15%. If the flights were international flights, the one percent increase in flights would lead to a 0.69% increase in revenue. This is a dramatic difference and implies airport officials should be substituting international for domestic and European flights as much as possible. However, this interpretation should be tempered since cost information is not included. If the marginal cost is the same for both types of flights, the interpretation stands, but should these costs differ, substitution should reflect differences in marginal cost.

Aircraft size also plays an important role in affecting revenue. As aircraft size increases the number of flights will change as well. For domestic and European flights.

Non-Aviation Revenue

The modeling of the linkages between flights and passengers and non-aviation revenue paralleled the investigation of aviation revenue. We separated these two sources of revenue since they are influenced by different factors. Non-aviation revenue is the revenue from non-airside activities. This would include revenue from concessions (food, clothing, other shopping items) parking and rental space to airlines, car rental agencies and other concessionaires. The primary driver of non-aviation revenue will be a passenger from different destinations (domestic, other Europe and outside of Europe) and of different types (business vs. tourist).

A number of models were estimated using different functional forms and combinations of variables. The model with the best statistical fit and providing plausible results is illustrated below. All variables are significant at least at the 10% level. A dummy variable was included for Frankfurt due to its use as a hub by Lufthansa. We wished to measure the different impact of tourist from different origins. The results are consistent with the literature in this area. The international traveler tends to add more revenue than domestic travelers do.

The elasticity of non-aviation revenue for German (domestic) and other European passengers is .23 while the elasticity of non-aviation revenue with respect to international passengers is .52. A 10% increase in non-international passengers leads to a 2.3% increase in revenue while a 10% increase in international passengers leads to a 5.2% increase in non-aviation revenue. As the proportion of passengers who are tourists rises, revenue also increases. Given other things, if 10% of passengers are tourists rather than business travelers, non-aviation revenue goes up by 1.9%. Therefore, when calculating the impact of changes in passengers on non-aviation revenue it would be the composite of these elasticities that would be used.

Input/Output Models

The two key indicators of an airport's importance are its impact on the economy and its transportation benefits. Economic impacts are the regional economic activities, employment and payroll that can be attributed, directly and indirectly to the operation of the airport. The three principal outputs from an economic impact study are measures of direct impacts, indirect impacts and induced impacts for employment, income and output.

Table 3-11: Estimates of Non-Aviation Revenue Related to Passenger Information

Variable Name	Estimated Coefficient	Standard Error	T-Ratio	Elasticity at Mean
constant	-39119	64420	-0.607	NA
German & European Passengers	0.00933	0.00329	2.836	0.23
International Passengers	0.07857	0.00809	9.712	0.52
Time	6618.6	1109	5.968	0.18
Proportion of Passengers Tourist	2563.6	1016	2.523	0.19
Frankfurt Dummy	16349	12210	1.339	NA

Adjusted R-Square = 0.9962

Direct economic impacts result from activities carried out at the airport by airlines, airport management, fixed base operators, air freight firms and other tenants. Employment, purchases of local goods and services and contracting for airport construction and capital improvements are examples of airport activities that generate direct impacts. The distinguishing feature of a direct impact is that it is an immediate consequence of airport activity.

Indirect economic impacts differ from direct impacts in that they occur entirely off-site. From the perspective of economic theory, indirect impacts are the jobs and income generated by the purchases of goods and services of firms dependant upon airport activity. The spending by these firms on goods and services represents output for other firms further down the production chain, bringing indirect employment, income, and tax activity.

Induced economic impacts occur as a result of spending on goods and services by the employees of firms and agencies directly tied to the airport.

As in the case of indirect economic activity, induced economic output leads to comparable induced employment, income, and tax flows. Induced impacts represent the multiplier of direct and indirect impacts. Multiplier effects are the increases in employment and income over and above the combined direct and indirect impacts generated by successive rounds of spending.

Although some of the induced impacts occur locally, some are felt outside the region because of the import components of the goods and services purchased. It is therefore important that the specific (induced) multiplier factors selected for any analysis take account of regional imports into the account.

IO models define, measure and diagnose the productive linkages and transactions among the key components of the national or state economic system, and therefore provide a realistic, technology based reading of what is really happening among the various sectors of the economy. When constructed accurately, IO definitions and measurement are totally compatible with macroeconomic models and with internationally agreed standards of national accounting. Given sufficient time, resources and data, any degree of precision can be attained by the IO methodology.

One can also distinguish between macro IO models (i.e. those incorporating large, national databases) and micro IO approaches (i.e. those diagnosing significant individual activities, such as an airport or subway). Under appropriate applications, the conventional macro IO and newer micro approach are compatible with each other.

IO analysis relies on the fact that economic systems are structurally interdependent and that these interdependencies can be recorded in an IO framework. Under such frameworks, the outputs (i.e. sales) of any sector and industry are distributed among all the other sectors and industries, where they become inputs (i.e. purchases). Allowing for producers and consumers, investment and capital depreciation, and interactions with other regions, a double-entry, consistent and precise tabulation and economic linkages can be constructed.

IO tables can vary in level of disaggregation. Higher levels of aggregation have fewer data requirements but also lose precise due to aggregation of the data. The IO technical coefficients matrix, expressed in either physical or monetary terms, are the key components of such models. A technical coefficient measures the amount of inputs (units in quantity or value) required from all industries in an economy to produce one unit of output (or a mark's worth of output) in a particular industry. The coefficients matrix derived from the IO model is a measure of the dollar value required for inputs for each dollar of sales of the final good or service. If the final sales of a good or service were to increase by some amount, three percent, this would lead to an increase in the demand for all the inputs.

Several critical assumptions are made regarding the technical coefficients used in standard macro IO analyses:

- *Each sector produces a single output, with a single input structure.* There is no automatic substitution between outputs of different sectors.
- *Fixed IO coefficients.* This is a rather restrictive assumption and if the technical coefficients are unstable, they lose predictive value. This occurs with significant changes in technology.
- *Linear-homogeneous production functions.* If this were not the case, variations from the scale of the applications would create distortions when using such models.

Under these assumptions IO models take the IO flows among sectors and industries at a point in time and treat the data, collected at this time, as representative of the economies production structure and linkages. IO models are re-calibrated on a 5 to 6 year basis precisely for the reason that the economy is dynamic and linkages will change over time.

Multipliers are taken from IO models to measure the impact that changes in airport activity will have on the level of income, output and employment. In the case at hand, a change in bilaterals would lead to an increase in the carrier and passenger demands for Hamburg Airport services. This in turn will lead to an increase in the demands for factors in the local Hamburg economy, like labor and services. This is said to have a multiplier effect because as each dollar is input into the Hamburg economy it will be used to purchase other goods and services in a form of a trickle down effect. For example, an increase in aircraft operations will lead to more baggage being handled. The baggage-handling firm will hire more labor. This labor receives its wages and will spend it in the local economy on food, clothing shelter, entertainment and transportation services. The local food market will receive these dollars and pay its own workers and will purchase goods and services from the local economy. This trickle down, in effect, multiplies through the system. The IO models provide a measure of these multipliers.

The multipliers from the *Empirica Study*[20] are as follows:

- Total indirect and induced effects 1.7;
- Metropolitan Region indirect and induced effects 1.3; and
- Airport Region indirect and induced effects 1.1.

All multipliers relate employment at the airport to employment of the airport.[21] Multipliers are generally disaggregated based on primary and secondary linkage organization. Tables of representative levels of disaggregation are illustrated below. Calculations are based on 1998 data. In Table 3-12 the level of employment in Hamburg economic region is illustrated for the years 1980 through 1994. In addition the employment at the airport and the Lufthansa facility are also displayed. Over time the relative importance of the airport as an employer has increased as the proportion of employment in the region has risen from four percent in 1980 to six percent in 1994. This entire growth has been due to activities at the airport proper rather than at the Lufthansa maintenance facility. One might therefore argue that the induced impacts from changes to the bilateral should focus on airport employment exclusively and not include the Lufthansa facility employment.

In Table 3-13, the employment impact using the multiplier from the IO study for Hamburg region is calculated. There are three different measures. The first is the total effect for the entire Hamburg region. Using these values it is evident that Hamburg airport provides a total of direct, indirect and induced employment of 20,636 people. If we focus only on the metro region the total employment is 15,781 while we a narrower area, the airport region is considered, employment total is 13,353. If a change in the bilateral governing access to Germany in general and Hamburg particularly, the increased activity will lead to more direct employment at the airport (this is considered in detail below) and will induce employment in the Hamburg region as well. It is this total effect that needs to be considered in assessing the value of such a change in policy.

Table 3-12: Employment in Hamburg Region and at Hamburg Airport 1980-1994

					Proportion of Regional Employment		
Year	Hamburg Region	Airport	Lufthansa Facility	Airport Total	Airport	Lufthansa Facility	Airport Total
1980	245,541	3720	7042	10762	0.015	0.03	0.04
1981	241,110	3741	6788	10529	0.016	0.03	0.04
1982	232,802	3623	6882	10505	0.016	0.03	0.05
1983	221,877	3679	6941	10620	0.017	0.03	0.05
1984	214,921	3755	6993	10748	0.017	0.03	0.05
1985	212,043	3959	7076	11035	0.019	0.03	0.05
1986	212,601	4095	7693	11788	0.019	0.04	0.06
1987	210,756	4264	7843	12107	0.02	0.04	0.06
1988	209,178	4599	8029	12628	0.022	0.04	0.06
1989	213,197	5095	8213	13308	0.024	0.04	0.06
1990	218,174	5371	8739	14110	0.025	0.04	0.06
1991	223,448	5577	8844	14421	0.025	0.04	0.06
1992	221,901	5600	8311	13911	0.025	0.04	0.06
1993	210,542	5890	7066	12956	0.028	0.03	0.06
1994	200,412	5796	6821	12617	0.029	0.03	0.06

Table 3-13: Employment Supported by Hamburg Airport - Total, Metro Region and Airport Region

Areas of Employment	Direct	Total Induced	Metro Region Induced	Airport Region Induced
Airport Corporation	1369	958	411	137
Airport Subsidiaries	320	224	96	32
Government Agencies	611	428	183	61
Airlines	1063	744	319	106
Import and Export Businesses	812	568	244	81
Restaurants and Catering Businesses	608	426	182	61
Car Rental	100	70	30	10
Repair and Maintenance	18	13	5	2
Fuel Companies	71	50	21	7
Travel Agencies	196	137	59	20
Retail and Banks	198	139	59	20
Security Services	372	260	112	37
Cleaning Services	27	19	8	3
Others	378	265	113	38
Subtotal Airport	6143	4300	1843	614
Lufthansa Repair and Maintenance Facility	5996	4197	1799	600
Total	**12139**	**8497**	**3642**	**1214**

Estimates were also made of the impact of changes in flight operations and passengers on the demand for employees at the Hamburg Airport. Over the last decade total airport employment has been relatively stagnant. In 1989 the employment at the airport was 5015 and in 1997 this figure was 5015. Employment at the Lufthansa maintenance center was 8213 in 1989 and 5904 in 1997. However, there has been a significant redistribution of people between jobs. In Table 3-14, the number of flights per employee and passenger per employee are illustrated. For airport employees, both flights and passengers have risen indicating an increase in labor productivity. A comparison with flights and passengers per airline employee is also provided. For airline personnel their productivity has risen as well. However, over the ten years airport productivity has risen more than airline productivity. For the airport there has been an increase of 27% in flights per employee and 41% in passengers per employee while the respective figures for airline personnel are 22% and 37%. Part of the explanation for airport labor productivity increases in the shift to contracting for services.

Table 3-14: Measures of Labor Productivity at Hamburg Airport

year	Flights per Airport Employee	Passengers per Airport Employee	Flights per Airline Employee	Passengers per Airline Employee
1989	33	2077	44	2824
1990	31	2018	48	3121
1991	28	1762	44	2724
1992	31	1977	44	2833
1993	35	2250	50	3235
1994	36	2401	46	3129
1995	37	2557	50	3437
1996	37	2569	60	4166
1997	42	2947	55	3869

To better understand how the demand for labor might change in the face of increased operations and passengers, we estimated some relatively simple regressions to determine how the demand for different categories of employees would change.[22] The results are presented in terms of elasticities. Four categories of employees were considered; airport employees, those working for concessions (food, beverage, car rental), service (repair, maintenance, fuel) and other (banks, travel agents, import and export, government). Table 3-15 shows the demand for airport labor tends to go down with respect to both passenger and flights but this is reflective of a trend to shift from own employees to contracting with firms that have a comparative advantage in each given area.

Table 3-15: Elasticity of Demand for Labor - Hamburg Airport

	Elasticity with respect to			
Labour Category	Passengers-Total	Domestic Passengers	Int'l Passengers	Flights
Airport	-0.50			-0.47
Service	0.37	0.33	0.05	
Concession	0.31	0.29	0.05	0.54
Other	0.42			0.67

The offset to the demand for the reduction in airport employment shows up in the increasing demand for all other categories of labor. There are differences with respect to flights as well as for domestic and international passengers for service and concession employment. Interestingly, domestic passengers (defined as all European including intra Germany) stimulate more employment than international passengers or flight operations.

Employment, Investment, Income and Tourism Impacts

Open markets and the reduction of barriers to trade provide opportunities for firm to exploit their competitive advantage. As aviation is liberalized, access to and from the German market is enhanced, German industries will also exploit their comparative advantage. Two related questions arise, how will increased access affect the local economy and, how will aviation intensive industries such as tourism be influenced. The two questions are dealt with in turn below.

Increased access and the local Hamburg economy Travel is a derived demand. The economy grows and develops increased trade and opportunities for trade lead to an increased demand for all factors of production including transportation. Therefore, a model of the demand for flights as it relates to economic growth must be developed. At the same time increased access, measured by increased flight frequency, broader choices of carriers and lower fares, will provide opportunities for firms to increase their exports to Europe and beyond. Thus, a model to explain the investment and employment impacts of liberalization is developed.

Ideally, we would like to relate information on the structure and growth of the economy to the demand for aviation services. Our data did not allow this and estimates were made at a more macro level. The data set was developed base don information provided by the German Association of Airports and the Institute for Economic Research. The airport data included the following airports; Frankfurt, Hamburg, Düsseldorf, Hanover, Munich, Nuremberg, Bonn, Bremen and Stuttgart. In addition to the operation, information on flights and passenger movements by domestic, European and world, information on the local economy was matched to the airport region. The data included; aggregate employment, aggregate investment, revenue from sales of all goods and services, a measure of GDP (Gross Domestic Product) or income and a measure of revenue from the sale of export goods and services. In some cases, data were available at a higher level of detail for a given airport or for the features of the economy surrounding an airport. However, to preserve the largest possible dataset for the modeling a higher level of aggregation was chosen rather than excluding airports from the data set. The panel of data covered the years 1987 through 1997.

In the modeling we wanted to distinguish, local economic drivers from those associated with broader trading in Europe or the world economy. We therefore distinguished domestic, European and world flights and passengers. We related these to total revenue (GDP) and revenue from export sales (GDP_{export}). In some cases, we also included dummy variables for some airports. Frankfurt, for example, was dummied since it dominates all other German airport since it is a hub for Lufthansa. Hamburg was dummied since that is the focus of the project.

A number of models were estimated in which GDP, or its components were related to numbers of flights. The model [provides measures of the responsiveness of flight activity (the derived demand for air service) as the economy grows. Table 3-16 summarizes these econometric estimates. T-statistics, measures of coefficient statistical significance are in parenthesis.

Table 3-16: Estimates of Relationship between Flights and Economic Activity

	Log of German Flights	**Log of European Flights**	**Log of World Flights**	**Log Total Flights**
Log GDP	0.02201 (1.94)	0.04416 (2.54)	0.00849 (1.99)	0.04940 (2.46)
Log GDP_{export}			0.11652 (1.77)	0.11645 (9.60)
Frankfurt	1.597 (4.76)	1.698 (2.81)	2.385 (2.49)	2.034 (6.83)
Hamburg	1.249 (3.35)	0.5058 (.753)	0.3915 (.036)	0.9951 (3.16)
Düsseldorf	1.0963 (4.24)	1.0889 (2.35)	0.6861 (0.826)	1.2464 (5.00)
R^2	.97	.96	.97	.99

The results can be summarized in terms of elasticities. The elasticity would measure the proportionate change in a type of flight with respect to a change in the level of economic activity.

A 10% increase in GDP would lead to a 0.2% increase in domestic flights, a 0.4% increase in flights within Europe and a 0.8% increase in flights outside of Europe. If we do not distinguish between types of flights, aggregate flights will increase by 0.5%. If we concentrate on that portion of the economy associated with sales for export, GDP_{export}, a 10% increase in this segment of the economy would lead to a 1.16% increase in flights outside of Europe. These results are quite intuitive. The low values for the elasticities for Domestic and European flights reflect the presence of substitute modes and greater us eof communication. These substitute modes are not available for destinations outside of Europe.

The next set of models examined the impact that increased accessibility and mobility provided by the liberal bilateral regime might have on the regional economy surrounding an airport and particularly Hamburg Airport. The two variables that are of particular interest are income (Y) (measured by GDP) and employment (L). Initially, we explored the direct relationship between income, employment and increased aviation access as measured by the number of flights. A number of models and specifications were examined but flights (F) was always insignificant. This led to the specification of the three equation model below.

The structural form of the model would be represented as:

$$Y=f_1(L, K)$$
$$L=f_2(Y, K)$$
$$K=f_3(Y, F, K_{t-1})$$

where K is the amount of investment, F is the number of flights and K_{t-1} is investment in the previous period. The first equation links aggregate income or sales to the two primary factors of production, labor and capital. Equation 2 links the demand for labor to the level of economic activity and the amount of capital in place. Equation 3 shows the demand for investment will depend on the level of economic activity, the amount of investment in the previous period and the availability of aviation services. It is in equation 3 that flights have their role. They influence income and employment through their impact on investment.

$$\Delta F \rightarrow \Delta I \rightarrow \Delta Y \text{ and } \Delta L \text{ and } \Delta Y \rightarrow \Delta I$$

The three key elasticities from this model are elasticity of income (or GDP) with respect to flights, $\xi_{Y,F}$, the elasticity of demand for labor with respect to flights, $\xi_{L,F}$, and , the elasticity of demand for investment with respect to flights, $\xi_{K,F}$. These elasticities are measured as:

$$\xi_{Y,F} = \xi_{Y,K} \bullet \xi_{K,F}$$
$$\xi_{L,F} = \xi_{Y,K} \bullet \xi_{K,F} \bullet \xi_{L,Y}$$
$$\xi_{K,F} = dK/dF \bullet (F/K)$$

The reduced form of the model is estimated on the panel of airport and regional economic variables using Seemingly Unrelated regression techniques. The basic results are reported below.

Results of Reduced form Estimation of Structural Economic Impact Model

$\text{Log } Y = 5.715 + 0.6877 \log K + 0.10649 \log K_{t-1} + 0.0621 \log L$
$R^2 = .61$
$\text{Log } L = -1.758 + 0.8976 \log K + 0.04742 \log Y$
$R^2 = .78$
$\text{Log } K = 3.0534 + 0.1135 \text{ Log } Y + 0.41423 \log F + 0.34956 \log K_{t-1}$
$R^2 = .89$
System $R^2 = .86$

The values of the elasticities of interest are:

$\xi_{Y,F} = 0.27$elasticity of economic output or income with respect to flights

$\xi_{L,F} = 0.03$elasticity of employment with respect to flights

$\xi_{K,F} = 0.41$elasticity of investment with respect to flights

Once we are able to estimate the expected changes in flight activity because of introducing a more liberalized international aviation regime in Germany we will be able to estimate the impact on the Hamburg region.

Impacts on Tourism We were also able to develop a tourism model that allows us to estimate the impact of changes in flights on the numbers of tourist passengers. We are also able to estimate the impact of changes in tourist passengers on the demand for labor. The models are partial models and are intended to only provide a order of magnitude estimate of the impact of liberalization. It would certainly be true that these estimates are minimum values. The final actual outcome would be larger if because of the liberalization Germany became relatively less costly to visit than other countries.

Two separate models were estimated. One related the number of tourist passengers to the level of income and the level of accessibility to the region measured by the number of flights. The second model related employment to levels of income and levels of tourist passengers. The model results are reported below. The relevant elasticities that can be calculated from these models are the elasticity of tourism with respect to flights, ξT, F, and the elasticity of employment with respect to tourism, ξ L, T.

$\text{Log Passengers}_{\text{Tourist}} = 9.4863 + 0.07973 \text{ Log } F_{G+E} + 0.06852 \text{ Log } F_W + 0.06493 \text{ Log } Y$
$R^2 = .93$
$\text{Log } L = -0.3698 + 0.04927 \text{ Log } Y + 0.02075 \text{ Log Passengers}_{\text{Tourist}}$
$R^2 = .56$

The values of the elasticities are:

$\xi_{T,F} = 0.08$ the elasticity of tourism with respect to flights,

$\xi_{L,T} = 0.02$ the elasticity of employment with respect to tourism.

Therefore a 10% increase in flights will lead to a 0.8% increase in tourist passengers and a 10% increase in tourism passengers leads to a 0.2% increase in employment, both rather small numbers. However we have indicated these are quite conservative numbers since they do not account for tourist switching destinations from other countries to Germany.

Summary

This section has provided the underlying models that will be used to calculate the impact of Open skies on the Hamburg airport and the Hamburg local and regional economies. Traditional impact analysis relies on input-output type models. We have used this approach here but the methodology makes some strong assumptions regarding the stability of economic linkages and the nature of the underlying production structure. Therefore, we extended the modeling to include estimates from econometric models describing both airport and economic impacts.

The airport revenue models distinguished revenue from airside activity from of non-aviation activity. The former, aviation revenue, is driven by the number and type of flights and size of aircraft. Non-aviation revenue , on the other hand, is influence by the number and origin of passengers and whether the passenger is traveling for business or non-business reasons. The elasticity of aviation revenue with respect to domestic and European flights was estimated to be 0.15 meaning a 10% increase in these types of flights would result in a 1.5% increase in aviation revenue. The comparable elasticity for International flights was found to be 0.69. Two elasticities of aviation revenue with respect to size were also estimated. The European aircraft size elasticity was -0.25, a 10% increase in size leads to a 2.5% decrease in revenue. This occurs because larger aircraft result in fewer flights so despite an increase in revenue from larger aircraft the reduction in the number of flights . The elasticity of aviation with respect to international aircraft size is 0.54; a 10% increase in size lead to a 5.4% increase in revenue.

The non-aviation model was used to develop elasticity estimates for key variables much like those for aviation revenue. We found the elasticity of non-aviation revenue with respect to increases in Domestic and European passengers was 0.23, a 10% rise in these type of passenger would increase non-aviation revenue by 2,3%. The comparable elasticity for international passengers was estimates to be 0.52. The much larger values reflects the greater propensity to spend among international travelers than domestic passengers. The impact of passenger type was also examined. As the proportion of tourists in the total passengers rose, revenue would increase. Specifically, the elasticity of non-aviation revenue with respect to increasing proportions of tourists was found to be 0.19. Thus, if passengers increased revenue would rise and if these passengers were tourists the increase would be augmented by a factor of 0.19.

Our models also focused on the impact of Open Sky on airport employment. Over time employment at the airport has been growing but with significant variation across types of work and the employers. For example, the airport proper has been reducing employees while employment in concessions, services and government related activities has been growing. Models were developed that provided elasticity of employment estimates with respect to changes in both passengers and flights. A division among the types of labor was also made but these ended up being relatively aggregate categories. The impact of changes in passengers ranged from 0.37 to 0.42, a 10% increase in passengers lead to increases in employment of particular types by 3.7 to 4.2%. The comparable flight elasticity ranged from 0.54 to 0.67.

Models linking airport activity to employment, output and investment in the local and regional economies were estimated using information for the major airports in Germany. The elasticity of output (or income) with respect to flights was found to be 0.49 - a 10% increase in flights led to a 0.5% rise in income. However, we also estimated the models in which output oriented for export was separated out. In this case the elasticity of income derivative from export oriented activity with respect to flights was 0.11. The elasticity of employment with respect to flights was found to be 0.03 and the investment elasticity was estimated as 0.41.

The final modeling effort was examining the impact of tourism. The two-stage model was used to first determine how Open Sky would impact tourism and a second stage was used to link the increase in tourism to employment derivative from tourism. We estimated that a 10% increase in flights would increase tourism by 0.8%, elasticity of 0.08, while the impact of this increase on employment was 0.02; a 10% increase in tourism leads to employment related to tourism by 0.2%.

---

[1] The modifications are made external to the model. That is, the competitive market structure remains while judgments with respect to the degree of competition and the effect of third country markets are made using secondary sources and available data to estimate the magnitude and distribution of effects.

[2] Armington, Paul S. (1969). "A Theory of Demand for Products Distinguished by Place of Production," IMF Staff Papers.

[3] Many trade policy analysts use the same neo-classical microeconomic approach found in the perfect competition model to measure consumers' and firms' benefits from policy changes. For a widely-accepted treatment of bilateral trade problems, the reader is referred to Dixit (1984), in which the author uses these same analytical tools. In particular, he uses the same concepts of consumer and firm surplus, as well as that of economic equilibrium.

[4] The cost benefit analysis discussed here is resource based and is not social cost benefit analysis which is often used for evaluating policy alternatives or project investment.

[5] Consumer surplus is the consumer welfare measure used.

[6] This approach meets the objectives outlined earlier and provides results that are generalizable rather than market specific. The consensus of the project team, developed at modeling seminars, supported this approach since the data requirements and the computational complexity associated with the bottom up approach would prove insurmountable for the time and resources allotted.

[7] Armington, Paul S. "A Theory of Demand for Products Distinguished by Place of Production." IMF Staff Papers, 1969.

[8] The relevant market is considered to be the OD.

[9] The basis of the Armington model, as applied to international air travel is as follows: The consumer engages in a two stage decision making process when considering the purchase of international air travel services: Stage One: Consumer chooses between travel over OD pair and all other commodities. Stage Two: Once the travel decision has been made, for a given OD pair, consumer chooses among various carrier-route combinations based on price and non-price factors.

[10] Form 41 data do not provide an accurate measure of the economic costs of capital invested in aircraft and therefore the block-hour costs need to be adjusted upward by the amount of interest cost on the capital tied up in the aircraft (opportunity cost of flight capital).

[11] For a comprehensive review of the empirical evidence related to parameter estimates see, Oum, Waters and Young (1992).

[12] The parameter estimates reported in the table encompass the range of values reported in Chapter 3. It is likely that these parameter values are market specific, however, these probability ranges are considered to encompass a credible eighty% confidence interval based on the secondary and primary research conducted.

[13] Caves, D.W., L. R. Christensen, and W.E. Diewert. "Multilateral Comparisons of Output, Input, and Productivity Using Superlative Index Numbers." *Economic Journal*, 92, 1982, pp. 73-86.

[14] Windle, Robert., "The World's Airlines: A Cost and Productivity Comparison." *Journal of Transport Economics and Policy*, 1991.

[15] Windle and Dresner, "Partial Productivity Measures and Total Factor Productivity in the Air Transport Industry: Limitations and Uses." *Transportation Research*, Vol. 26, 1992.

[16] Oum, T.H. and C. Yu. "A Comparative Study of Total Factor Productivity of World's Major Airlines." *(Forthcoming, Journal of Transport Economics & Policy, 1996).*

[17] We would also like to differentiate between a change I flights due to a given carrier increasing frequency and a change in flights resulting from an increase in the number of carriers serving the airport. The reason is they would impact revenues (and expenses) quite differently.

[18] The model was estimated using the a pooled time-series cross section estimation method that takes account of both cross equation variation as well as serial correlation. The pooling technique employs a set of assumptions on the disturbance covariance matrix that gives a cross-sectionally heteroskedastic and timewise autoregressive model. Estimates are obtained using Generalized Least Squares.

[19] The negative sign also has the interesting interpretation that as size increase revenue goes down since the number of flights would decrease. This is a tradeoff for airports when dealing with increases in demand. Airlines may decide to accommodate the increased passenger demand by flying less often in larger aircraft. This would be most likely true at tourist dominated airports.

[20] Economic impact study of Hamburg Airport, 1997.

[21] Other multipliers that could be used are expenditure and income multipliers.

[22] Models were estimated using ordinary least squares with corrections for serial correlation using the arima method.

4. Country Data Analysis

Introduction

A number of different OD markets were analyzed as part of this study. The countries were determined during the initial steering committee meeting in conjunction with representatives of the Wirtschaftsbehörde Hamburg, the Hamburg Airport, the Bundesverkehrsministerium (BMV), the Arbeitsgemeinschaft Deutscher Verkehrsflughäfen (ADV), and representatives of a number of Bundesländer.[1] Criteria for the selection was to include countries that have significant market size for Hamburg Airport, as well as represent varying levels of restrictiveness in their current bilaterals. The intend behind the later criteria was to be able to apply the results to other countries with bilaterals of similar nature. However, the results of the study show that there is little to no impact on the results based on the current level of restrictiveness of the bilaterals. This result is in line with other studies (Dresner & Windle 1992) that showed that there is little positive effect from partial liberalization. As long as some market restrictions remain and adjacent markets are liberalized, traffic diversion will take place and denying significant positive effects from partial liberalization. The main factor of the impact is the current level of supply, i.e., frequency and aircraft gauge, as well as the size of the travel market between Germany and the country in question.

Countries Selected for Analyses

The following countries were selected.

Table 4-1: Countries Chosen and Level of Bilateral ASA Restrictiveness

Country	Bilateral level of restrictiveness
Canada	Low
China	Moderate
Japan	High
UAE	Low
Ghana	Moderate
Russia	High
Thailand	Low
Chile	Moderate
Ukraine	High

Details of the bilateral agreement between Germany and the respective country are listed in Table 4-2.

Table 4-2: Detailed Bilateral ASA Review

Countries	Designation	Tariff	Capacity Flgts/Wk	5th Freedom Rights
Canada	Multiple	Double Disappr		Yes
Chile	Multiple	Double Approval	6/98 – 7 11/99 - 9	Limited Routes
Japan	Multiple	Double Approval	Detailed	Yes, with limitations
Thailand	Triple MOU Multiple	Country of Origin	20 plus 10 w/o points beyond	Yes, based on LVA
Ghana	Multiple	Double Approval	2	No 5th Freedom
Russia		Country of Origin	Detailed	Limited
UAE	Multiple	Country of Origin		Yes
China	4, one of which has to be Cargo	Double Approval	19999 – 14/7 2000 – 16/7 2001 – 18/7	Limited
Ukraine		Country of Origin	Detailed	Individual Approval
USA	OPEN SKY			

Data Set for Hamburg Open Sky Project

General Comments:

- The base case covers the status quo as of 1997.
- The passenger data was assembled using both the material provided by the Airport as well as schedule information taken from the OAG database. The numbers were rounded and somewhat approximated in addressing the breakdown between carriers serving the same routes. Indirect flights provided by other European carriers or carriers from other third countries were covered by creating a Proxy carrier. This was the only way to handle this traffic in the calculations. Carriers like BA, KLM, etc fill less than five percent of their available seats on flights to the covered countries with transfer passengers from Germany. Including the individual carrier with such low utilization rate results in unreasonable fares. The appropriate way to address this would have been to expand the model to cover all of Europe; however, the level of effort required

would have been well outside of the scope of this analysis. The results for the Proxy carrier in the alternate case can be reallocated to the underlying carriers based on their base case marketshare. I.e., if BA makes up 43% (32,500/75,000) of the Proxy for Canada, its alternate case number of passengers was assumed to be 30,800 (0.43*71,114). The frequency and aircraft gauge for the Proxy carrier was chosen to yield reasonable utilization rates on the given routes.

- The fare data was an approximation based on information derived from carrier information and travel websites such as Expedia.com and Travelocity.com. Further, an assumed leisure/business traveler split was used based largely on the results of Hamburg Airport's 1998 passenger.
- In all cases American Airlines was used as the new entrant to simulate competition by a new carrier with a superior productivity and cost structure.
- The analysis for Thailand, Chile, and Ukraine yielded some unique results. Chile is particularly problematic and should be viewed as an exception. There were no non-stop flights between Chile and Germany in 1997. The flights stopped in either Argentina or Brazil many of the passengers disembarked in those countries. This resulted in utilization rates for Chile of approximately 25%. Fares change drastically in the alternate case to reach reasonable utilization rates.

Comments for individual Countries:

Canada:This case contains Canada 3000 as an existing low fare carrier, providing no business class. An entering scheduled service carrier such as American would come in at a higher average fare structure due the three classes of service. The model results indicate that Canada 3000 would be able to raise fares. This result is misleading. If only leisure fares and capacities would be considered the result can be expected to be different.

Japan:It should be noted that both LH and JAL provide non stop service from Frankfurt to Tokyo and Osaka as well as non stop service from Munich to Osaka. Aircraft gauge, fare, and/or frequency are different on the routes. Hence, both carriers are listed with separate inputs in the model.

UAE:For the Emirates a similar situation as with Canada exists. This is due to the presence of LTU, a German low cost carrier that essentially provides scheduled charter service. In order to arrive at a reasonable result for the alternate case fare for LTU, the carrier preference for this carrier had to relatively low. One can interpret this as a average preference with a business traveler preference for this carrier that approaches zero due to the booking limitations. The low preference for LTU in turn resulted in a higher alternate case fare for LH which should be viewed as a modeling exeption.

Ghana:The only relevant connecting passengers fly via Amsterdam. Hence KLM was used as the only other carrier and there was no need to use the proxy carrier.

Russia:No aircraft in block hour cost was available for Aeroflot's Tupolev aircraft. Aircraft data for Boeing 727 was used to approximate the values for the Tupolev.

Data Sources

In order to populate ALM and the Airport Choice models data from a number of different sources was utilized, such the German aviation database,[2] as well as data from both ICAO and OAG sources.

---

[1] The authors are thanking Dr. Bartowsky and Dr. Mürl of the BMV as well Mr. Kuhne of the ADV for their participating in the Steering Committee.

[2] The authors like to express special thanks to Mr. Ringen of Hamburg Airport for his support in the data collection efforts.

5. Analytical Results

The analysis results from each of the three models, the Air Liberalization Model, the Airport Choice and Demand Distribution Model, and Economic Impact Model are presented in this section. The first and second models estimate the impacts on air travel demand by airport from a policy change. The third model estimates the impacts on airports, the regional economy, and tourism from a change in air travel demand. Results from each model are presented in turn.

Country Level Aggregate Results

To address the question whether Germany will realize gains from liberalization, an analytical model was developed which simulated the impacts on consumers, producers, and the aviation system resulting from a change in bilaterals. A number of different OD markets, determined during the initial steering committee meeting in conjunction with representatives of the Wirtschaftsbehörde Hamburg, the Flughafen Hamburg, the Bundesverkehrsministerium, and the Arbeitsgemeinschaft Deutscher Flughäfen (ADV), were analyzed as part of this study. The countries selected are Canada, Chile (including Honk Kong), China, Ghana, Japan, Russia, Thailand, UAE, and Ukraine, since the ASAs between Germany and these countries represent a cross-section relatively liberal to restrictive agreements. This selection was made to allow for extrapolation of the results to other countries, since it was demonstrated that the results are not depended on the level of restrictivness of the agreements. The year 1997 was chosen as the base year, as it was the most recent year with a complete dataset at the time of the study.

The Air Liberalization Model reports results in two principal ways. First, the model estimates the new market equilibrium based on the assumed policy changes. This new equilibrium is described in terms of total traffic carried, average fares, consumer and produce surplus (welfare impacts). The consumer benefits are measured by using the standard consumer surplus methodology while producer benefits are simply the impact on segment profits. The results of the analysis are presented in Table 5-1.

Table 5-1: Air Liberalization Model Aggregate Results for Germany

	Canada	Chile	China	Ghana	Japan	Russia	Thailand	UAE	Ukraine
Current Annual Passengers (000)	512	45	382	23	430	600	390	170	80
New Annual Passengers (000)	574	116	423	36	496	678	438	193	109
Percentage Change	**12%**	**157%**	**11%**	**55%**	**15%**	**13%**	**12%**	**14%**	**36%**
Current Average Fare	$964	$1,500	$2,500	$1,000	$2,058	$763	$1,910	$912	$1,000
New Average Fare	$922	$769	$2,350	$827	$1,927	$739	$1,819	$888	$883
Percentage Change	**-4%**	**-49%**	**-6%**	**-17%**	**-6%**	**-3%**	**-5%**	**-3%**	**-12%**
Current Travel Expenditures ($M)	$344	$68	$980	$23	$885	$458	$745	$155	$80
New Travel Expenditures ($M)	$374	$89	$1,004	$30	$956	$502	$798	$172	$96
Percentage Change	**9%**	**32%**	**2%**	**28%**	**8%**	**10%**	**7%**	**11%**	**21%**
Current Consumer Surplus ($M)	$289	$17	$1,029	$13	$666	$362	$727	$134	$63
New Consumer Surplus ($M)	$337	$62	$1,183	$24	$807	$427	$852	$159	$95
Percentage Change	**17%**	**258%**	**15%**	**81%**	**21%**	**18%**	**17%**	**19%**	**52%**
Current Producer Surplus ($M)	$219	$16	$837	$16	$740	$361	$619	$118	$67
New Producer Surplus ($M)	$250	$38	$886	$21	$793	$404	$667	$136	$81
Percentage Change	**14%**	**137%**	**6%**	**32%**	**7%**	**12%**	**8%**	**15%**	**21%**

The total effects for all nine countries combined are as follows:

- The average fare declines by 12 percent,
- The annual travel expenditures increase by $283 million or 8 percent,
- The annual consumer surplus increases by $646 million or 20 percent, and
- The annual producer surplus increases by $283 million or 9 percent.

It has to be noted that these figures are based on an ex post analysis and do not represent a forecast, i.e., the results indicate what would have been the case in 1997 if the ASAs between Germany and the nine countries would have been liberalized at that point in time. One can expect that the results would increase over time based on the general trend of traffic growth in the aviation industry. Hence, if the analysis were to be conducted based on current figures the above figures would be even more favorable.

Simulating the 'Open Sky' Scenario

To determine the impacts of an 'Open Sky' policy for all German airports, we started with an ex post analysis of 1997 air transport in Germany. In a second step, we assumed a scenario in which 'Open Sky' is established in the year 1997 for selected markets outside the European Union. At the same time, the ceteris paribus conditions is assumed to hold, i. e. no changes were assumed for air transport concerning the countries neighboring Germany, neither in their air network existing in 1997 (routes, frequencies, prices), nor in the situation of their airports (capacities, handling fees, etc.). In addition, 'Open Sky' liberalization was applied only for air transport between the selected markets (Table 5-3) and Germany. Routes between Germany and other areas were kept constant. Effects caused by a change in mode choice between air and ground transport modes where not considered. For Russia and the Ukraine ground transport to/from Germany is marginal; for the other markets examined, it does not exist at all. The overall procedure of our work task is depicted in Figure 5.1 illustrating the different working steps, databases and models used.

Figure 5.1: Procedure

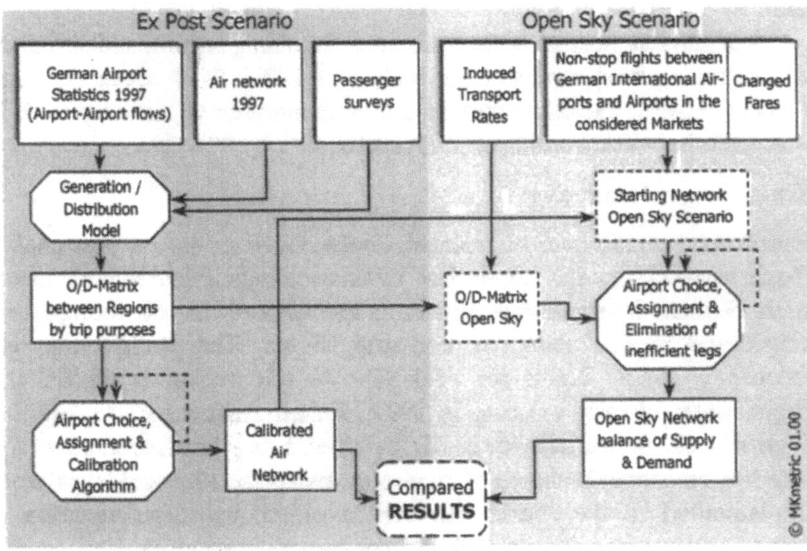

Ex post analysis

To establish a base case of 1997 an ex post-analysis of air transport in Germany was undertaken. This included creating a stylized network and representing scheduled and charter flights to/from all airports (international and regional) in the European Union. This network was enriched by all flights to/from European hub airports, to represent all possible routings inside Europe and from Europe to intercontinental destinations. Attached was the existing network to/from European international and regional airports. In total, the digital network represents air transport between more than 400 airports.

By using airport choice routines, passenger flows from the German air transport statistics for 1997 were transformed into an airflow matrix from regions in Germany and its neighboring countries to regions in the markets examined for the 'Open Sky' simulation. Information generated from numerous passenger surveys on several German airports were used, for splitting the passenger flows into business and non-business trips.

To assign these regionalised passenger flows to the air network, it was supplemented by links representing ground transport between the regions and the airports, including airport access/egress by private car as well as by public transport. In addition, the single airports were augmented by connecting links, which allow us to simulate connecting-times between different flight routes, when a plane change is required to reach a destination. In the end, the size of the air network which originally consisted of about 10 tsd. links was increased to more than 100 tsd. links in total.

Assignment results were calibrated by using airport and route choice algorithms to best represent the reality of 1997. With focus on Hamburg Airport (HAM) the difference in the total number of passengers at HAM was 1.6% between simulation and statistics.

Simulation of 'Open Sky'

Based on the reference air transport network from the ex post analysis, a 'basic network' for the 'Open Sky' simulation was implemented connecting each German international airport to the airports in the foreign markets considered in this study by non-stop flights. The inaugurating default frequency was 99 flights per week. The default frequency applied also for flight routes already existing in 1997, if their frequency was less than 99 flights/week. As the number of flights offered to a destination plays a major role in a consumer's choice of an airport, using the identical level of service implemented in the 'basic network' avoided any discrimination of an airport and ensured the reflection of consumer preferences.

Table 5-2: International Airports in Germany

Airport	TLC*	Airport	TLC*
BERLIN-SCHONEFELD	SXF	HAMBURG	HAM
BERLIN-TEGEL	TXL	HANOVER	HAJ
BERLIN-TEMPELHOF**	THF	LEIPZIG	LEJ
BREMEN	BRE	MUNSTER/OSNABRUCK	FMO
COLOGNE/BONN	CGN	MUNICH	MUC
DRESDEN	DRS	NUREMBERG	NUE
DUSSELDORF	DUS	PADERBORN	PAD
ERFURT	ERF	SAARBRUCKEN	SCN
FRANKFURT	FRA	STUTTGART	STR

* = Three-Letter-Code

** = THF was not equipped with new routes in the basic network, due to its capacity constraints.

The international airports of Germany were connected with the airports, representing the markets considered in this study, shown Table 5-3.

Table 5-3: Considered Markets and their Representative Airports

Country, considered in 'Open Sky' Scenario	Airports, representing the Country
Canada	Calgary, Edmonton, Halifax, Toronto, Vancouver
Chile	Santiago de Chile
China	Peking, Shanghai
Ghana	Accra
Hong Kong	Hong Kong
Japan	Nagoya, Osaka, Tokyo
Russia	Moscow, Novosibirsk, St. Petersburg, Samara
Thailand	Bangkok
United Arabic Emirates	Abu Dhabi, Dubai
Ukraine	Kiev

Connecting the 17 international airports in Germany with the 21 representatives of the markets under consideration, means 357 new/upgraded connections in the basic network compared to the reference network of the year 1997.

For the 'Open Sky' simulation in 1997 passenger airflows were augmented by destination specific shifts, representing induced passenger flows, which are generated by changing relative prices between transport and other goods. Transport prices are expected to fall due to increased competition on the considered routes and the additional capacity. Table 5-4 shows the increase in passenger flows for each market considered.

Table 5-4: Induced Transport Rates through 'Open Sky' in 1997 by Country

Country	Induced Demand Elasticity	Percent Change in Fare	Quantity, the Induced Demand
Canada	0.048	-4.4%	+0.211%
Chile	0.033	-48.7%	+1.607%
China	0.094	-6.0%	+0.564%
Japan	0.096	-6.4%	+0.614%
Russia	0.045	-3.0%	+0.135%
Ghana	0.203	-17.3%	+3.512%
Thailand	0.055	-4.8%	+0.264%
UAE	0.085	-2.6%	+0.221%
Ukraine	0.003	-11.7%	+0.035%

Source: Prof. Dr. Gillen.

The passenger flows from the ex post analysis were supplemented by the market-specific factors for the induced demand and assigned to the basic network. According to the result of assigning these new passenger, airflows to the 'Open Sky' network, routes inaugurated for the 'Open Sky' scenario, were adjusted in their level of service (frequency) due to the computed demand on the specific routes. In some cases, when the load of a single route was to low to offer that route economically with a minimum frequency of one flight per week, the route was omitted.

The adjustment of frequencies was carried out using an iterative process, until the number of seats offered on each route and the corresponding trip purpose specific passenger demand came into balance. Finally, there were 83 routes left that could sustain non-stop service of at least once per week. Considering charter flights to holiday destinations, there may exist some routes, which could be served economically during summer time every second week, but these were not considered in this study. [1]

Interpretation Framework of the 'Open Sky' Results

Before presenting the results, it is useful to discuss the alternative hypotheses that are being considered. This is clearly useful in interpreting the results.

First, the effects described in the following two sections are based on a comparison of the status quo situation in 1997 and an assumed ex post 'Open Sky' scenario for Germany in 1997. So the scenario analyses a 'what if' question concerning the potential demand under ceteris paribus conditions (incl. capacity restrictions, e. g. at Frankfurt Airport) in 1997. For example, what demand would have existed at Hamburg Airport, if a number of markets had been liberalized. To answer this question, we show the potential demand in these markets for Hamburg Airport.

The 'Open Sky' scenario itself (only) considers 10 markets that are currently regulated in different ways and would be fully liberalized as a hypothesis of the scenario. Other, potential non-liberalized markets, interesting for Hamburg, like Central Europe (due to the expected EC membership of some countries the liberalization will take place automatically) as well as hubbing points for specific markets could not be considered in this study. Similarly, we could not consider spillover effects that are most likely to occur when Germany obtains first mover advantages (see task of this project). We provide some insights as to the magnitude of such effects since we restricted ourselves to the 10 markets and the main effects caused by the given scenario for Germany and the neighboring regions abroad.

It should be noted that our results are computed for the year 1997 and density effects generated by passenger volume, based on the higher productivity of the airports, can only be partially reflected (e. g. price reduction). The airlines and consumers will capture most of the gains, with a time lag, in some quantitative and/or qualitative way (i. e. increase in the level of service, comfort or reduced parking, ground handling & retail fees – in general increased airport attractivity). In addition, low charges and fees attract, in mid and long term, regional and low cost carriers serving markets other than the focus of this study. On the other hand, one also has to consider the time it will take until other countries will follow such massive liberalization activities. [2]

We faced an even more complex problem in the 'Open Sky' scenario when considering aircraft movements since there were a large number of strategic responses. We therefore imposed two possible supply strategies. The first is highly restrictive and forces airlines to reduce frequencies and to use large aircraft to be able to inaugurate new services. This strategy is based on the hypothesis that competition is so intense that airlines have to run their services at minimal profit to avoid the possibility that a competitor enters the market. As a consequence, aircraft movements will decrease significantly.

The airport's airside revenue from landing and passenger fees will depend on the mixture of aircraft assumed (indeed, imposed) by such a restrictive hypothesis (ceteris paribus the aircraft distribution given by the Hamburg Airport statistics). On the other hand this strategy leads to an overestimate of the beneficial environmental effects. As the Hamburg Airport is in the privatization process, obviously the first scenario is interesting for investors from a financial perspective, but this scenario does not reflect what we observe in the market.

We therefore introduced a second aircraft movement scenario that considers alternative airline strategies. When observing the air market one simply notes that new intercontinental routes are not inaugurated with the largest equipment, instead airlines prefer to operate with smaller long haul aircraft operating at a higher frequency to build the market.[3]

Finally, one must recognize that airlines cannot be forced to offer a new service even if the demand exists. Therefore, claims have been made that some 'Open Sky' impacts may be thwarted by alliance partnerships. While this is true, one also must recognize there is a strong competitive environment that forces airlines to respond to a market competition. At the moment the structure of airline alliances and the given market framework still allows a concentration process towards the hubs for intercontinental routes (e. g. in Germany FRA and MUC). However, as the development/growth rate of the smaller airports (e. g. Paderborn,

Dortmund, Munster-Osnabrück, Baden Airport) accelerates, it acts as a countervailing force to the concentration of activity at international hubs. If we consider that with liberalization and supporting regulation, competition among airports as well as strong competition between airline alliances will force airlines to decentralize intercontinental services.

As the ability of an airport to market their capabilities are still limited, one can only support the process stated above, by assigning more freedoms to the airports to increase their flexibility to trade their resources on the basis of market prices. This allows airports to be more proactive in the development of air services and it will strengthen the overall competitive environment. In general, one should keep in mind that the policy towards liberalization, deregulation and privatization serves the economic welfare of Germany overall, not the single airports and airlines.

Having considered the most important hypothesis of this study, we now move to the presentation of the results. In the context of this study, we applied the 'system approach' (Mandel 1999) that allows to analyze the 'Open Sky' scenario effects in detail for each airport in the network. Here, we depict the results for Hamburg Airport in detail and show the effects on the passenger volume for Germany.[4]

Results for Hamburg Airport

In this section we illustrate and describe the effects of 'Open Sky' on Hamburg Airport. The numbers shown for the 'Open Sky' scenario are calculated including induced traffic flows, caused by decreasing tariffs for flights to/from the considered markets.

The values reported are based on the total effect, i. e. the sum of the embarking and disembarking passengers, as well as arriving and departing and transfer passengers at an airport. Accordingly, the numbers given in route-specific analysis are the total effects for both directions; passenger volumes on routes include OD as well as transfer passengers.

The analysis of results considers the development on each route to the considered markets, for both, the number of passengers and the change in the number of aircraft movements. Later, we analyze the effects for Hamburg's catchment area.

Passenger Demand

Assuming 'Open Sky' existed in Germany in 1997, Hamburg would have attracted about 149 tsd. additional passengers.[5] From these 149 tsd. passengers 17 tsd. are hubbing at Hamburg, so the route performance (of IATA-passengers) is 166 tsd. Additional total passengers.[6]

Analyzing new passengers by their trip purpose (Figure 5.2), 37% of the new passengers travel for business reasons, while 63% belong to the holiday/vacation/other private trips travel purpose. The highest growth in passenger numbers takes places for Thailand and Hong Kong, each with more than 70 tsd. passengers. This is because, there were no non-stop flights to those destinations in 1997. Some losses occur on the Canadian routes, due to new non-stop flights offered by other German airports in the 'Open Sky' scenario. Due to the extensive level of service on these flights (just one per week from May to October) the service is not attractive for business travelers. So the total demand on this route consists by more than 90% of leisure trips. Passenger flows to other markets remain almost constant. For these, the numbers are unchanged in the flights offered. Some minor changes are the result of demand reactions of passengers, choosing non-stop flights, instead of hubbing at Hamburg Airport.

Not all of the direct markets we considered are sustainable even under an Open Sky regime. In Ghana and Chile, for example, total demand to/from Hamburg in 1997 was just 4.132 passengers for Ghana, resp. 5.554 passengers for Chile.

Countries having sufficient passenger volume to inaugurate a route to Hamburg, may also be limited in terms of the number of airports served. For example, although Japan is a big enough market to be connected with Hamburg directly, this would only apply for the airports of Tokyo and Osaka, but not for Nagoya. Here one should note that not only new services are inaugurated, existing ones will also be reduced. Therefore, slots will still be used like before but just for another route.

Table 5-5: Changes through 'Open Sky' in 1997 at Hamburg Airport

Hamburg Airport to & from	Additional Passengers in Total [tsd.]	Additional Route Passengers [tsd.]	Transfer Passengers in HAM [tsd.]
Canada		-4.2	0.0
Chile		0.0	0.0
China		50.8	6.8
Ghana		0.0	0.0
Hong Kong		70.5	4.1
Japan		86.0	6.3
Russia		15.9	-0.3
Thailand		72.2	2.4
UAE		0.2	0.0
Ukraine		17.5	0.3
Germany		-5.6	-9.2
EU		-137.8	7.0
Other		0.5	0.0
Grand Total	*+148,5*	*+166.0*	*+17.4*

One outcome of the analysis showed a decrease in passenger demand for the inner European routes: This is the result of people, who formerly reached their final (intercontinental) destination by feeder flights from Hamburg to an European hub like London, Amsterdam, Vienna, etc. Although the majority of passengers prefer non-stop flights offered at Hamburg, there remain passengers (esp. in business travel) who still prefer feeder flights to a hub, due to the higher frequency offered by these via-flights (e. g. daily, instead of a non-stop flight once or twice per week). Even so, no route (destination) is omitted in the 'Open Sky' scenario due to the passengers switching to the new non-stop flights offered to the markets considered in this study. The passengers with a final destination located in the areas of such European hubs and high share of business travelers on these routes ensure the existence of such flights and routes with a high level of service.

The same holds true for domestic flights from Hamburg to Frankfurt. Although numbers shown for domestic markets decrease slightly, the losses on the Frankfurt route are compensated for, by passengers to/from other German airports, who now change at Hamburg Airport.

When adding the differences caused by the 'Open Sky' scenario shown in Table 5-5 to the number of passengers in the considered markets as they existed in, we obtain the total numbers for Hamburg Airport and the change of demand percent.

Table 5-6: Total Passenger Numbers for Hamburg Airport, Ex Post and 'Open Sky' in 1997 by Route Destinations

Hamburg Airport	Route Passengers 1997 (official statistics) [tsd.]	Route Passengers 1997 'Open Sky' [tsd.]	% Change in Number of Passengers
Canada	21.6	17.4	-19.4%
Chile	0	0	0%
China	0	50.8	n. a.
Ghana	0	0	0%
Hong Kong	0	70.5	n. a.
Japan	0	86.0	n. a.
Russia	90.5	106.4	+17.6%
Thailand	0	72.2	n. a.
UAE	7.6	7.8	+2.4%
Ukraine	0	17.5	n. a.
Germany	3575.3	3569.6	-0.2%
EU	3505.6	3367.8	-3.9%
Other	1311.6	1312.1	+0.0%
Grand Total	*8512.1*	*8678.1*	*+1.9%*

Another perspective in analyzing the changes in passenger demand is to consider the change in the catchment area of Hamburg Airport. Figure 5.2 shows the differences on county level.

Hamburg Airport gains most additional passengers in the 'Open Sky' scenario from the area of the Hanseatic City of Hamburg itself (+64 tsd.). Other areas where Hamburg has a remarkable growth in the number of passengers are the counties of Ostholstein (+6 tsd.), Hanover (+8 tsd.) and Bremen (+11 tsd.). Although the last two counties have their own airport (BRE and HAJ), a remarkable share of passengers from these areas prefer to use newly inaugurated non-stop flights from Hamburg Airport, instead of reaching their final destination by using a connecting flight from HAJ or BRE to a hub like Frankfurt, Amsterdam or London.

Figure 5.2: Changes by 'Open Sky' in the Catchment Area of Hamburg Airport

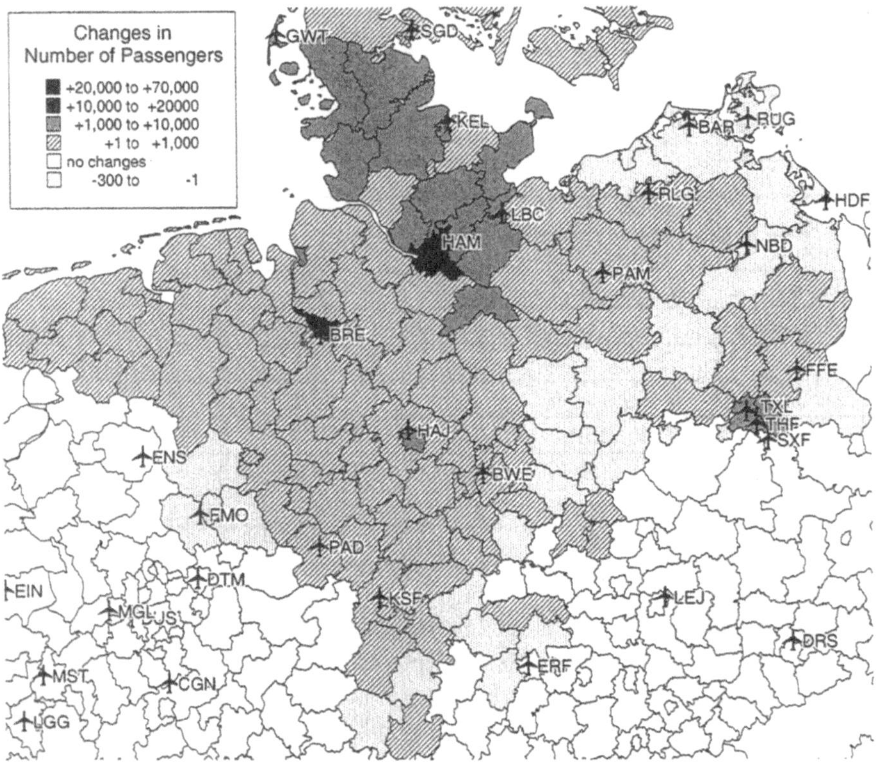

In addition, Hamburg gains some new passengers from all counties in the Federal States of Schleswig-Holstein and Niedersachsen, and new demand also arises from parts of Hessen, Brandenburg, Berlin and parts of Mecklenburg-Vorpommern. Acquisition of new passengers for Hamburg Airport takes place even in the neighboring countries of Denmark and the Netherlands.

In general, Hamburg Airport gains passengers for those destinations for which there are new inaugurated flights, while it loses some passengers on routes that already existed at Hamburg, but now are also offered at other airports like in Berlin (TXL, SXF), Munster-Osnabrück (FMO) or Erfurt (ERF). The net result of these offsetting effects can be positive or negative, depending on a number of factors. They include the local demand in the specific county, the number of additional markets served from Hamburg and the change in supply at competitive airports. These are the reasons why Hamburg Airport wins some passengers in total, e. g. in the area of Berlin, while it will lose some passengers, e. g. in several counties located between Berlin and Hamburg.

Some small decrease (less than 300 passengers each) in Hamburg's sphere of influence appear for some counties situated around the airports of Munster-Osnabrück, Berlin and Erfurt, as these airports – beside Hamburg – are also winners of an 'Open Sky' scenario. The same is true for several counties in Mecklenburg-Vorpommern, as the Berlin airports are chosen first in the airport choice from these regions, when travelling to destinations regarded in the 'Open Sky' scenario. But, as the population density of those areas is quite low, these effects are not very strong.[7]

Aircraft movements To illustrate how 'Open Sky' would have affected the number of aircraft movements in 1997, we decided to show the effects for two different scenarios, as described in the section above. Airport strategy I is used for the computation of the demand potential shown previously. In a/c strategy II we hold demand constant However, we know that consumers are elastic with respect to service levels so, higher frequencies will have a positive effect on the demand and vice versa.

In the simulation of aircraft movements, we used five different classes of aircraft types. An important consideration in simulating aircraft movements is to decide which aircraft types come into service on which route. We analyzed which of the defined classes of aircraft are used to serve the routes between Germany and the distinct markets considered and found there is no single type of aircraft that is used on the routes to each market. For flights inside the European Union a wide range occurs in the number of seats an aircraft is equipped with. The class of aircraft used doesn't only vary with the flight distance. Other factors, like the total number of passengers, the trip purpose (business, vacation) of the majority of travelers on a route, the number of competitors serving a route, etc. has a significant impact on the number of flights offered. Ultimately the type of aircraft selected is one that permits a profit maximizing level of service given the level of passenger demand and their response to fare and service level changes. Table 5-7 shows the result of this analysis that is in addition the base to calibrate our aircraft choice model.

Table 5-7: Class of Aircraft used on Routes to the Considered Markets

Destination	Class I	Class II	Class III	Class IV	Class V
Canada				x	x
China				x	x
EU	x	x	x	x	
Hong Kong				x	x
Japan				x	x
Russia		x	x	x	
Thailand				x	x
UAE			x	x	x
Ukraine		x	x		
Germany	x	x	x	x	
Other	x	x	x	x	x

To assure that these aircraft types are representative of what is offered at Hamburg Airport, we defined them with respect to the existing mix of aircraft in 1997, as it is indicated in Table 5-7.

In the first scenario, we assumed a strategy that is characterized by strong competition with minimal yields which forces the airlines to adjust the number of aircraft movements strictly in line with the changes in the number of passengers on each route, as the load factors have to be kept high. This applies for the flights on the new routes as well as on those feeder flights with decreasing number of passengers. In addition, the airlines do not have complete flexibility in varying the size of aircraft on the feeder flights affected, as the numerous OD-business passengers prefer particular flights, with a schedule best fitting their travelling plans (e. g. outbound in the early morning, inbound in the afternoon).

Although the total number of passengers at Hamburg Airport rises by 'Open Sky', the total number of aircraft movements diminishes in this (first) scenario. The decrease in aircraft movements is caused by the different mix of aircraft types used on routes to the specific markets. Given the hypothesis above, on long distance routes larger equipment is used. On short-haul flights, especially for feeder flights from Hamburg to several hubs, carriers adjust their services. Thus, the change in the number of aircraft movements directly reflects the different levels of demand on long haul and short-haul flights to and from Hamburg Airport.

Table 5-8: Aircraft Classes and their Hamburg Specific Representatives

Class	Representatives (order by HAM 97)		Average Seats per a/c	Weighted Average Seats per a/c, HAM 97
V	DC10	McD.-Douglas DC 10	370	372.0
	B747	Boeing B 747	390	
	A330	Airbus A 330	390	
	MD11	McD.-Douglas MD 11	408	
IV	A300	Airbus A 300	273	273.3
	IL86	Ilyushin IL 86	316	
	A340	Airbus A 340	290	
	L101	Lockheed 1011 Tristar	280	
III	B757	Boeing B 757	203	201.5
	A321	Airbus A 321	169	
	A310	Airbus A 310	247	
	MD83	McD.-Douglas MD 83	166	
	B767	Boeing B 767	238	
	B727	Boeing B 727	172	
II	B737	Boeing B 737 200-500	104 - 155	125.2
	A320	Airbus A 320	147	
	MD87	McD.-Douglas MD 87	118	
	DC9	McD.-Douglas DC 9	116	
	FK10	Fokker 100	102	
	RJ10	Avro RJ 100	97	
	TU54	Tupolev TU 154	140	
	A319	Airbus A 319	130	
	MD82	McD.-Douglas MD 82	147	
I	DH8	DHC Dash 8 100 + 300	36/50	50.6
	CRJ	Canadair Regional Jet	50	
	RJ85	Avro RJ 85	80	
	BA46	BAe 146	83	
	FK50	Fokker 50	50	
	AT42	ATR 42	50	
	E120	Embraer Brasilia EMB 120	30	
	SB20	Saab 2000	50	
	AT72	ATR 72	64	

We point out that in reality the number of aircraft movements can be higher than indicated in the restrictive first scenario, as smaller aircraft types could be used by the airlines on the new routes. One reason is that if demand decreases, airlines still want to ensure high frequencies on the inner European or domestic routes to hubs for the remaining OD-business passengers. To avoid losing business class passengers on short-haul routes to competing airlines and ground modes (high-speed trains) the airlines might keep frequencies high on such routes and switch equipment (e. g. from Boeing 737 to Canadair Jet) according to the decreasing number of passengers, compliant with their overall yield policy. Another strategic issue of airlines concerns the general policy regarding grandfather rights on slots.

For these reasons, we assumed in the second scenario[8], a strategy that airlines operate a mix of aircraft, which allows them to offer higher frequencies on the inaugurated routes and to maintain their service levels on routes with decreasing passengers. The result is that the overall number of aircraft movements diminishes only slightly. New intercontinental routes, in general, are served by aircraft of class IV (273 seats in average) in this scenario, while using class V aircraft (372 seats in average) is the exception.

Table 5-9: Total Numbers of Aircraft Movements for Hamburg Airport

	Aircraft Movements 1997 (official statistics)	Aircraft Movements Strategy I	Aircraft Movements Strategy II	Differences to Statistics 1997 Strategy I	Differences to Statistics 1997 Strategy II
Canada	68	50	50	-18	-18
Chile	0	0	0	0	0
China	0	259	191	259	191
Ghana	0	0	0	0	0
Hong Kong	0	263	358	263	358
Japan	0	352	430	352	430
Russia	1,490	1,397	1,465	-93	-25
Thailand	0	266	361	266	361
UAE	52	52	52	0	0
Ukraine	0	127	204	127	204
Germany	56,375	56,454	56,454	79	79
EU	50,352	47,648	48,561	-2,704	-1,791
Other	18,708	18,708	18,708	0	0
Grand Total	*127,045*	*125,575*	*126,833*	*-1,470*	*-212*

When comparing the results of the two strategies, we can see that the first strategy would cause a decrease of aircraft movements at Hamburg Airport by almost 1.500 for the year 1997, while the second strategy keeps the number of aircraft movements almost constant (-200 a/c movements/year).

Considering the weekly performance at the airport instead of movements per year, strategy 1 corresponds to a reduction of 14 departures per week, while strategy 2 results in only two fewer departures per week less. The figures below show the changes in aircraft movements by class of aircraft under the two different strategies.

The changes in aircraft movements shown in Figure 5.3 reflect passenger demand from feeder flights to the new inaugurated non-stop flights quite clearly, as the number of departures of Class I aircraft diminishes by about 20 per week, while Class V aircraft departures increase by 6 per week.

Figure 5.3: Changes by 'Open Sky' on Aircraft Movements Starts per Week (Strategy I)

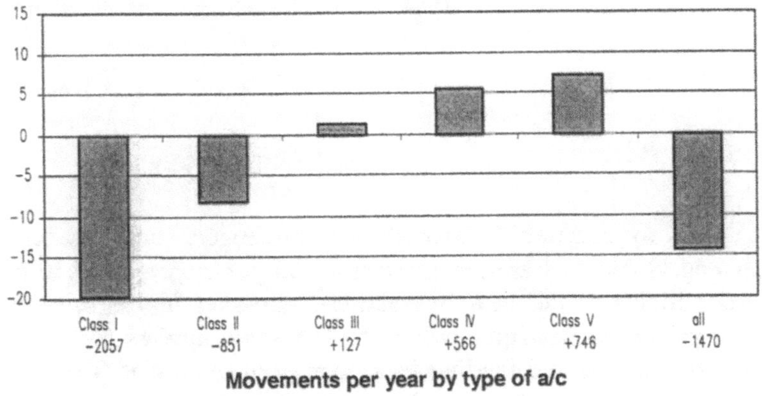

Figure 5.4 clearly shows what would happen if the airlines have full scope in switching between different types of aircraft to serve the specific routes: Class II aircraft (-14 departures/week) will be partly replaced by Class I equipment to minimize the decrease in flight frequencies. In addition, Class IV (+11 departures/week) instead of Class V aircraft (+2 starts/week) is the 'standard' type to serve the new inaugurated routes.

Both scenarios have in common that, although the number of feeder-flights will diminish, none of those routes will be dropped, as the number of passengers to London, Copenhagen, Paris, etc. will remain high enough to operate several flights to each destination per day.

As the absolute number of aircraft movements decreases (-1.5 tsd. in strategy I, -0.2 tsd. in strategy II) as well as there are changes in the aircraft mixture (for strategy I largest decrease in Class I and increase in class V, for strategy II largest decrease in Class II and increase in Class IV), environmental issues are also affected. The noise contours, pollution and fuel consumption at Hamburg airport will change. Under both strategies there are fewer aircraft movements, non-stop services replace hubbing and therefore a passenger travels fewer passenger-miles on a given OD pair. Consequently, environmental resources are used more efficient.

Figure 5.4: Changes by 'Open Sky' on Aircraft Movements Starts per Week (Strategy II)

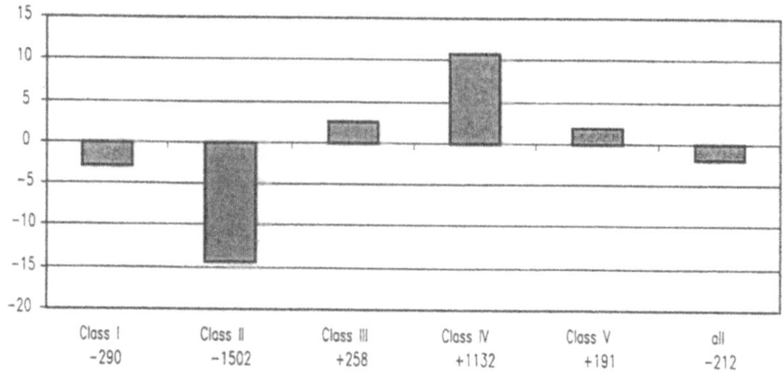

Due to additional international passengers and former domestic passengers that now appear as international passengers (shift from domestic feeder flights to the new international non-stop flights) airport revenues from passenger handling will rise. The same applies for revenues from aircraft handling and landing fees: more movements of wide-body aircraft will compensate for the reduction caused by reducing the numbers for small types of aircraft (given the fee and charge structure at Hamburg airport in 1997).[9]

If one assumes that the average mix of aircrafts within the considered classes will be the same in the 'Open Sky' scenario than it was in 1997 and one applies the same average handling costs and passenger charges, revenue from the aviation sector for Hamburg Airport would increase slightly (+6 mill. DM).[10] In addition, one would expect, that due to the transfer passengers and higher rate of intercontinental passengers retail revenues increase (see economic effects in this report).

Results for Germany in Total

In this section we show the total effects for Germany of an 'Open Sky' Policy for the considered markets concerning the passenger volume. Passengers numbers will be analyzed from the point of origin and destination and of the routing passengers chose with and without an 'Open Sky'.

The numbers are based on the total effect in Germany, i. e. the sum of the embarking and disembarking passengers, as well as the arriving and departing transfer passengers only at the German airports. It does not include changes that apply to airports abroad. Accordingly, the number given in route-specific analysis means the total effects of both directions together, for the routes from, to and between German airports, not the changes which apply to routes between airports abroad.

As a result of introducing 'Open Sky' in Germany the demand at German airports would rise by 277 tsd. passengers for the year 1997. This growth consists of travelers, who:

- Embark or disembark at a German Airport, instead of using a foreign airport, due to the better connections the new inaugurated flights offer.
- Change planes at a German Airport.
- Make additional trips to/from the considered markets (induced transport).

Table 5-10 shows these effects in detail.[11] While the new non-stop routes will generate about 190 tsd. additional passengers, the reduced fares on flights to the 'Open Sky' markets will also increase the demand by 85 tsd. trips. For transfer passengers, there will be a change: due to the new non-stop flights offered, which replace a number of transfer connections, the number of domestic-international[12] transfer passengers will decrease by more than 380 tsd. On the other hand, the new routes will attract more than 200 tsd. transfer passengers from neighboring regions of Germany (6th freedom traffic). These results, of course, are conditional with respect to competitive reactions of airports outside Germany and the consideration of airline alliance effects (ceteris paribus hypothesis).

Table 5-10: Change in Passenger Demand on German Airports

Changes by 'Open Sky' on German airports by	Air Network Effect	Induced Transport	Grand Total
Embarking/Disembarking Passengers	+369.2	+50.0	+419.2
Domestic-International Transfer Passengers	-383.2	+30.4	-352.7
International-International Transfer Passengers	+205.2	+4.9	+210.2
Total	+191.2	+85.4	+276.7

While the reasons for the changes in the number of transfer passengers are obvious (non-stop flights versus transfer flights, changing plane in Germany becomes more attractive for foreign passengers), Table 5-11 points out, where the new embarking/disembarking passengers come from. They sum up to 369 tsd. passengers (without induced traffic). 'Open Sky' mainly shifts passengers from Dutch airports, especially Amsterdam Schiphol (more than 200 tsd. passengers) to German airports, while hubs in other countries lose only a few travelers.

We know which route people take without an 'Open Sky' policy in Germany, and it is important to determine if these routing change, or other passengers' routing changes with Open Sky. Are these travelers to/from Germany, or if the German airports also gain travelers, whose origin or destination is in a neighboring country.

Table 5-11: Former Airports used by New Passengers in Germany

Country Airports	Percentage of use
Dutch	64.0%
Swiss	10.0%
Danish	9.0%
Belgian	5.0%
French	5.0%
Austrian	4.0%
Luxemburg	3.0%
other foreign	0.5%

Table 5-12 shows the differences in the number of passengers of the sphere of influence of all German airports in total. The result is separated by the origin/destination of the travelers by countries.

Almost 50% of all passengers who chose a German airport in the 'Open Sky' scenario start or end their trip in Germany. This shows how much the attractiveness of the German airports could rise. It is also evident that travelers from the Netherlands and Belgium will benefit from an 'Open Sky over Germany.'

Table 5-12: Origin of New Embarking/Disembarking Passengers in Germany

Origin	Percent
Germany	47%
Netherlands	31%
Belgium	16%
France	3%
Luxemburg	1%
Denmark	1%
Other	3%

Finally, we point out the developments on the single routes, when analyzing the passenger shifts. Table 5-12 numbers for passengers are separated by trip purpose. In addition the changes for aircraft movements are given.

'Routes' are non-stop flights offered between Hamburg Airport and the airports in the considered markets. The number of passengers on each route (e. g. Hamburg – Hong Kong, non-stop) consists of travelers to that final destination (Hong Kong) as well as transit passengers with a different final destination (e. g. Hamburg – Hong Kong – Sydney) – the same holds for Thailand with Bangkok as transfer point for the Asian/pacific market.

Table 5-13: Change in Demand for Germany in Total by Routes

Germany	All Route Passengers [tsd.]	Germany	All Route Passengers [tsd.]
Canada	+39,4	Thailand	+187,9
Chile	+125,0	UAE	+21,5
China	+127,3	Ukraine	+161,6
Ghana	+31,9	Germany	-337,8
Hong Kong	+271,9	EU	-259,9
Japan	+208,9	Other	-15,4
Russia	+52,2	*Grand Total*	*+614,5*

For Germany in total, corridors with the highest growth in an 'Open Sky' scenario are the routes between Germany, Hong Kong and Japan. And what has already been stated for Hamburg Airport concerning the increase of passengers numbers and the decrease of aircraft movements, will also apply in the 'Open Sky' scenario for Germany in total. Despite having additional passengers, there are fewer flight movements, due to the consumer's switch from domestic or inner-European feeder flights (with small aircraft) to the new non-stop flights especially when intercontinental destinations are served. And although the number of feeder flights will diminish, there will be no route between a German airport and an European hub, which will be omitted. So the overall accessibility of Germany increases.

Conclusions and Remarks

As the detailed results for Hamburg and total results for Germany show, the outcomes are quite different according to destinations, embarking versus transfer passengers and passenger demand versus aircraft movements. Not all German airports would profit from an 'Open Sky' policy in the same way. There will be winners and losers.

Big winners are airports, situated in highly populated areas, which today do not have an adequate supply of flights to destinations, where there is demand potential, such as Cologne, Stuttgart, Munich, Berlin and, Hamburg. For those airports the same effects according to revenues and environmental issues will apply as for Hamburg Airport.

Not all German airports can be called a winner of the 'Open Sky' scenario. In particular, Frankfurt Airport would have 1.2 million fewer passengers than in 1997, which was 40.3 million passengers. About 700 tsd. of those 1.2 million are transfer passengers (counted twice), who now prefer a non-stop flight from an airport closer to their origin. The others are embarking/disembarking passengers who take one of the new non-stop flights in the 'Open Sky' scenario from/to an airport located closer to their origin/destination, instead of undertaking a time-consuming trip to/from Frankfurt Airport by ground transport.

However, this loss of 1.2 million passengers under the 'Open Sky' policy is a loss of only three percent. In light of the existing capacity problems at Frankfurt Airport an 'Open Sky' policy may give the German hub the necessary freedom to develop its capacity under reduced time constraints.[13]

In addition, some smaller airports without sufficient demand to be served by non-stop flights resulting from the 'Open Sky' scenario, lose passengers on their connecting flights to Frankfurt and other European hubs. Bremen, Paderborn and Leipzig belong to this group. This does not mean that the total number of passengers on these airports will decrease in future. To the contrary, it is expected that passenger numbers continue to grow due to dynamic growth. What this analysis shows is simply that under the scenario considered their passenger numbers in 1997 would have been lower than what they were under the current regulatory situation.

The results cover all German passengers and passengers from neighboring countries for the markets considered in this study. Further relations, e. g. Russia-Canada where not taken into account as German airports are currently not used as transfer points for these routes. The inclusion of such relations in the analysis of 'Open Sky' scenarios will most probably increase the resulting passenger figures as 6th freedom traffic will be attracted .[14]

On the other hand, the figures shown will diminish, if an 'Open Sky' policy, as described in this study for Germany, is also established in neighboring countries, as about 50% of the additional passengers have their origin or destination in countries around Germany. So the decision to introduce 'Open Sky' in Germany should be made soon to seize available first mover advantages.

A key result of the 'Open Sky' policy is the increase of passenger numbers while aircraft movements decrease. Air transport therefore becomes more efficient. In addition, this means environmental effects, like noise and air pollution can be expected to be positively affected, despite some additional air travel induced by lower fares. Travels also benefit from having a greater proportion of direct flights (time savings).

Finally, new (intercontinental) destinations offered at different international airports in Germany will strengthen its position in the global economy as the accessibility of its regions and its polycentric organization of the economy will increase overall. In addition, redirected passenger flows (spill-over effects, 6th freedom traffic) and the induced passenger volume indicate consumer advantages which have economic impacts as well. Together, this will benefit the total economic welfare and strengthen Germany's, as well as, the regions competitive position in attracting investors, tourists, etc. in the global context.

Economic Impact Analysis

Chapter 4 provided the estimates of the models that will be used in measuring the impact of the change sin flights and passenger movements at Hamburg airport. There are a number of factors to consider in the analysis. First, is the distribution between business and leisure passengers. The tourism model makes this an important distinction as well as the non-aviation revenue forecasting model. Second, is the distribution between domestic (within Germany), European and International flights. Even if aggregate flights decrease that may not mean that the airport and local economy are worse off because the impacts of flights are not homogeneous. Third, we make a distinction between passenger types in the same categories as types of flights. Fourth, the gauge or size of aircraft can make a difference in both service as well as airport revenues and is taken into account in the analytical results.

Impacts on Airports

In the modeling we made a distinction between aviation and non-aviation revenue. Aviation revenue is airside revenue obtained from landing, parking and gate fees. They are directly tied to aircraft operations and aircraft size. Non-aviation revenue is revenue from all other sources but mostly from parking, concessions (food, shops, car rental etc.), leases and terminal rentals to airlines and associated aviation related activity.

Aviation revenue (AR) was affected primarily by flights and aircraft size. The model estimated distinguished between domestic, European and International flights as well as the size of aircraft used in the flights. By inserting values for each of the variables in the model we are able to measure the impact of changes resulting from liberalizing the bilateral between Germany and [select] other countries. In developing the impact measures we focus on the combination of changes (operations by type, passenger by type and gauge of aircraft) rather than on a particular variable of interest and hold other variables at their mean values. This is intended to illustrate the net effect of the sum of variables. It is certainly possible to simulate the outcome if a particular variable takes on a new value. In fact, this exercise may be useful for airport management in terms of pointing them in a certain direction for marketing strategies.

As a result of the liberalization, Open Sky, there is a marginal decrease in domestic and European flights, a five percent increase in International flights and a five percent and three percent increase in average seats per flight for European and international travel respectively. As a result airside revenue can expect to rise approximately five percent. The most significant contributors to this revenue increase are increases in the number of international flights and increases in the gauge of aircraft.

Non-aviation revenue can also be expected to rise. In section 3.6.3 we developed a model to assess changes in passengers activities and airport activities on non-aviation revenue. The model linked non-aviation revenue to numbers and types of passengers as well as their trip purpose - business and non-business travelers were distinguished. Using this model in the same way as the aviation revenue forecasting, the change in non-aviation revenue as a consequence of changes in bilaterals can be assessed.

The impact of Open Sky on route passengers (Official statistics) and the distribution between business and tourism across German, European and International enplaned passengers would result in a 9.3% increase in non-aviation revenue. The outcome is a result of an increase in EU passengers and a significant increase in international passengers. The other important contributing factor is the major shift to a greater proportion of tourist traffic to 63% tourist.

Airside revenue has fallen from a high of 80% of total airport revenue in 1989 to 72.5% in 1997. Using this proportion as a weight to calculate the weighted average increase in airport revenue, the liberalization of bilaterals would result in an increase in total revenue of 6.7%. One might regard this as a conservative estimate since it takes existing strategies as fixed. One might expect airports would alter their marketing and operations strategies in response to changes to the bilateral and attract more revenues. The long-haul connecting hub is an example of such a strategic shift in behavior.

Impacts on the Regional Economy

The impact on the regional economy can be assessed using the models estimated and reported in section 3.6.5. The first impact can be assessed using the elasticities contained in Table 5-14. The impact on labor demand at Hamburg airport can be estimated from the information contained in Figures 3, 4 and 5 of Mandel et al. (1999) and on the distribution of employment across categories at Hamburg Airport. Table 5-14 reports the changes. The net impact is to increase employment by 19 people due to changes in passenger demand and by 28 due to increased flights. A total of 47 people. A point of explanation is in order here. Recall from the modeling section, we found aggregate airport employment was growing over time but some categories of employment were falling. Most notably we found the airport was reducing the number of employees. This is precisely what one would expect from a modern management approach at the airport. As in other industries there are firms that offer services for which they have a comparative advantage. It makes no economic sense for the airport to undertake activities for which they have no special skills or are not a part of their value chain. As in other industries the airport will focus on those activities where it can add customer value and contract out to other firms where they can purchase these services. Hence we see airport employment going down but other categories of employment going up for a net positive increase with Open Sky. If the impact on the Lufthansa facility is included, the total employment effect rises to 208. Again this might be regarded as a conservative figure since it does not account for strategic repositioning by the airport.

Table 5-14: Impact of Bilateral Change on Labor Demand at Hamburg Airport

Categories of Employment	1994	Passengers	Flights
Airport Corporation	1534	-15	-10
Airport Subsidiaries	NA	NA	NA
Government Agencies	611	4	5
Airlines	1177	9	10
Import/Export Businesses	766	6	7
Restaurants and Catering Businesses	569	3	4
Car Rental	66	1	1
Repair and Maintenance	22	1	1
Fuel Companies	52	1	1
Travel Agencies	142	1	1
Retail and Banks	154	1	1
Security Services	168	1	1
Cleaning Services	101	1	1
Others	434	3	4
Subtotal Airport	5796	19	28
Lufthansa Repair and Maintenance Facility	6821	54	59
Total	12617	74	87

Next the impact on output, investment and employment in the Hamburg region are measured. Using the elasticities calculated from the economic impact model the affects on the economy are presented in Table 5-15. Output (or income) increases by almost two million and employment rises by 126 people. Interestingly, the value for the increased employment is relatively close to the value one obtains by multiplying the change in airport employment by the total induced and indirect effects from the *Empirica* Economic Impact Study. Using this technique the value would be 71 new employees in the region.

Table 5-15: Impact of Bilateral Change on Regional Output, Employment and Investment

	1999	Impact	Value in 1999+t
Output	DM 367.890.812	DM 1.986.610	DM 369.877.423
Employment	210.433	126	210.559
Investment	DM 6.727.855	DM 55.168	DM 6.641.723

Impacts on Tourism

Impacts on the amount of tourism as well as the employment impacts for tourism can be calculated using the elasticity values developed in section 3.6.5.2. The results follow a two stage approach. Increases in flights and lower fares resulting from the liberalization will increase tourist traffic to Germany. As a result of the increase in tourism, employment in the tourism industry in the Hamburg area will rise.

In 1997 Hamburg Airport handled a total of 8,512,124 passengers.[15] Of this total, approximately 30% were non-business, 2,553,637. In 1997 Hamburg airport handled 127,045 operations, excluding Germany and EU operations this would be 20,318 international flights. Under the Open Sky liberalized bilateral the net increase in International flights would be 5.37%.[16] Using the elasticity of tourism with respect to flights, 0.08, this would result in an increase in tourists by 10,970 and increase employment in the tourism industry by approximately 20 persons; the elasticity of tourism employment with respect to tourism is 0.02. Part of the increase can be explained by the shift from 30% to 60% of passengers travelling for non-business reasons.

Summary

The Open Sky proposal has the potential to have a significant impact on the Hamburg Airport and Hamburg economy. The analysis began with an assessment of what would be the outcome for the German economy with a change in the rules governing bilateral trade in aviation services between Germany and other countries. The outcome for changes in passengers and flights was distributed across the major German airports as a result of both increased aggregate demands and induced traffic flows. Route passengers increased by 165,970 with 17,000 of these hubbing. There was a decrease in flows from Canada, other EU countries and within the domestic economy but, there were gains on all other routes examined. The most significant increases came in Japan, Thailand, Hong Kong and China with 85,957, 72,209, 70,459 and 50,796 passengers respectively. Flight operations had a net decreases. This was a result of a reduction in a large number of smaller feeder aircraft moving away from Hamburg and a net increase in larger aircraft. Flights from Canada were down by 14 but average aircraft size was up. Similarly, Germany and the EU reduced flights but all other countries increased flights. International flights (non-EU and non-domestic were up by over 1200 flights annually. The other significant shift was from business travel to non-business travel; 63% of new passengers are on non-business trips.

The impact of these changes are felt on airport revenue from airside and non-aviation sources as well as on the level of economic activity in the local and regional Hamburg economy. Airside revenue increases by about five percent as a result of an increase in the number international flights and because larger aircraft are used on these flights.[17] Non-aviation revenue also increased by 9.3%. This revenue came from concessions, and the growing proportion of tourists in the passenger growth. Overall, airport revenue increases by 6.7%. This is a weighted average of aviation and non-aviation revenue and the fact that non-aviation revenue is a growing proportion of aviation revenue.

Airport employment was also affected. There was a net increase of 47 jobs due to Open Sky. If the impact on the Lufthansa Maintenance base is included this increases to 208 new jobs. There is a shift from airport employment to concession, airline and service employment. Restaurants and catering and freight brokers account for a sizeable proportion of the increase in employment.

The output oft the Hamburg economy rises by a small amount, about 0.03% or $783,316 US. Employment increases are small at only 78 people; a non-significant amount in an employment population of over 200,000 workers. The increase in investment is also in the order of 0.5%, about $21,000 US.

Tourism impacts are somewhat more encouraging as tourism is labor intensive and the increasing proportion of new passengers are in the non-business type. Because of the increase in international flights and passengers, tourism increases by approximately 11,000, about 0.4%. As a result of the growth in tourism, tourism employment increases with 20 new jobs to accommodate the tourism increase.

The numbers reported here may appear small, yet they represent perhaps the floor of the impact of Open Sky. The analysis does not take account of what would occur should the airport take a more proactive role in marketing the airport and building connections with other countries. A strategic initiative in this direction will augment all of the numbers reported by a non-trivial amount.

[1] Examples for such a route are the existing charter-flights between some regional airports in Germany and Puerto Plata, Santo Domingo and Punta Cana in the Dominican Republic, which take place, every second week, between May and September, combining one or two regional airports in Germany with one or two destinations in the Caribbean Sea to a three- or four-stop round-trip.

[2] If one reflects on the history concerning the USA-Netherlands agreement one can expect a fast reaction as such bilaterals are of strategic importance.

[3] The same applies for other routes under competition where airlines operate with smaller aircraft to keep their slots active instead of reducing the frequency. For example, when one considers the Delta service in Hamburg, Sabena switched to smaller aircraft and added one frequency at the time Delta was changing their alliance to Air France and closing down the Hamburg – Atlanta direct service.

[4] Note, that we only considered 10 markets in the 'Open Sky' scenario definition and that the results are based on a ceteris paribus ex post scenario analysis for the year 1997 (and not upon an ex ante forecast).

[5] Non-IATA passengers: - transfer passengers are counted once.

[6] IATA passengers: - transfer passengers counted twice.

[7] Berlin can easily compensate the few number of passengers they lose (to Hamburg) from the area of Berlin itself (2.000) by raising their market shares in the south of Berlin, additional passengers changing plane in TXL or SXF and the induced demand to the markets considered.

[8] Please note that consumers are sensitive to survive attributes like frequency or gauge of aircraft. In consequence to produce a consistent result out of the scientific point of view one should apply the system approach assuming strategy II, as the models are linked and interact. So changes in service frequency will influence the total demand, its distribution, the competition among modes, the airport-, slot- and access/egress choice (see Mandel 1999). Obviously it exceeds the scope of this study as the focus is on demand potentials when liberalisation takes place and not on the analysis of airline/alliance strategies on the demand. To allow a direct comparison of the two a/c strategies we here impose that the demand does not change.

[9] In comparison with other airports, Hamburg's aircraft fee structure ´97 is one of the most expensive specially for large a/c, but in passenger charges the reverse is the case. For the following years significant changes were announced by the management.

[10] Revenue rises even if airlines act as assumed in strategy I (- 1.5 tsd. a/c movements).

[11] Numbers shown include all passengers embarking and disembarking; transfer passengers are counted twice at the transfer airport and counted once more, if embarking or disembarking at a German Airport (Example: a passenger from Hamburg to Hong Kong who changes the plane at Frankfurt Airport is counted once, when entering the plane at Hamburg, a second time when arriving at Frankfurt and a third time when entering the plane to Hong Kong at Frankfurt Airport).

[12] 1st leg domestic – 2nd leg international transfer passengers.

[13] Concerning the results stated above for Frankfurt Airport, we want to stress in this context that the analysis is focusing on Hamburg and in the study we considered just 10 markets and the effects for Germany and the direct neighbouring regions abroad. Of course there are still potentials left for Frankfurt to compensate the losses by a diversification of the services as well as in attracting 6th freedom traffic from regions we could not consider in this study.

[14] As stated earlier the study considers 10 markets and not all these markets are to be liberalised. Therefore to generate a first rough estimation for an overall liberalisation, one could consider the different markets as representatives of different market types. According to the results shown one can then estimate the total effects. But the consistent way to approach the problem would be an extended 'Open Sky' study considering all markets to be liberalised based on at least an European scope (incl. EU demand matrix, world air network).

[15] Mandel et al. (1999) Figure 4.

[16] Op Cit, Figure 5.

[17] Landing and parking fees increase with aircraft weight and carrying capacity.

6. Strategic and Policy Implications

Policy Recommendations

The general analysis of the effects of ASAs (chapter 3) as well as the simulation results for Germany as a whole (chapter 4) show, that liberalization of international air transport is an opportunity rather than an impediment to enhance social welfare of the German economy. Early liberalization may generate a first-mover advantage for the German air transport system vis-à-vis its EU rivals, while a delay of liberalization might work in favor of other EU countries. Hence, the German government should promote the shift to deregulation as quickly as possible. A slow move to liberalization will permit established airlines and airports to entrench their current position.

The experiences with deregulated air transport markets have also shown that, although competition in liberalized air transport markets is workable, there might be a role for competition policy after liberalization to ensure ongoing contestability of airlines' routes and networks. Furthermore there might a role for international safety standards. These both might be important areas for international coordination of air transport policy. The aim should be to establish a global institutional framework for air transport, which ensures fair and ongoing competition between carriers in the future.

In principle, liberalization could be obtained by

- Unilateral action by the German government which would have to open its own markets without demanding anything in exchange;
- Bilateral negotiations with trading partners,
- Multilateral liberalization under the auspices of the WTO and its GATS; or
- Multilateral liberalization by creating a conditional liberalization club whose members obtain most favored nations concessions and national treatment (non-discrimination) only on the condition of granting these rights to all carriers of all other club members as well.

In the following, the pros and cons of each of these alternatives will be explored in detail.

Unilateral Liberalization of Restrictive Bilaterals

In general, unilateral trade liberalization will be beneficial to the domestic economy if it happens vis-à-vis all trading partners. The results of an opening of international air transport markets can be internalized by the national economy via lower prices of imported air services and by enhanced efficiency of the national air transport system as a result of increased competition on international markets. Additional rents will emerge in the long run, when the domestic economy will react to the emergence of new trade relations by structural change according to the specialization pattern given by comparative advantages, and by the corresponding transfer of national resources to branches with export opportunities. It is conceivable in this context that Germany specializes in the production of other goods and services while it accepts to be served with air transport services entirely from abroad.

There exists an exceptional case where unilateral liberalization might result in a reduced aggregate welfare level of the national economy: If the German government restrict unilateral liberalization to apply only vis-à-vis one single country, while not exterminating restrictive ASAs to other countries in that region, this country may perhaps restrict German airlines ability to compete on equal terms with that country's carriers. In such a situation Germany may perhaps find itself trapped in a situation where the flag carrier of that trading partner could exert monopolistic power on bilateral routes, which would clearly disadvantage not only German airlines, but the national economy as a whole.

However, the emergence of such a situation is limited to the case of a market structure which is to a high degree exogenous. If instead the still protectionist country has to face a serious threat of traffic diversion (including adverse spillover effects on interconnected markets) Germany would be much less subject to monopolistic exploitation by the protectionistic country. Such a threat of traffic diversion might be either generated because either the bilateral in force grants appropriate 5th freedom rights to airlines of third countries serving the relevant market, or because 6th freedom rights permit traffic diversion via third countries' hubs. Accordingly, if the structure of the relevant market should become endogenous by competing liberalization efforts of neighboring countries, traffic diversion might loom in the very neighborhood. Resident carriers would have little to lose then from liberalization without reciprocal concessions, but domestic secondary airports might acquire additional traffic. Hence, any major shift towards endogenous bilateral market structures improves the prospects of unilateral preferential liberalization. The recent trend of more and more intra-regional liberalization agreements in various parts of the world has already enhanced the prospects of success of unilateral liberalization.

From the general perspective of free trade, however, the logic of unilateralism is directed towards reaping welfare gains from intensified competition on international markets by liberalizing trade relations not vis-à-vis a single, but vis-à-vis all, or at least a sufficiently large group of, trading partners, which exert a threat of traffic diversion to each other. In such a case, problems of exogenous market structures could be avoided.

Bilateral Liberalization

As past experience and also the political-economic context within which the design of air transport policy takes place suggest, the German government may be very hesitant with regards to liberalization without any concessions in return. It would have to face strong vested interests of highly organized interest groups, which might make unilateral liberalization vis-à-vis all (or at least a large group of) countries not appropriate from the view of the policy makers. Instead they might prefer to negotiate concessions by others for granting own concessions to weaken resistance or vested interests against liberalization. Moreover, in the case of an attractive domestic market, reciprocity can be deployed as an engine and driving force for trade liberalization not only at home but also elsewhere. Under these circumstances, non-unilateralism may provide an opportunity to open up additional foreign markets and to make use of reciprocity as a bargaining chip. Hence, what are the prospects of a policy approach that relies on bilateral liberalization?

Bilateral liberalization has already been intensively used by the U.S. in opening Trans-Atlantic and Trans-Pacific routes. The official reading was that this approach should serve the end of exporting US liberal aviation policy as pursued after the 1978 domestic liberalization (Kasper 1988: Ch. 5). But of course the approach contained also a mercantilist component of strengthening US carriers' position in world air service markets. In doing so, the US government tried to use the existing bilateral agreements as a tool to tear down existing foreign market barriers which hindered US carriers from expansion and realization of economies of scope and traffic density. The approach that the U.S. followed can be characterized as 'aggressive bilateralism'. Nevertheless, evaluating the determinants of success of the US-strategy helps to assess the prospects of success of bilateral liberalization as far as Germany is concerned.

The explicit US strategy in liberalizing international air transport services on a bilateral plane was based on reciprocal concessions of additional market penetration opportunities, whereby reciprocity did not mean strictly identical concessions on both sides but an exchange of less state intervention and of granting additional traffic rights of different quality as suggested by the single case. At the end of the 1970s, the US held extensive 3rd and 4th freedom route rights, but had given so far their European and Japanese counterparts only limited concessions for gateways to the large US market. On this base the US strategy consisted of offering foreign countries (and their carriers) access to additional US gateways in exchange for 5th-freedom rights for US carriers, for relaxation or even elimination of price controls, and for liberal capacity regulations so that US carriers would be free to feed traffic from all over Europe resp. Asia without any regulatory restrictions (Kasper 1988: 76). The concession on the US side was more limited: Access to her large domestic market via additional traffic rights to/from additional gateways, with access being limited to cross-border traffic. Although cabotage rights were not granted by the U.S., the opportunity to serve additional gateways was an attractive 'carrot' for European and Asian counterparts. The U.S. deployed this 'carrot' in the course of a sophisticated 'divide et impera' strategy through 'beachhead agreements' with single partners (in the case of Europe: the Netherlands). This strategy aimed at encircling restrictive countries with liberal agreements, thus exercising a threat of traffic diversion to the disadvantage of protecionistic trading partners, and by this means forcing such countries to follow up in liberalizing their agreements with the US, too. Hence, traffic diversion served as an appropriate 'stick' and counterpart of the 'carrot.'

In the case of the European trading partners, the US government was quite successful in achieving more liberal air service agreements. Negotiations with the Netherlands in 1978 ended in a new agreement which provided for additional US gateway access rights granted to the Dutch KLM in exchange for 5th freedom rights beyond Amsterdam all over Europe granted to US carriers, as well as for prize liberalization.

Just to outline the bargaining positions: For KLM the additional 3rd/4th freedom rights to/from the U.S. were an asset to increase her share in long haul North Atlantic traffic vis-à-vis European rivals and to strengthen her position in interconnected European markets by increasing economies of traffic density in the own route network. Given the already existing dense route network of KLM within Europe, the costs of additional competition by US carriers on European routes were lower for her than the benefits of enhanced access to Trans-Atlantic traffic. For US carriers, the 5th freedom rights to carry traffic to/from Amsterdam from/to other European destinations in combination with access to the domestic US market could be exercised to enhance their competitive position against European rivals, too.

The agreement with the Netherlands was soon followed by a similar one with Belgium. These two threat 'sticks' of traffic diversion were sufficient to drive the United Kingdom and Germany towards negotiations with the U.S. In late 1980, the U.S. had succeeded in negotiating more liberal agreements with both countries. Moreover, an attempt of the US Civil Aeronautics Board to question the IATA price cartel's antitrust immunity in 1978 ended in an multilateral agreement between the USA and the European Civil Aviation Conference, representing aviation authorities of more than twenty European countries. The essence of this agreement was a partial price deregulation in Trans-Atlantic traffic by introducing double disapproval pricing zones.

Vis-à-vis Japan, the USA deployed a similar carrot/stick-strategy including the technique of encircling the target country by liberal agreements with competitors, but the story runs a little bit differently. More liberal agreements were signed with a couple of other Asian countries. But in the case of Japan, another element of the bilateral air transport relations made things more difficult: First, the existing agreement was already somewhat more liberal than the European ones insofar as the legal text permitted multiple designation of carriers in bilateral air transport as well as 5th freedom rights. Second, Japan, felt being treated unfair under the old agreement as regards 5th freedom rights and followed a strategy of obstruction when US carriers wanted to exercise existing carrier designations and traffic rights under the old agreement. In this situation, both the traffic rights' restrictions for Japanese airlines under the current bilateral and the threat of anti-competition trials before the CAB were applied as 'sticks', whereas additional access to the USA was the corresponding 'carrot'. The 'carrot and stick' strategy served the end to respond to Japan's blocking of the seamless exercise of the existing agreement. Finally, multiple designation and 5th freedom rights could be used more intensively in US-Japanese air transport, but in this case the strategy served the end to bridge the gap between the rights granted in the agreement and their actual exercise as had so far been conceded by Japan's authorities.

In the 1990s, the U.S. continued their aggressive bilateralism by persuading their European and Asian partners to revise the respective bilaterals towards the standard of 'open skies' agreements, i.e. free access and unlimited capacity for 3rd and 4th freedom as well as for unlimited traffic rights to all landing points in the other country. The strategy was largely the same: The liberalization was based on discrimination against third parties and confined to the respective trading partner. The U.S. started to enter into a series of negotiations with neighboring countries, whereby the threat of traffic diversion acted as an incentive mechanism for other trading partners to negotiate own 'open skies' agreements with the USA. Again the Netherlands were the preferred beachhead in Europe, with an 'open skies' agreement being signed in 1992. Agreements with other EU members followed in 1995 for Sweden, Luxembourg, Finland, Denmark, Belgium, and Austria, and in 1997 for Germany. But also nearby non-EU members were included: Switzerland, Norway and Iceland in 1995 and the

Czech Republic in 1997. For the Asia/Pacific region, the respective list of countries and dates reads as Singapore, Brunei, Malaysia, Taiwan and New Zealand in 1997 (Oum 1998: 128). In 1998, quite a liberal agreement could be reached even with Japan. This ASA granted unlimited 5th freedom rights, more liberal code sharing options and removed capacity restrictions for incumbent carriers (Elek et al. 1999: 144). But it should also be mentioned that the strategy was not entirely successful in Europe in the 1990s: 'Open skies' agreements still do not yet exist with respect to the United Kingdom and France which still have resisted the competitive pressures though negotiations are currently underway between the U.S. and the United Kingdom.

The lesson from the American experience in using the bilateral policy approach as a means to gain better market access opportunities and less regulation elsewhere in the world is threefold:

- A country must be in a position to offer a valuable asset in terms of attractive traffic rights to her trading partner, otherwise the leverage effect will not work. Even the only limited access to some additional landing points of the large American market with its huge demand potential was sufficient to wake European countries' interest in re-negotiations of agreements. Compared to the rather unique position of the U.S., it must be questioned, however, whether Germany would be successful if she would deploy a similar strategy for opening up the rest of still restrictive bilaterals in the current situation, given
    - the limited size of the domestic market;
    - the existence of the liberalized intra-European and North Atlantic markets, which means that valuable 5th freedom rights have already been absorbed; and
    - the difficulties for trading partners to obtain intra-European traffic rights.
- If the threat of traffic diversion is quite a realistic outcome of successive negotiations, this can be an effective tool to drive hesitating countries towards concessions on their own. This means that a system of restrictive bilateral agreements is no longer stable, if the first, or at least the second, domino has fallen.[1] This explains why the U.S. were successful in persuading European countries to agree to 'open skies' agreements. The threat of traffic diversion in the actual European context was, and is all the more realistic considering that North-Atlantic and other intercontinental traffic to and from secondary European airports can be served by European airlines using solely 6th freedom rights via hubs in other European

countries, provided that distances and travelling times on these alternative routes are short enough to make traffic diversion a realistic option.

- For a country with bargaining power, the threat of withholding concessions may be necessary in the course of retaliatory action against attempts of withdrawal of existing rights by the trading partner. In this case. bilateralism is likely to result in effective retaliation as suggested by chapter 2.

The bilateral liberalization strategy, however, is one of high transaction costs, because already liberalized bilaterals could be again transformed into restrictive ones.

In sum, bilateral liberalization may work to a certain extent. However, one should be aware of its limits. Although the U.S. as the most prominent example of the bilateral approach did succeed in opening up foreign markets by getting access rights for their own carriers, the network of 'open skies' bilaterals that emerged did not led to entirely open access to all markets. Market opening has been confined to the routes between the U.S. and their individual European or Asian trading partners, whereby the US carriers automatically got 5th freedom rights to build up feeder systems in Europe and Asia, while European/Asian carriers got free access only on their respective direct routes to US airports (and potentially beyond). Thus, a series of 'open skies' agreements with one country serving as the 'hub' (such, for instance, the U.S.) does not necessarily lead to open skies among the trading partners, unless the countries at the end of the spokes co-operate among each other. This suggests to push ahead air transport liberalization by a multilateral approach.[2]

Multilateral Liberalization

Multilateral liberalization of traffic rights in air transport could either be conducted within existing structures such as the General Agreement on Trade in Services (GATS) of the World Trade Organization (WTO) or, alternatively, might require an extra liberalization forum. An extra forum would eventually be preferable due to shortcomings of the GATS as regards air transport and to regulatory requirements from the sphere of anti-trust as well.

The WTO as a Forum for Liberalization of Bilaterals? In principle, no obvious reason can be found why international air transport should be treated differently from other services with respect to global liberalization.[3] So far, however, the provision of international air transport services and the access to domestic airports is a matter of the bilateral ASAs, and therefore explicitly exempt from multilateral liberalization procedures of the GATS agreement under the auspices of the WTO. According to paragraphs 2 and

3 of the Annex on Air Transport Services to the GATS legal text, only secondary services (aircraft repair and maintenance, selling and marketing of air transport services, and services rendered by computer reservation systems) are covered by the GATS rules (WTO/CTS 1998: 1 f.), in particular

- The general rules of unconditional most favored nation (MFN) treatment (Art. II), transparency (Art. III), reciprocity,[4] independent dispute settlement (Art. XXIII) and progressive liberalization (Art. XIX), as well as
- The specific rules of domestic market access (Art. XVI) and national treatment of foreign suppliers (Art. XVII) which apply only to those services for which bound concessions have been made in national commitment schedules (Art. XX).[5]

The reason for this exemption from GATS has exactly been the existence of the bilateral agreements:

- It would have taken too much time to include this sophisticated network of agreements on traffic rights into a multilateral GATS agreement when the GATS was negotiated at the end of the Uruguay Round 1994; and
- In particular the U.S., but also other countries did not accept the application of unconditional MFN treatment to market access in air traffic because they feared free-rider conduct of less liberal-minded trading partners (Knorr 1998a: 387).

Accordingly, traffic rights as the 'hard rights' in aviation were explicitly singled out as controversial issues for future action.[6] Given the fact that any future amendment to the liberalization process under the GATS has to be approved by the WTO members, a consensus among them is necessary in order to cancel the explicit exclusion of air traffic rights from GATS.

A forum for such amendments is the Ministerial Conference, which is held at least once every two years.[7] The WTO's 3rd Ministerial Conference, scheduled to be held 30 November – 3 December 1999 in Seattle, Washington, USA, will launch the next major world trade negotiation round due to start early in 2000. So far, aviation seems not to be among the most prominent issues on the agenda for the Seattle meeting itself or for the WTO negotiation round to be launched. However, several members are pointing in their ex-ante communications to an automatic revision process of the air transport annex: As is the case for member states' MFN exemptions from Art. II GATS, the air transport annex which excludes traffic rights from GATS has to be reviewed regularly by the

Council for Trade in Services, at least 5 years after GATS went into operation, i.e. no later than in the year 2000 (WTO/CTS 1998: 2).

The EU and Argentina are explicitly referring to this procedure in their communications for the future GATS agenda, while Australia, New Zealand, Chile, and Switzerland are stressing the merits of a further liberalization in general (WTO/GC 1999a-d). Interestingly, no explicit hint at air transport services can be found in the US government's communication.[8] This is in line with former reservations against granting unconditional access to the domestic market (even for gateways for 3rd and 4th Freedom traffic, leaving cabotage aside) on a multilateral base: In the period before formation of the WTO and the enactment of the GATS, the US government had denied to negotiate multilaterally under the former GATT umbrella. The reason was that she would have been forced to grant traffic rights unconditionally also to protectionist trading partners and would have not necessarily been able to acquire foreign traffic rights in exchange. At best, it was argued at that time that unconditional MFN treatment would slow down negotiations substantially (Kasper 1988: 95 ff.).

Concluding, one may well doubt whether traffic rights in air transport will play a major role in the GATS round to be launched in the year 2000 although there are some hints that a limited number of countries would like to start negotiations on traffic rights under the GATS umbrella. To be sure, multilateral liberalization under a WTO umbrella would be preferable to any plurilateral agreement of smaller size. The very advantage of GATT/GATS negotiations in the past has been that a huge number of participants have simultaneously negotiated reciprocal concessions according to the MFN principle. These simultaneous negotiations increased the number of potential liberalization deals and, hence, the probability, of a true progress in liberalization.[9]

However, multilateral GATS negotiations on air traffic rights would be a cumbersome and time-consuming effort, given the heterogeneous interests of the various participants which apparently have not changed since the Uruguay Round. Thus, it is well conceivable that a multilateral approach below WTO level would be more successful for the medium term. This has led various researchers, among them Knorr (1998a), Drysdale et al. (1998), Australian Productivity Commission (1999) and Elek et al. (1999) to propose the model of an open liberalization club[10] as a device for liberalizing international air transport markets. It should be mentioned that making use of this alternative approach does not mean to leave aside the WTO altogether.

Liberalization Clubs Compared to a truly multilateral approach under GATS, a liberalization club (LC) is only a second-best solution. This disadvantage can be offset in the longer run, if the club concept encompasses options for progress towards multilateralism. Formally, there are two kinds of LCs perceivable: First, the co-operative approach by which a number of 'small countries' form a liberalized area among themselves and merge their bargaining power to obtain concessions from a 'big country' in bilateral negotiations, and second, the all-embracing open peer club in which every member willing to accept the club charter is entitled to obtain the benefits of liberalization on a conditional most favored nations base, the condition being strict reciprocity of liberalization. Both kinds of LCs might well be thought upon as an en-suite effort: Enhancing the own bargaining power against a large country, such as the U.S., might be advisable to small countries willing to acquire foreign traffic rights for their domestic carriers in the first place. But once this co-operation would be working, it could well be transformed into an all-embracing peer LC provided that options exist and incentives are set to allow additional members to join, and that the former large trading partner becomes a member of the club. In any case, the formation of a LC rests on the utilization of bargaining power and takes the existing bilateral agreements as a starting point with the objective of arriving at more open world markets in the end. On this avenue, the LC would serve as a tool to open up foreign markets by granting concessions to the access to the domestic market. Thus, discrimination against trading partners is used to broaden the support for open markets. However, without institutional safeguards a LC might lead to a segmentation of air transport markets rather than to progressive liberalization. If the LC movement would come to a standstill at the first stage of the co-operative approach, the club might well exhibit all detrimental features of regionalism in trade:[11]

- As a matter of fact, any regional trade liberalization approach discriminating against third countries outside the still existing external trade barriers has to be assessed by the balance between the positive trade-creation and negative trade diversion effects in the sense of Viner (1950). Beneficial trade-creation effects for the members of a free-trade area (resp. a customs union) have to be balanced by the negative trade-diversion effects, when trade with (possibly more efficient) partners outside the liberalization area is substituted by trade with suppliers within the area.
- Any regional customs union has to cope with the danger of limiting the benefits to core members by following a 'closed shop' approach. The EU Single Market's example of the 'fortress Europe' demonstrates that there are strong incentives inherent in

regionalism to block outsiders even if the markets inside the customs union are going to be liberalized.

- The regional bloc may well be tempted to exert market power at the expense of trading partners, although retaliation is looming around the corner in most cases and will leave both sides worse off than before.
- A regional bloc is more susceptible to lobbying in favor of interests from within the club than a multinational organization is.

With regards to air transport, a tendency towards market segmentation might be realistic (Elek et. al. 145): Members could raise administrative barriers against non-members once a LC has been formed. Based on a 'closed shop' model of a LC and spurred on by intra-bloc competition, member carriers could try to become dominant suppliers on bloc-external routes. While efficiency gains due to intra-bloc competition would clearly be advantageous, potential exertion of market power on bloc-external routes might lead to welfare losses all the more considering that bloc-external carriers could not compete on equal terms and could not act as countervailing power.

The danger of constraining instead of liberalizing air transport on a global scale cannot be ruled out initially. Hence, the LC model of conditional reciprocal liberalization of markets has to be supported by an additional institutional element: Openness of the club to all outsiders willing to join it on acceptance of the basic rule of mutual liberalization. If a trade liberalization club is open for accession by third countries which are, for the time being, discriminated by the conditional MFN treatment, even the detrimental effects of discrimination in a static welfare perspective (i.e. trade diversion to less efficient suppliers) may transform into beneficial dynamic effects. To be sure, the outsiders suffer losses from trade diversion and less foreign trade on their behalf; at the same time, they are offered the option to become insiders and to be compensated for the losses. Schmieding (1988: 518 ff.) who proposed the LC model for any trade negotiations points to the dynamic force of discriminatory treatment: The trade diverting effects serve as a mechanism by which outsiders get incentives to alter their deteriorating situation. But he makes clear at the same time that openness is a conditio sine qua non for a workable LC from the beginning, because the unconstrained option to join the club is the means by which the trade diverting effects are transformed into trade creating ones.[12] Hence, a LC has to be defined by its charter to be an open liberalization club (OLC).

The emphasis on openness is indeed the essence of the proposal of Elek et al. (1999). Their model of an OLC for air transport combines conditional

MFN treatment in granting free market access with the rule that no country from outside may be excluded from joining the clubs if it grants similar concessions to all club members.[13] For this purpose,

- The traditional GATT/GATS principle of *non-discrimination* should be applied only on a conditional base among club members, but it should be supplemented by the principles of (ii) *accession* to the club, i.e. openness;
- *Transparency*, being another GATT/GATS principle should be applied universally to facilitate accession; and
- *Review*, which means an option to improve club rules according to constructive suggestions from new members, should also be ensured by institutional safeguards.[14]

Equipped with these features, a LC would be less subject to the danger of concentrating on limited liberalization and market segmentation. Moreover, an OLC would be more in line with GATS rulings, because it would offer the option of transforming the plurilateral approach of participants into a truly multilateral one, i.e. the inherent principle of discrimination of non-members would become the more insignificant the more members would join the OLC, and conditional MFN would transform into unconditional MFN once all GATS members would be members of an OLC in air transport as well.[15]

Incentives to join an OLC Although the principle of openness may at first sight keep off countries with an explicit neomercantilistic policy attitude (because domestic airlines suffer a loss of profits due to increased competition after a country has joined the club), there are several incentives which could drive them to join an OLC after all. Disregarding the indisputable advantages of liberalized air transport markets for domestic consumers, domestic producer interests may be met by the membership in an OLC as well: Domestic airlines gain from increased efficiency which results from improved network structures in a larger liberalized area and the corresponding economies of scope and density; and also from achieving specialization rents in the case of distinct comparative advantages of some airlines in serving specific markets.

As the OLC grows in size, incumbent carriers can balance the risk of additional competition within the club with the prospects of serving additional attractive markets. On the other hand, newcomers have an incentive to join, because incumbent countries' airlines have a first-mover advantage in improving their own efficiency.[16] By this mechanism, an OLC could grow from a plurilateral body in the beginning via inclusion of larger countries with attractive markets to a genuine multilateral structure.

A further advantage of an OLC may be seen in its suitability as platform for possibly required supra-national competitive action. An OLC could well serve the end of defining and implementing rules and enforcement mechanisms for correcting perceived competitive 'fouls,' committed either by carriers, by airport authorities or by countries. It would be up to the basic charter of the club to provide the required institutions and organizational units. This option of subordinating international air transport to an independent and plurilateral anti-trust legislation and control body might be an additional incentive for countries to join an OLC, because it would diminish the danger of unfair trade practices from the side of third parties.

The optimal forum for an OLC Once an OLC is thought upon as the best solution towards attaining multilateral air transport liberalization, the next question arises regarding implementation. Elek et al. (1999: 147 ff.) discuss the option of taking an existing regional institutional structure as a starting point and propose to found an OLC among the Asian countries under the umbrella of the Asia Pacific Economic Cooperation (APEC) movement which provides similar principles for attaining freer trade in this region. While this may be an option for air transport policy in Asia, the question for European countries arises whether it would be a superior strategy to rely on the European Union as an existing germcell of air transport liberalization. The European Single Market covers aviation which has been completely liberalized since 1997. Principally, also for Europe an organization as well as an institutional setting already exists which might be transformed into an OLC.

The question is, however, whether an EU club would be able to develop from the first stage of co-operation to a genuine OLC which will become (and will remain to be) open for other countries as well regardless of their geographical origin. Doubts can be raised whether it would be appropriate to use the EU as a nucleus for an OLC:

- A strong argument against the EU is her rather limited open-mindedness for trade-liberalization vis-à-vis countries from outside the customs union ('fortress Europe'). Although the internal liberalization records both for the Single Market and for EU competition policy look acceptable for recent years, external liberalization has not been pursued with the same intensity, and discriminatory action is widespread, e.g. by an increasing use of anti-dumping measures.
- A further (more legal) argument against the EU is its regional focus which limits the Union's activities to European interests.[17]

- Despite all efforts to widen the EU by granting membership to new (European) members, an equally important objective of the Union is deepening, i.e. acquiring competencies at the expense of the member states. Under these circumstances, the danger of external protectionism increases, and openness to third parties may be further neglected.
- Even if not the EU as a legal body, but the member states by virtue of their still existing national airspace sovereignty would form an OLC, the initially independent club might sooner or later be attracted institutionally by the EU. What makes this issue a delicate one is the fact that the European Commission is indeed attempting to drive member states towards transferring the right to negotiate bilateral agreements with countries from outside the EU exclusively to the Commission. If member states would surrender their national airspace sovereignty to the EU layer, this might just result in the limited co-operative club model instead of openness to third parties,[18] because the EU would become negotiating party obliged to advocate the interests of the European suppliers.

In sum, substantial reservations may be raised against the EU as a nucleus for an OLC. Admittedly, the APEC for Asia may be in a somewhat more comfortable position because of its inherent features of openness. However, the danger of limiting liberalization to regionalism should be counteracted from the beginning. This could be achieved by pursuing an avenue towards associating an OLC for air transport to an exiting truly multilateral body.

One candidate might be the ICAO. It is an United Nations' body and hence can act independent of single states. Furthermore it is highly acquainted with sector-specific issues of aviation and also provides the option to use an already existing dispute settlement mechanism. The feature of an independent arbitration service is an inevitable element of an OLC anyway (Schmieding 1988: 523). However, the ICAO dispute settlement mechanism has been hardly utilized so far (Knorr 1998a: 384). Moreover, the ICAO is (at least for the past) not known as the most thorough proponent of liberalization.

Here again, the WTO enters the stage. Although comprehensive negotiations on air traffic rights in the next GATS round are, as has been argued above, not likely to occur in the foreseeable future, the option exists to subordinate an OLC to WTO rulings by means of a plurilateral agreement whose concessions apply only to the signatories.[19] There have been several plurilateral agreements for a limited number of commodities under GATT in the past (on subsidies, government procurement, harmonizing of technical standards). They were drafted for those cases where during the negotiation round an agreement among all GATT members could not be attained, but where future negotiations might succeed in providing multilateral approval. The above-mentioned plurilaterals on subsidies and technical norms could be incorporated into GATT and GATS in the Uruguay round, whereas new plurilaterals have been agreed upon (trade in civil aircraft, dairy products, and bovine meat products) waiting to be incorporated in future rounds (Knorr 1998a: 387).

According to this proposal, a loose connection to the WTO could be tied which would provide a number of advantages (ibid.: 386):

- Except unconditional MFN the GATS principles and procedures could be applied, in particular the binding of concessions;
- The OLC could make use of existing WTO dispute settlement procedures;
- Subordination of an OLC under WTO would sufficiently provide for openness to members regardless of their geographic origin and largely prevent unbalanced negotiate power; and
- An international competition agency which might become necessary because of the progressive emergence of airline alliances is not precluded in this case.

In addition, the disadvantage of a sector-specific approach (i.e. the non-availability of inter-sectoral concessions) might lose some of its relevance, because the expectation of a future merging of air transport liberalization with the GATS might pave the way for additional concessions and provide additional incentives for countries to join the OLC.

In an overall perspective, the Knorr (1998a) proposal for a plurilateral air transport liberalization club affiliated to the WTO is very much in line with that of Stehn (1993) who had pleaded for reforming GATT by applying conditional MFN treatment and openness to third parties in order to make use of the driving power of trade diversion. It combines the elements of an OLC with the well established institutions of an international organization.

Conclusions

Summing up, a plurilateral OLC approach towards liberalization of international air transport appears to be a superior solution in terms of both welfare gains and feasibility. Once the option of unilateral liberalization is disregarded (which is a quite realistic assumption), among the remaining alternatives the OLC model qualifies for the most advantageous benefit-cost-ratio. Pursuing a strategy of bilateral liberalization might be workable, but presumably less successful than in the case of the U.S.: Germany may not be in the same comfortable position with regard to valuable traffic rights as the U.S. were when they successfully pursued their bilateral liberalization strategy. Moreover, obtaining a large bundle of sufficiently attractive traffic rights in exchange appears to be connected with high transaction costs, in particular for additional 5th freedom rights. Among the plurilateral alternatives, the truly multilateral WTO/GATS approach would be the first choice with respect to welfare gains and trading options for different bundles of concessions. But equally, this solution seems to be the one with the least probability of realization, at least currently. Hence, the option of a liberalization club would be a practicable detour. It would deploy the threat of trade diversion under regionally limited liberalization schemes as an incentive mechanism towards overcoming regionalism and might pave the way towards truly multilateralism. But a necessary condition for this concept to render the expected results is strict openness of the club to all outsiders willing to join and to accept the basic condition of liberalization. The crucial role which openness plays in this approach makes an independent and explicitly open club the superior solution vis-à-vis entrusting the EU with the task of liberalizing: In this case, the stage of regionalism might not be overcome. Finally, once an open liberalization club is considered, it may prove advantageous to affiliate it loosely to the WTO. this would provide the option of directing the detour via an OLC to the original target, i.e. a truly multilateral liberalization.

Airport Specific Recommendations

The analytical results from our models provide a set of recommendations that relate to a strategic direction for Hamburg Airport and policymakers in the local and State economy. The recommendations are not aimed at specific instruments nor do they provide recommendations for specific actions on an operational level.

Position on Liberalization

- Regulation tends to raise the cost of air transport to the detriment of air transport users. Empirical evidence also shows that deregulation does not affect the airlines' safety records negatively. Integrating these results, it may be concluded that deregulated air transport markets show no tendency to produce systematic market failures. A need for sector-specific regulation does therefore not exist - *Hamburg Airport and Hamburg Region should support increased national air liberalization.*
- EU members that are successful in attracting international traffic flows will reap the greatest benefits from the liberalized EU air transport markets. Liberalization of international air transport is an

opportunity rather than an impediment to enhance social welfare of the German economy as a whole. Early liberalization may generate a first-mover advantage for the German air transport system vis-à-vis its EU rivals, while a delay of liberalization might work in favor of other EU countries - *Hamburg Airport and Hamburg Region should promote the shift to deregulation as quickly as possible. A slow move to liberalization will permit established airports and airlines to entrench their current position.*

Position on Airport Strategy

- Liberalization provides an opportunity for airports to actively engage in air services marketing. Airline choice, passenger, and cargo marketing are all components of this package - *Hamburg Airport can maximize the value of its scarce resources by being pro-active in attracting carriers and developing routes for passengers and cargo based on analysis of market potential in currently restricted markets.*
- As the revenue burden shifts from airside to non-aviation sources, it increases the risk exposure of the airport but it also increases the opportunities for the airport to increase aggregate revenue through pricing and providing customer value by actively developing more routes and carrier choice - *Hamburg Airport needs the opportunity for greater commercial freedom under an Open Sky environment to protect itself from carrier exploitation and to take advantage of new opportunities. It must lobby State and Federal Authorities to provide this freedom either directly or through institutional change.*

Position on Local and Regional Economic Development

- Airports cannot create economic activity but they can play a role in redistributing it. The ability of an airport to assist in making a regional economy more attractive is their service offering relative to others - *the State of Hamburg should develop complementary policies that induce airport utilization.*
- Airports change competitive advantage through greater carrier choice, higher frequency and, for some market segments, lower fares. Hamburg needs to understand which variable has greater appeal - *the State of Hamburg needs to promote accessibility. Increased access will result in a broader network and the halo affect that accompanies it.*

- Airports affect direct employment and subsequent income in the region by increasing numbers of carriers, flights, and passengers, in that order. International flights increases employment more than domestic or European flights - *the State of Hamburg needs policies that are complementary to attracting International passengers since they increase income and employment more than domestic passengers.*

The results of our analysis clearly show that the airport has much to gain from liberalization. Revenue from both aviation and non-aviation sources rises as does employment and the opportunities for new services. The benefits that we have measured do not take account of a pro-active approach the airport might adopt to enhance the gains available under Open Sky.

The benefits to the State of Hamburg are not direct, but can be significant. Industry and tourism depend on accessibility to a region. Certainly, accessibility provided by the airport is not a sufficient condition for local economic development but it will be necessary to ensure no change in competitive advantage relative to other regions. There is value to the local economy from liberalization but these benefits will depend to some extent on the State of Hamburg adopting business policies that are complementary to airport development.

---

[1] If the first country is willing to grant extensive or even unlimited 5th freedom rights, at least a second one at the end of the 5th freedom routes which agrees to this new traffic is required to make effective the new rights.

[2] C.f. also Elek et. al. (1999: 145).

[3] Another network industry, telecommunications, is already subject to WTO liberalization procedures under the GATS.

[4] Reciprocity is an essential pillar both of GATT and GATS negotiations, although it has never been explictly defined by the legal text of the agreements (cf. Stehn 1933: 7).

[5] The delicate role of restrictions in trade of services has led to a rather modest interpretation of these principles: "The GATS has three basic principles: first it covers all services except those provided in the exercise of governmental authority; second, there should be no discrimination in favour of national providers - the national treatment principle; and third, there should be no discrimination between other Members of the Agreement - the most-favoured-nation (MFN) principle. These are very powerful principles. No tariff or other generalized protection mechanism is applied in services, *but* the agreement does provide for *important exceptions. First,* governments can *choose* the services in which they *make market access* and *national treatment commitments*; *second,* they can *limit the degree of market access and national treatment* they provide; and *third,* they can *take exceptions even from the MFN obligation,* in principle only for ten years, in

order to give more favourable treatment to some countries than to WTO Members in general." WTO (1999, italic emphasis added).

6 The WTO Committee on Specific Commitments summarises that "In conclusion the Chairman stated 'A number a of delegations felt that it should be possible to include certain less controversial issues - the so-called soft rights - in the multilateral agreement, leaving the more difficult issues - the so-called hard rights - aside at this stage.'" (WTO/CSC 1997: 2).

7 The Ministerial Conference is the highest decision-making body of the WTO, representing all members.

8 In fact, the U.S. communication (WTO/GC 1999e) is devoted primarily to procedural proposals and general guidelines for future negotiation rounds. While other service sectors, such as telecommunciation, energy services, electronic commerce or financial services, are mentioned explicitly throughout the communication, this is not true for transport in general, with the exception of "express delivery services" in the passage on sectoral negotiation modalities (ibid.: 3, para. 14) and the following reasoning on the role of services to enhance productivity growth: "Efficient transport and distribution helps farmers get their products to market without spoilage and ensures that manufacturing components reach the factory in time for production" (ibid.: 1 f., para.4).

9 The limited scope for reciprocity is a major disadvantage of all sector-specific as opposed to multisectoral negotiations, and in aviation it is a direct consequence of bilateralism (Knorr 1998a: 384). Including aviation in the next GATS round would render the opportunity to trade unilateral concessions in air traffic rights for unilateral concessions in other sectors. See also Oum (1998: 129) who deplores that sector-specific liberalization approaches in air transport might lack the necessary success because of the absense of the option of trading inter sectoral reciprocal concessions.

10 The idea of a trade liberalization club is not new for trade theory. For example, the model of a trade liberalization club without reference to a particular sector has been put forward by Schmieding (1988). The proposal of Stehn (1993) to change GATT rules from unconditional to conditional MFN treatment is on the same line.

11 Cf. also Stehn (1993: 3ff.) and Knorr (1998a: 384 f.).

12 "From a dynamic perspective, openness is the decisive criterion. Closed arrangements may well lead into a *cul de sac*. Arrangements which are open to outsiders clearly deserve the praise" (Schmieding 1988: 519).

13 Cf. Stehn (1993: 16) and the literature cited therein for similar reform proposals for the whole GATT system combining conditional MFN treatment with open access. Stehn justifies his proposal by two shortcomings of GATT: First, the declining willingness of negotiating parties to make concessions (free rider problem) which drives major exporters such as the USA to turn to bilateralism, and second, the lack of an effective mechanism within GATT to force retarding large importing countries to give up their resistance to liberalization (foot dragger problem).

14 Cf. Elek et al. (1999: 145 ff.). It should be noted, however, that their fourth principle — review — might be at odds with the liberalization movement insofar as a revisable club charter might again become subject to protectionist lobbying. The charter should contain

adequate safeguards that the liberalization movement is irrevocable (Schmieding 1988: 521 f.), maybe according to the Art. XIX GATS principles of progressive liberalization and binding commitments.

[15] According to the GATS legal text, Art. VII:1 provides the opportunity for WTO members to mutually recognise qualifications of suppliers of professional services via agreements or unilateral action. This may be interpreted as an example for a LC, since the recognition comes into force only between the signatories. In addition, Art. VII:2 calls for openness of such an agreement (or unilateral provision) so that other WTO members can join. Hence, at least for this specific case the GATS provides a similar set of rules as the OLC approach (Elek et al. 1999:145, Fn. 6). Another exemption from unconditional MFN treatment can be found in Art. V bis on labour market integration. One should add that an OLC for air traffic would be consistent with GATS rules not because it could rest on similar explicit exemptions in the legal text, but simply because air traffic rights are still not covered by GATS at all. Art. V:1 which allows WTO members to engage in service liberalization agreements and which was agreed upon to cover the European Single Market, calls for substantial sectoral coverage in terms of number of sectors. Hence, an OLC for air traffic on its own would not be covered by Art. V:1. This would mean that founding an OLC on the one hand and negotiating on air traffic liberalization in the next WTO round would be conflicting strategies for the participating countries, unless the negotiations would lead to an amendment of the GATS legal text with an explicit exemption of air traffic from unconditional MFN.

[16] C.f. chapter 3.3 and also Elek et. al. (1999: 150).

[17] However, market liberalization had already been exported to non-members (for instance to EFTA countries) and the Union Treaty imposes on the Union the obligation to contribute to a stepwise liberalization in world trade. In principle, an extended EU Single Air Transport Market could offer limited membership via the associate membership model.

[18] In the context of an OLC, the negotiation mandate for traffic rights is implictly transferred to the club management as well. This serves the end of improving the attractiveness of the club to outsiders and the power of the constrained MFN treatment. The access (and the potential denial of access) to a common market offers more incentives for membership and reciprocity than the single members' ones. In contrast to the EU, an OLC offers the option of exit, so that the club management can be urged to adhere to liberalization.

[19] The proposal to form an OLC for air traffic among liberal-minded countries on the legal base of a plurilateral agreement under WTO rulings has been put forward by Knorr (1998a: 387). Elek et al. (1999: 145) agree (at least implicitely) to this proposal by emphasizing the danger that a simple LC might raise protectionist barriers against outsiders in the absense of WTO-type limits on discrimination.

References

ABC World Airways Guide (1996). Juli. Dunstable.

ADV (Arbeitsgemeinschaft der Deutschen Verkehrsflughäfen) (1997). *Sicherung und Optimierung des Luftverkehrsstandortes Deutschland. Situationsanalyse und Beiträge zu Problemlösungen.* Stuttgart.

Anonymos (1992). End of MoU Could Lead to End of IATA. *Avmark Aviation Economist* 9: 2-4.

Arbeitsgruppe Verwaltung und Recht (1980). Niederschrift über die Sondersitzung der Arbeitsgruppe Verwaltung und Recht des Länderausschusses Luftfahrt am 4. Juli 1989 in Düsseldorf (unpublished).

Aring, J. (1998). Der Flughafen Hamburg als Wirtschafts- und Arbeitsplatzfaktor. Zur Bedeutung des internationalen Großflughafens für die Großstadtregion. In W. Pfähler und B. Tiedemann (Hrsg.), *Häfen, Transrapid, Telekommunikation. Wachstumsmotoren für die Hamburger Metropole?* Frankfurt am Main.

Atzkern, H.-D. (1992). *Die regionalwirtschaftliche Bedeutung von Flugplätzen im ländlichen Raum der Bundesrepublik Deutschland unter besonderer Berücksichtigung des Regionalluftverkehrs. Eine Wirkungsanalyse raumbedeutsamer Effekte.* Bayreuth.

Association of European Airlines (without year). *Yearbook 1999.* Brussels.

Bauer, P.W. (1987). Airline Hubs: A Study of Determining Factors and Effects. *Economic Review (Federal Reserve Bank of Cleveland)* 23: 13-19.

Bayerisches Staatsministerium für Wirtschaft und Verkehr (o.J.). Information zum Gutachten 'Wirtschaftliche und verkehrliche Auswirkungen des neuen Flughafens München auf sein Umland. o.O.

Ben-Akiva M., Lerman S.R.: Discrete choice analysis; London; 1985.

Berry, S. (1990). Airport Prsence as Product Differentiation. American Economic Review 80: 394-399.

Beyhoff, St. (1994). *Vielfliegerprogramme und der Wettbewerb im Luftverkehr.* Köln.

Bhagwati, J.N. (1990). Departures from Multilateralism: Regionalism and Aggressive Unilateralism. *The Economic Journal*, 100: 1304-1317.

Bittlingmayer, G. (1986). Efficiency and Entry in a Simple Airline Network. *International Journal of Industrial Organization* 8: 245-257.

Bletschacher, G., H. Klodt (1992). *Strategische Handels- und Industriepolitik. Theoretische Grundlagen, Branchenanalysen und wettbewerbspolitische Implikationen.* Kieler Studien,244. Tübingen.

Borenstein, S. (1989). Hubs and High Fares: Dominance and Market Power in the U.S. Airline Industry. *Rand Journal of Economics* 20: 344-365.

Borenstein, S. (1990). Airline Mergers, Airport Dominance, and Market Power. *American Economic Review* 80: 400-404.

Borenstein, S. (1991). The Dominant-Firm Advantage in Multiproduct Industries: Evidence from the U.S. Airlines. *Quarterly Journal of Economics* 56: 1237-1266.

Borenstein, S. (1992). The Evolution of U.S. Airline Competition. *Journal of Economic Perspectives* 6: 45-73.

Borenstein, S. and N. Rose (1994). Competition and Price Dispersion in the U.S.Airline Industry. *Journalof Political Economy* 102: 653-683.

Boss, A., C.-F. Laaser, K.W. Schatz et al. (1996). *Deregulierung in Deutschland. Eine empirische Analyse*. (Authors: E. Bode, H. Böhme, A. Boss, E.-J. Horn, C.-F. Laaser, A. Rosenschon, B. Sander, K.-W. Schatz, R. Schmidt, H. Sichelschmidt, J. Stehn and H. Wolf). Kieler Studien 275. Tübingen.

Box G. E. P., Cox D. R.: An Analysis of Transformations; Journal of the Royal Statistical Society, Series B 26; 1964.

Bremiker, B., P. Klemmer und A. Ortmeyer (1982). *Analyse der regionalen Produktionsgesetzmäßigkeiten in der Bundesrepublik Deutschland.* Bonn.

Brueckner, J.K. and P.T. Spiller (1994). Economies of Traffic Density in the Deregulated Airline Industry. *Journal of Law and Economics* 37: 379-415.

Brueckner, J., N. Dyer and P. Spiller (1992). Fare Determination in Airline Hub-and-Spoke Networks. *Rand Journal of Economics* 23: 309-333.

Butler, G.F. and M.R. Keller (1994). International Aviation Policies: Is It Time for Change? *Transportation Quarterly* 48: 367-380.

Butler, R.V. and J.H. Houston (1991). The Location of Airline Hubs. *Southern Economic Journal* 57: 975-981.

Butler, R.V. and J.H. Houston (1993). Airline Hubs in the Single European Market: A Benchmark Analysis. *Review of Industrial Organization* 8: 407-417.

Button, K., K. Haynes and R. Stough (1998). Fyling into the Future. Air Transport Policy in the European Union. Cheltenham,UK and Northampton/Mass.,USA.

Caves, D,W., L.R. Christensen and M.W. Tretheway (1984). Economies of density versus Economies of Scale: Why Trunk and Local Service Airline Costs Differ. *Rand Journal of Economics* 15: 471-489.

Congress of the United States of America (1980). International Air Transportation Competition Act of 1979, Public Law 96-192 of Feb. 15, 1980: 94 Stat. 35-49.

Corden, W.M. (1974). *Trade Policy and Economic Welfare*. Oxford.

Deutsches Institut für Wirtschaftsforschung (1996). *Verkehr in Zahlen.* Berlin.

Dixit, A.K. (1984). International Trade Policy for Oligopolistic Industries. *The Economic Journal Conference Papers*, 94: 1-16.

Doganis, R. (1991). *Flying Off Course. The Economics of International Airlines.* London.

Doganis, R. (1993). The Bilateral Regime for Air Transport: Current Position and Future Prospects. In OECD (ed); *International Air Transport: The Challenges Ahead.* Paris.

Doganis, R. and G. Thompson (1973). *The Economics of British Airports.* Transport Studies Group, Department of Engeneering, Polytechnic of Central London.

Doganis, R. and A. Graham (1987). *Airport Management. The Role of Performance Indicators.* Transport Studies Group, Polytechnic of Central London.

Doganis, R., A. Graham and A. Lobbenberg (1995). *The Economic Performance of European Airports.* Research Report 3. Department of Transport. Cranfield University, Bedford.

Dresner, M. and T. H. Oum (1998). *The Effect of Liberalized Air Transport Bilaterals on Foreign Traffic Diversion.* Journal of Transport Economics and Policy, Volume 32, Part 3, 317-30.

Dresner, M, and R. J. Windle (1992). *The Liberalization of US International Air Policy: Impact on US Markets and Carriers.* Journal of the Transportation Research Forum, 32, 273-85.

Drysdale, P., A. Elek, H. Soesastro (1998). Open Regionalism: the Nature of Asia Pacific Integration. In P. Drysdale, D. Vines (eds.), *Europe, East Asia and APEC: a Shared Global Agenda.* Cambridge: Cambridge University Press, 103-135.

Elek, A., C. Findlay, P. Hooper, T. Warren (1999). 'Open Skies' or Open Clubs? New Issues for Asia Pacific Economic Cooperation. *Journal of Air Transport Management*, 5: 143-151.

Evans, W. and Kessides, I. (1994). Living by the 'Golden Rule': Multimarket Contact in the US Airline Industry. *Quarterly Journal of Economics* 109: 341-366.

Findlay, C., G. Hufbauer and G. Jaggi (1996). Aviation Reform in the Asia Pacific. In G. Hufbauer and C. Findlay (eds.); *Flying High. Liberalizing Civil Aviation in the Asia Pacaific.* Washington D.C.

Flughafen Frankfurt/M. AG/Marktforschung (1999). *Monatsbericht zur Verkehrsentwicklung (September).*

Gaudry M.I.J., Lestage P., Guélat J., Galvan P.: TRIO-Tutorial, Version 1.0; Centre de recherche sur les transports, University of Montreal; CRT-902; 1993.

Gaudry M.I.J.: Asymmetric shape and variable tail thickness in multinomial probabilistic responses to significant transport service level changes. Forthcoming paper in Transportation Research B; 1992.

Ghobrial, A. (1989). Competition between U.S. and Foreign Air Carriers: An Econometric Approach. *International Journal of Transportation Economics* 16: 19-33.

Giersch, H. (1985). Perspektiven der Weltwirtschaft. In Verein für Socialpolitik (Hrsg.), *Probleme und Perspektiven der weltwirtschaftlichen Entwicklung*. Jahrestagung in Travemünde 1984. Schriften des Vereins für Socialpolitik, N.F., 148. Berlin: Duncker & Humblot, 595-616.

Gillen, D. (1997); Deregulation and Privatization: The Role of Advancing Trade in Services under WTO. In F. Flatters and D. Gillen (eds.); *Competition and Regulation. Implications of Globalization for Malysia and Thailand.* Ontario.

Gillen, D., R. Harris and T. Oum (1996). *Assessing the Benefits and Costs of International Air Transport Liberalization. Research Report to Air Policy Group.* Ottawa (Transprt Canada).

Grande, M. (1985). Der Luftverkehrsmarkt der Bundesrepublik Deutschland. In Lufthansa (ed.). *Lufthansa-Jahrbuch 1985*. Köln.

Gresser, K. und P. Kessel (1983). *Auswirkungen von Flughäfen auf die regionale Entwicklung*. Freiburg/Breisgau.

Hübl, L. und U. Hohls (o.J.). *Regionalwirtschaftliche Bedeutung des Flughafens Hannover-Langenhagen. Bestandsaufnahme und zukünftige Anforderungen.* Gutachten im Auftrag der Flughafen Hannover-Langenhagen GmbH (Bearbeitungszeitraum: August 1983–März 1984).

Hübl, L., U. Hohls-Hübl und B. Wegener (1990). *Berliner Flughäfen und ihre Bedeutung als Wirtschafts- und Standortfaktor*. Berlin.

Institut der deutschen Wirtschaft (1992). *Zahlen zur wirtschaftlichen Entwicklung der Bundesrepublik Deutschland.* Köln.

Institut der deutschen Wirtschaft (1998). *Zahlen zur wirtschaftlichen Entwicklung der Bundesrepublik Deutschland.* Köln.

International Air Transport Association (IATA) (1998). *World Air Transport Statistics*. Montreal, Geneva, London.

International Civil Aviation Organization (ICAO) (various years). *Civil Aviation Statistics of the World.* Montreal.

International Civil Aviation Organization (ICAO) (1998). International Civil Aviation Vocabulary. Document OACI No. 9713.

Kasper, D.M. (1988). *Deregulation and Globalization: Liberalizing International Trade in Air Services.* The American Enterprise Institute Trade in Services Series. Cambridge (Mass.): Ballinger.

Keeble, D., P.L.Owens, C. Thompson (1981). *The Influence of Peripheral and Central Locations on the Relative Development of Regions.* University of Cambridge, Department of Geography. Cambridge, Mass.

Keeble, D., P.L.Owens, C. Thompson (1982). Regional Accessibility and Economic Potential in the European Community. *Regional Studies*, 16: 419-432.

Keeler, T. (1992). Airline Deregulation and Market Performance: The Economic Basis for Regulatory Reform and Lessons from the U.S. Experience. In *Transport in a Free Market Economy.* Basingstoke, Hampshire.

Kleit, A. (1992). Airline Networks as Joint Goods: Implications for Competition Policy. *Journal of Regulatory Economics* 4: 175-186.

Knorr, A. (1997). Wettbewerb und Flugsicherheit — ein Widerspruch? eineökonomische analyse am Beispiel des amerikanischen Luftverkehrsmarktes. *Zeitschrift für Verkehrswissenschaft* 68: 94-122.

Knorr, A. (1998a). Bilaterale, regionale oder multilaterale Liberalisierung des Luftverkehrs? *Internationales Verkehrswesen* 50 (9): 383-387.

Knorr, A. (1998b). Zwanzig Jahre Deregulierung im US-Luftverkehrs — eine Zwischenbilanz. *ORDO Jahrbuch für die Ordnung in Wirtschaft und Gesellschaft* 49: 419-464.

Krugman, P.R. (1984). Import Protection as Export Promotion: International Competition in the Presence of Oligopoly and Economies of Scale. In H. Kierzkowski (ed.), Monopolistic Competition and International Trade. Oxford: 180-193.

Laaser, C.-F. (1991). *Wettbewerb im Verkehrswesen. Chancen für eine Deregulierung in der Bundesrepublik.* Kieler Studien, 236. Tübingen: Mohr.

Laaser, C.-F., J. Stehn (1996). Marktwirtschaft und Subsidiarität: die föderative Arbeitsteilung auf dem Prüfstand. *Zeitschrift für Wirtschaftspolitik*, 45 (1): 58-91.

Langner, S. (1996). *The Allocation of Slots in the Airline Industry. A Transaction Cost Economics Analysis.* Baden-Baden.

Last J., Mandel, B.: VIA Systemkomponenten – software documentation; Karlsruhe; 1997.

Lawrence, R.Z. (1990). Discussion In R.Z. Lawrence, C.L. Schultze (eds.), An American Trade Strategy: Options for the 1990s. Washington, D.C.: 134-138.

Leigh, L. (1990). Contestabilty in Deregulated Airline Markets. Some Empirical Tests. *Transportation Journal* 30: 49-57.

Levine, M. (1987). Airline Competition in Deregulated Markets: Theory, Firm Strategy, and Public Policy. *Yale Journal of Regulation* 4: 393-494.

Levine, M. (1989). Towards Open Markets. *ITA-Magazine* (January/February): 3-8.

Mandel B.: Airport Choice & Competition - a Strategic Approach; proceedings of the 3rd Air Transport Research Group (ATRG) Conference 1999, in Hong Kong.

Mandel B.: Measuring Competition in Air Transport ; Airports and Air Traffic - Regulation, Privatization and Competition; editors Pfähler W., Niemeier H.-M. and Mayer O.G.. pp 71-92; Peter Lang Press; 1999.

Mandel B.: The interdependency of airport choice and travel demand; Taking Stock of Air Liberalization; editor Gaudry M., Mayes R., pp 189-222; Kluwer Academic Publishers, Dordrecht, 1999.

Mandel B., Gaudry M., Rothengatter W.: A disaggregate Box-Cox Logit mode choice model of intercity passenger travel in Germany; The Econometrics of Major Transport Infrastructures; editor Quinet E., Vickerman R., pp.19-44; MacMillian Press, London, 1997.

Mandel, B., Gaudry M. I. J., Rothengatter, W.: A Disaggregate Box-Cox Logit Mode Choice Model of Intercity Passenger Travel in Germany and its Implications for High Speed Rail Demand Forecast; The Annuals of Regional Science, pp. 99 - 120; Springer Verlag; 1997.

Mandel, B.: Schnellverkehr und Modal-Split; Nomos Verlag, Baden-Baden, 1992.

Manski C. F., McFadden D.: Structural Analysis of discrete data with econometric applications; London; 1981.

Mauldin, G. (1990). *Hub Dominance and Pricing in the Airline Industry.* PhD thesis, University of California.

Meier, E. (1991). Der Luftverkehr braucht eine bessere Infrastruktur. In Deutsche Lufthansa AG (Hrsg.), *Lufthansa Jahrbuch '91.* Köln.

Morrison, S. and C. Winston (1986). *The Economic Effects of Airline Deregulation.* Brookings Studies in the Regulation of Economic Activity. Washington, D.C.

Morrison, S. and C. Winston (1990). The Dynamics of Airline Pricing and Competition. *American Economic Review* 80: 389-393.

Morrison, S. and C. Winston (1995). *The Evolution of the Airline Industry.* Washington, D.C.

Nuutinen, H. (1992). Regulation: The Tortuous Path to Plurilateralism. *Avmark Aviation Economist* 9: 14-19.

Organization for Economic Co-operation and Development (OECD) (1997). The Future of International Air Transport Policy. Paris: OECD.

Oum, T. (1998). Overview of Regulatory Changes in International Air Transport and Asian Strategies Towards the US Open Skies Initiatives. *Journal of Air Transport Management* 4: 127-134.
Oum, T. and M. Tretheway (1992). *Airline Economics: Foundations for Strategy and Policy.* Vancouver.
Pagnia, A. (1992). *Die Bedeutung von Verkehrsflughäfen für Unternehmungen: Eine exemplarische Untersuchung der Flughäfen Düsseldorf und Köln/Bonn für Nordrhein-Westfalen.* Frankfurt am Main.
Productivity Commission (1998). *International Air Services.* Report No. 2. AusInfo. Canberra.
Schmieding, H. (1988). What about a Liberalization Club for an Open World Economy? *The World Economy*, 11 (4): 515-527.
Siebert, H. (1988). Strategische Handelspolitik — Theoretische Ansätze und wirtschaftspolitische Empfehlungen. *Aussenwirtschaft* 43: 549-584.
Siebert, H. (1994). *Außenwirtschaft*, 6. Auflage. Stuttgart.
Siebert, H. (1999). *The World Economy.* London.
Sichelschmidt, H. (1991). Im Zeichen der Golfkrise. *Die Weltwirtschaft* (2): 219–223.
Sichelschmidt, H. und H. Wolf (1993). Die Liberalisierung des EU-Luftverkehrs: Entwicklung, Stand und Perspektiven. *Die Weltwirtschaft* (2): 167–185.
Sorgenfrei, J. (1989). *Regionalflughäfen: Funktionen und Wirkungen.* Göttingen.
Spencer, B.J., J.A. Brander (1983). International R&D Rivalry and Industrial Strategy. *Review of Economic Studies*, 50: 707-722.
Spengler, J. (1950). Vertical Integration and Anti-trust Policy. *Journal of Political Economy* 58: 347-352.
Spiller, P. (1989). A Note on Pricing of Hub-and-Spoke Networks. *Economic Letters* 30: 165-169.
Statistisches Bundesamt (various years). *Fachserie 8: Reihe 6: Luftverkehr 1992.* Stuttgart.
Stehn, J. (1993). America's Departure from Multilateralism. Highway or Dirt Road to Freer Trade? Kiel Discussion Papers, 212. Kiel: Institute of World Economy.
Tretheway, M. and T. Oum (1992). *Airline Economics: Foundations for Strategy and Policy.* Vancouver.
Vaubel, R. (1993). Perspektiven der Europäischen Integration: Die Politische Ökonomie der Vertiefung und Erweiterung. In H. Siebert (Hrsg.), *Die zweifache Integration: Deutschland und Europa.* Workshop zur Strukturberichterstattung. Tübingen, Mohr: 3-32.
Viner, J. (1950). *The Customs Union Issue.* New York.

Warren, T. amd C. Findlay (1998). Competition Policy and International Trade in Air Transport and Telecommunications Services. *The World Economy* 21: 445-456.

Wolf, H. (1996).*Grundsatzfragen einer Flughafenprivatisierung in Deutschland. Gutachten im Auftrag des Bundesministeriums für Finanzen.* Kiel.

World Trade Organization, Committee on Specific Commitments (WTO/CSC) (1997). A Brief Analysis of Cases of 'Ad Hoc Scheduling' in Past Service Negotiations. Note by the Secretariat, S/CSC/W/11 of 9 October 1997. Geneva (available from Internet).

World Trade Organization, Council for Trade in Services (WTO/CTS) (1998). Air Transport Services. Background Note by the Secretariat, S/C/W/59 of 5 November 1998. Geneva (available from Internet).

World Trade Organization (WTO) (1999). General Agreement on Trade in Services. The Design and Underlying Principles of the GATS. Geneva (available from Internet: http://www.wto.org/ wto/services/services.htm of 15 July 1999).

World Trade Organization, General Council (WTO/GC) (1999a). Preparations for the 1999 Ministerial Conference, EC Approach to Services. Communication from the European Communities, WT/GC/W/189 of 2 June 1999. Geneva (available from Internet).

World Trade Organization, General Council (WTO/GC) (1999b). Preparations for the 1999 Ministerial Conference, Objectives for GATS 2000 Negtiations. Communication from Australia, Chile and New Zealand, WT/GC/W/204 of 14 June 1999. Geneva (available from Internet).

World Trade Organization, General Council (WTO/GC) (1999c). Preparations for the 1999 Ministerial Conference, Services. Communiction from Argentina, WT/GC/W/231 of 6 July 1999. Geneva (available from Internet).

World Trade Organization, General Council (WTO/GC) (1999d). Preparations for the 1999 Ministerial Conference, Negotiations on Services. Communication from Switzerland, WT/GC/W/262 of 21 July 1999. Geneva (available from Internet).

World Trade Organization, General Council (WTO/GC) (1999e). Preparations for the 1999 Ministerial Conference, Further Negotiations As Mandated by the General Agreement on Trade in Services (GATS). Communication from the United States, WT/GC/W/295 of 5 August 1999. Geneva (available from Internet).

Zantke, S. (1976). *ABC des Luftverkehrs.* 3., überarbeitete Auflage. Hamburg.

References

Zhang, Anming (1996). *An Analysis of Fortress Hubs in Airline Netwoks.* Discussion Paper 96-09. Department of Economics. University of Victoria. Victoria, British Columbia.

For Product Safety Concerns and Information please contact our EU representative GPSR@taylorandfrancis.com Taylor & Francis Verlag GmbH, Kaufingerstraße 24, 80331 München, Germany

Batch number: 10725802

Printed by Printforce, the Netherlands